Spiral Into Love

**HOW TO STOP FALLING IN
LOVE WITH THE WRONG ONES...
AND STAY IN LOVE WITH THE
RIGHT ONES**

**PHILIPPA
WALLER**

WITH ADDITIONAL MATERIAL
BY **TOM BRUNO MAGDICH**

Published in 2012 by FeedARead.com Publishing – Arts Council funded

First Edition

A CIP catalogue record for this title is available from the British Library.

"It makes so much sense and is so easy to read and digest and yet seems so eye opening. It's cool how it can be applied to any relationship not just a sexual one. I enjoyed the research context you provide as well."

Monica Beletsky – Hollywood movie and TV writer

CONTENTS

THE AUTHOR

Ever since I can remember I have been fascinated by relationships. From the junior school playground, where kiss chase was more of a slobber scrum; to Sixth Form, when I realised that every girl but me and my twin sister seemed to have taken a class in flirting; through to adult life, where suddenly I was in my mid-thirties, single and wondering where the time had gone.

As a writer and a communications coach I am by necessity fascinated with humans and their relationships. I spent most of my adult life searching for the almost perfect relationship. In doing so I had exciting relationships, sweet relationships, kind relationships, hideous relationships, French relationships, holiday relationships, long relationships, too-short-to-mention relationships. I failed at relationships, worked out a lot more about successful relationships, looked for relationships, avoided relationships, talked to people looking for relationships, helped some triumph through rocky relationships, celebrated their wonderful relationships and supported a fair few out of damaged relationships.

I wrote films about love, poems about love, songs about love, an entire stage musical about love, and over a period of ten years travelled the world performing in improvised comedy shows about love – where real people got to meet and fall in love. Some actually got married.

I then went on to study human psychology, counselling and CBT, as well as work with leading edge, innovative thinkers in human behaviour and development.

Now approaching the age where life apparently begins, I find myself understanding a lot more about what it means to love, to be in love and, perhaps more importantly, to stay in love.

This book is about communication and how we communicate with each other in relationships based on what we most value in life. It brings together all my research and study, reading and discoveries, experience and passion on the subject of how we humans search for, fail at and succeed in love. And more importantly – how we can all learn to *spiral into love*.

One other thing. When I read a book I always appreciate the author suggesting how I use their book. Some say read it one chapter at a time; others say feel free to dip in and out. When it comes to *Spiral into Love* it may be tempting to take the Personal Profiler and skip to the bits that feel most relevant to you. But this is a book that grows and builds, revealing layers of understanding through each relationship combination and partnership dynamic. You may feel one relationship dynamic speaks to you more at this point in your life, but the truth is we shift and change from relationship to relationship and even from day to day. So, the first time you read this book – read it all. Then, by all means, go ahead and dip away!

Match Me a Match

We humans love to love. As online dating sites like singlesover60.co.uk and laterlife.com show, we won't give up until we find it. However, there's no doubt that finding the love of your life isn't always easy.

Even in an internet age of uber-connectivity, where Facebook friends can number in the thousands, it is becoming increasingly hard to find our special soul-mate for life. There are many fine books, full of helpful advice telling us why lasting love is so hard to find. We read that it may simply be down to differing personality traits, cognitive differences, hormonal imbalances or which planet we're from. We discover why men marry bitches, how to be a good husband and are even given advice on the sixty-minute marriage. While such books offer us some useful insights, they don't necessarily show us the entire picture.

If men are from one planet and women from another, how is it that in some cultures women behave more like the archetypal western male and men more like the archetypal western female?[1a,1b] If it's only down to gender why do gay relationships and same-sex friendships break down? If love comes down to whether we both speak the same language how is it we can sometimes completely understand the language the other person is speaking and still never want to see them again? If love is actually about *Why Men Marry Bitches*, why are we also encouraged to pop *Why Men Divorce Bitches* into our shopping baskets? If a man needs to read a book like *How to be a Good Husband*, should he also read *Women Really Do Love Bastards*? And should we be advising people to read *The Sixty Minute Marriage* or *Fit to be Tied: Making Marriage Last a Lifetime*?

The reality is that much advice around relationships focuses in on one of the many aspects of human interactions – a single, misinterpreted but commercially lucrative scientific soundbite. But *Spiral into Love* is about none of these things. Or rather, it is about *all* of these things.

The search engine

If you're reading this book then I'm guessing you're either single and looking for a relationship, engaged and questioning a relationship, married and resuscitating a relationship or blissfully happy and only reading this to reaffirm your own romantic success.

If it's any of the above then congratulations. You're either looking for a new way to find love or are taking positive steps to rejuvenate or maintain the love that you have. Most importantly, you're looking for a few more answers to this thing called love, a different approach – something concrete that can help you make a rational and informed decision in a rational and informed age, while still enabling you to energise your relationship with enough fun and romance to keep the love very much alive.

It all starts with what we're typing into our Google search box. When it comes to the real Google search box, we're probably all pretty good at finding a decent local pizza delivery service or cut-price holiday to Kephalonia, but when it comes to the metaphorical Google hunt for romance, are we really any good at searching for the love of our lives?

Imagine for a moment that your love life is like a computer. (You may know a few people who feel their love life actually *is* a computer. If so, you might like to lend them this book when you're done.) Now picture yourself sitting at your desk or kitchen table, staring at your computer screen. The Google page is up, as is your heart rate, and you're about to embark on the most important search of your life: the search for love.

So what words will a man or woman type into that box? They may well be very different – no surprises there. Often they'll go something like:

THE MAN: Out of my league, under 40, no facial hair or nagging.
THE WOMAN: Gsoh, honest, mentally and financially stable, hygienic, all own teeth.

These are all important factors, no doubt – let's take that as read. But are they really the foundations of lasting love? Are we asking the right questions when it comes to choosing our life partner? Do we truly know and understand the life partner we already have?

> *'Usually couples seem to hook up on the basis of quite skin-deep similarities and see if it works out afterwards'*
> *Dr Luisa Dillner, Love By Numbers.*

Today we understand more about human nature than ever before, but many of us don't seem to be putting this knowledge into practice when it comes to love . . . and it's not like we're getting better at it. Let's take a look at the stats – the 'science bit', if you will – but we won't stay too long on this section – it's no trip into rom-com land. As any good psychotherapist will tell you anyway, it's better to merely glance at the past and move quickly into a more positive future. However, I think it's worth reminding ourselves of the current love climate, even if it is a little stormy and overcast right now.

Online or offline – there's an awful lot of people in the world today looking for love, but whether you meet your mate on the world wide web or on a world-wide cruise, the number of failed relationships is on the rise.

All you wonderfully intoxicated romantics out there brace yourselves. Here's a sobering look at some less than cuddly statistics on the state of relationship play today. From loving alone to living alone, from the heady engagement to the head on divorce.

Welcome to . . .

The LOVE stats

- ▶ Over 14 million people in the UK are single.
- ▶ Five million of them use online dating sites.

- ▸ The UK online dating industry is worth over £300 million.
- ▸ Globally, the online dating industry is worth over $4 billion.
- ▸ One in five people in the UK say they have broken off an engagement.
- ▸ The UK has the fourth highest divorce rate in the world.
- ▸ The USA has the highest divorce rate in the world.
- ▸ Over half of marriages in the UK will end in divorce.
- ▸ Most over-16s are single, divorced or widowed.
- ▸ Statistics reveal many people stay in unhappy marriages for the children, because of finances, because of guilt or because they don't want to be alone.
- ▸ 15–20% of couples are in a sexless relationship.
- ▸ £20 billion a year is spent as a consequence of relationship breakdowns.
- ▸ Over half the meals consumed in the UK are eaten alone.
- ▸ Single people spend on average £250,000 more over a lifetime than couples.
- ▸ In twenty years, people living by themselves will be the largest group – 44% – of the adult population.

Whichever way you look at the stats above, it's not great. Over half of all marriages end in divorce? If you were headed into an operation with a fifty-fifty chance of survival, you'd consider that a pretty critical and terrifying condition, and probably not an occasion to be ordering a £2,000 ivory silk dress and a six-tier sponge cake with crystalised pink roses. (Though a silk-clad pre-op cake fest might, in fact, be money just as well spent.)

Clearly our relationship search criteria aren't operating as effectively as they could be. In fact, if Google's search criteria worked on the same principles as our own search for love, we'd be better off using the Yellow Pages. Or phoning a friend. Or even asking the neighbour. Anything would be more reliable. Of course, Google doesn't operate on the basis of throwing up a chaotic selection of irrelevant and unhelpful options.

Google's search criteria are based specifically on our individual needs. It even offers us a glimpse into new, improved suggestions and options that we may never have even thought of searching for. This is because it identifies who we are, what we like, what we've looked for in the past and MOST IMPORTANTLY – WHAT DRIVES AND MOTIVATES US. In other words, our VALUES.

This is all down to the power of the cookie – those little electronic trackers that sites like Amazon love to pop into your computer to get to know you a little better, find out what you're looking for and see if they can find the perfect products to match your consumer desires. Love them or hate them, those cookies are there to hunt down and find out exactly what you value . . . even when you don't know exactly what you value yourself.

So what are 'Values?'

Our values are unique to each and everyone of us. They are the things we care about in life, that motivate us everyday. They are made up of the beliefs we hold, the rules by which we live and the behaviours we deem important or necessary. Our values are both inherited from our family as well as learned from the cultural conditioning of our society. The values we hold may change throughout our lives. As infants we value survival above anything else. As teenagers we might value freedom and the right to express ourselves as individuals. As adults we may go on to value stability, honesty, success, friends, family, financial security, loyalty or global peace.

Understanding what you and any potential partner truly values is the first step to a whole new way to find and stay in love! So perhaps it's time to put a little values cookie in your heart, your very own relationship search engine, to help you find the perfect partner who shares, or at least understands, your values, wants and desires. And that's exactly what *Spiral into Love* is here to help you do.

When it comes to love, we've been going in blindly. We need to stop listening to those old proverbs! If love is blind, is it any wonder we stumble, trip and crash to the ground, a bleeding wreck in its pursuit?

We need to stop groping in the dark in search of love, because, judging by the stats, it isn't working. The old way is broke. And we need to fix it.

It's time to place some value on love.

It's time for a new proverb: *Those who know they value love, love to know their values!*

For all the poems, songs and self-help books ever written, the research, along with my personal experience, in the field has revealed that lasting romantic happiness, relationship success and marital bliss depends on one factor more than any other: *values*!

Yes, what you and your chosen partner individually value will determine the length and quality of your relationship more than any other aspect. Have you ever been head over heels in love with someone and they've suddenly stopped returning your calls or been in a long and seemingly successful relationship that abruptly ends? If so, it's easy to feel unworthy, question your own attractiveness or even develop low self-esteem. But here's the thing, it might not be that he or she just isn't that into you. There's every chance they think you're fabulous. But if the two of you have totally incompatible wants, needs and values then however beautiful, intelligent, kind and wonderful you are, the relationship is not the one for you. So walk away knowing you're fabulous, that it wasn't YOU he wasn't into, it could be that your values simply didn't match at this time in your lives.

As grim as some of the love stats may appear, the future is far from hopeless. In fact, if you're ready to understand your values and the values of any potential or current partner, your future could be very, very rosy indeed!

Spiralling Into Love

Spiral into Love offers you a unique approach to finding new love – or keeping your current love alive and vibrant. Relationships can be challenging, we all know that. Very few partnerships survive without facing difficult periods and managing conflict. But the truth is, we argue over what we care about. We fight when our boundaries are crossed. We do what we do because of our belief in our values.

The first step to this new approach to love is for us to understand our values and the values of our loved ones. By understanding our own and our partner's values, we may well be able to stop the fighting before it even begins, and we'll certainly be able to start building a loving, supportive and exciting relationship – for life.

This book contains an easy to use values diagnostic – the SPIRAL PROFILER – which you will find on page 257. The Spiral Profiler is a simple and highly effective values-based assessment tool.

Based on research around values in human development and relationships, we can identify five key sets of values, or, in other words, value systems.

The profiler will help you identify which of the main five value systems is most dominant for you, i.e. what you most value in life. By knowing what your dominant values are, you can begin the journey towards understanding how and why you think, feel and react the way you do when it comes to love.

After that, you can read about how each of the five value systems responds to each other when they are in a relationship together. In that section I outline how each combination of values creates its own unique dynamic and experience. Some value combinations find aspects of a relationship easier to handle than others and they all have their strengths as well as their challenges. Under each combination we will take a look at the six key areas of any relationship and how your values and the values of your partner will impact on how you feel as a couple.

These key areas are:
1) Dating and early romance
2) Long-term and marriage
3) Kids and family
4) Friends and social life
5) Money
6) Sex

Dating and early romance
As much as we might enjoy the heady cocktail of early dating, it may be important to quickly assess whether a relationship is going somewhere – particularly as we get older and the biological clock starts ticking. More and more men and women are still looking for

their life partner well into their late thirties when there's simply less time to waste. When we start dating someone, it is essential to be able to work out their values before we commit to a long-term relationship with them. Understanding each other's values will tell you a lot about how compatible you both are and whether the relationship is headed towards a wedding ring or a dead-end fling.

Long-term and marriage

Both men and women report that they get frustrated when the same arguments come up again and again and never get resolved. It makes being in a long-term relationship so much harder and chips away at our feelings of love. By truly understanding why these conflict patterns occur, you can start to shift and even eradicate unnecessary fights and move towards keeping the love alive and energised every day.

Kids and family

When it comes to raising children, everyone is unique. Your personal value set will determine whether you're a hands-on or hands-off parent and why that is, what kind of rules you lay down or why you might not like to lay down any rules at all. How you bring up a child may be different to how your parents raised you. It may be different to how your friends bring up their children. That doesn't make it wrong. You will parent based on your own values, so it's good to know what those values are and the impact you have on your family and partner.

Friends and social life

I've discovered that most available research around whether relationships succeed or fail only looks at the couple themselves, often in isolation from the rest of the world. We now know, however, that the friends and social contacts a couple is surrounded by will have a big impact on the relationship.[2] Some people value a few close-knit friends, some value meeting as many new people as possible and some simply value being left alone. The value you place on friends and socialising will hugely impact the dynamic between you and your partner.

Money

Money causes more stress and arguments between a couple than any other factor.[3] For all the fights over finances, I wonder how many of us actually take the time to ask why these conflicts occur. Nowadays, fewer and fewer couples pool their money.[4] In fact, most couples rarely discuss their feelings towards money at all, when money is overwhelmingly the most conflict-ridden area of any relationship. Few of us would take a job without discussing money, whereas most people will enter into a life-long relationship with not so much as a mention of it.

We sometimes forget that money is a hugely emotional issue. Our attitude to it is very much tied up with our deepest emotions and values. Money can mean power in a relationship, and even leave one partner feeling disempowered. Managing money is often about control. It can also be responsible for us gaining or losing respect; a couple's personal and social life can suffer or become complicated if neither or only one of them has money. Money issues can even lead to a breakdown in a couple's sex life.

Money can be the root of many relationship problems, so understanding your own and your partner's attitude towards money, based on both your deepest values, is one of the most effective ways you can begin to reduce any tension within your relationship.

Sex

Needless to say, sex has a massive impact on the health of any loving relationship. We all have different attitudes to and expectations of our sex life. Sometimes communication over sex breaks down entirely and the relationship can become platonic. We can feel rejected if our partner refuses sex, guilty if we've done the rejecting and resentful if we have sex unwillingly. All of these feelings can begin to erode the very foundations of our relationship. By understanding how your partner thinks about sex and the values that are – or aren't – tied up with it, we can ensure that our sex life begins to build and strengthen our love for one another.

Once we've looked at the dynamics of the various value set combinations, we then look at how we can begin to understand and manage our relationships from a whole new perspective – the Rainbow Perspective.

The truth is, while we may have a dominant value set, we will often express other values at different times of our life or even different times of the day. Different people will surface different value systems within us. We have, if you like, a rainbow of values. The Rainbow Perspective is about understanding these values in ourselves and others.

From high up in the Rainbow Perspective, we can see and acknowledge the full range of values that both we and our partners hold and express – while not allowing ourselves to be hijacked by any single one of them. Well, not for too long at least!

From this new way of looking at your relationship, you will be able to identify and manage the different values and attitudes as they arise within yourself and your partner. Taking the Rainbow Perspective really puts you in the driver's seat and enables you to author your own, lasting happiness.

We'll then look at the importance of communication within a relationship and how to effectively talk to your partner, depending on their values. The key to a vibrant, long-lasting connection is learning how to communicate with our other half at the deepest level of their personal values. In this way, both you and your partner can get more of your fundamental needs met. When your needs are met, your love can continue to grow, build and spiral into the future.

When we're in a difficult stage or challenging moment in a relationship, we don't have time for a ten-year self-development or partner-awareness programme. Time is ticking by and whether you're single in a void or married and annoyed, relationship stresses are mounting. What we need is instant self-understanding, immediate knowledge of our partner and some practical tools and tips we can put into practice straight away, and that's exactly what *Spiral into Love* is here to do.

If you're looking to find new love, rekindle old love, or check whether your latest flame is the one for you, then read on. You've probably realised that, when it comes to the most important aspect of your life – love – it's time to stop crossing your fingers and hoping for the best. It's time to stop blindly falling in love. It's time to open our eyes and our hearts to a whole new way of finding and holding onto love.

What Is Love?

We casually bandy the word 'love' around every day of our lives. Whether we're talking about our partner, a new pair of jeans or our preference for cottage cheese with pineapple chunks. We've become very much accustomed to this word 'love'. So, before we go any further, let's have a look at what we even mean by love.

Neuroscientists Andreas Bartels and Semir Zeki investigated the neural activity associated with romantic love by using fMRI scans to observe how subjects' brains reacted when they were shown pictures of loved ones. Their study highlights which areas of the brain are stimulated when faced with the object of their affection. They concluded that 'by showing that a unique set of interconnected areas becomes active when humans view the face of someone who elicits a unique and characteristic set of emotions, we have shown that underlying one of the richest experiences of mankind is a functionally specialised system of the brain'.[5]

To physician-philosopher Raymond Tallis, this is a crude way to explore human love. Tallis says, 'Love is not like a response to a single stimulus, such as a picture. It's not even a single enduring state, like being cold. It is a many-splendored and many-miseried thing.' This state of love includes hope, jealousy, kindness, lust, guilt, delight and moments of not feeling in love at all.

A wealth of research has been carried out on the phenomenon of love to try to discover exactly what it is and what it means. Historically, people have referred to love as an emotion and even sometimes an illness! More recently, neuroscientific research has revealed that the 'feeling' of love is very much tied up to an area of the brain that deals with motivation – the same part of the brain, in fact, that deals with addiction. So when someone tells you they're addicted to love, they may in fact be telling it exactly how it is.

A number of neuroscientists studying the phenomena of love now call the experience of love a 'goal-orientated motivational state'.[6] They liken the feeling of love to the feeling we have when some of our basic drives – such as hunger, thirst and sex – are satisfied. We humans like the feeling we experience when our drives are being satisfied. The relief of a cool drink on a hot day, the satisfaction of a good meal after a prolonged period of hunger and the release and physical satisfaction we can feel after sex. It's at times like this, when our fundamental needs are met, that all those lovely 'happy' chemicals like oxytocin, serotonin and dopamine are released into our brain.

What's interesting about this research is that it reconfirms what we instinctively know: the feeling of falling in love doesn't last! It's a temporary, chemically-induced feeling we experience in the early stages of finding someone attractive. In order to maintain this feeling, we need to satisfy both our own and our partner's key motivators on a regular basis. Falling in love can feel wonderful for a while, but there are two important things we need to know when it comes to love:

1) The initial feeling of euphoria will fade. It has to. For anyone who's been in an over-extended passionate love affair, you'll know that although it can be addictive, it's unsustainable and utterly exhausting.
2) It is by understanding our needs and our partner's needs that we can begin to work towards sustaining the feeling of love. Rather

than expecting that feelings of love will remain consistent, we must take control and help to keep recreating the feelings of love in our relationship. By understanding what each other values and what's important to us, we can truly begin to work towards a lifetime filled with love.

So, we need to take control and stop blindly falling in love.

Falling in love

Before we can spiral into love, let's take a look at the well-worn phrase 'falling in love'. The phrase to 'fall in love' was first coined by the English Renaissance scholar John Palsgrave[7], sometime in the early 1600s, when he wrote a poem about a young girl whose corset he no doubt fancied his chances of getting into. But how accurate, useful or romantic is this phrase?

To fall in love suggests we tripped or stumbled into love. To fall in love feels like an accident, and an unfortunate accident at that. After all, what else do we fall into? We fall ill, we fall down, we fall over, we fall into a trap, we fall into error, we fall into sin, we fall and hurt ourselves, we might even fall into conversation but mainly we fall because we weren't concentrating or got unlucky. We fall if it's dark, we fall if we're blindfolded, we fall if we're pushed, we fall if we want to throw ourselves from a great height to our certain death. They say love is blind and if we keep insisting on falling into it then it's hardly any wonder we wake up three months into a relationship shocked, bruised, exhausted and convinced we'll never make the same mistake again. And then do. Again and again. And maybe even yet again.

If we keep falling and tumbling and tripping and stumbling into love, surely we can only expect ongoing hurt and disappointment. We don't fall into success. We don't fall into happiness or excitement. We never knowingly fall into peace and contentment. Why do we think falling in love will land us in relationship bliss? As we keep falling, the relationship failure rate will keep soaring. It's time to stop *falling* and start *spiralling* into love.

Spiralling into love – the conscious and ongoing creation of a loving relationship based on the understanding and support of both partners' primary values and needs.

The truth is, if we don't address what is of primary importance to us and our partner, we will continue to stumble blindly into and along in relationships that are at best unsatisfactory and at worst destructive.

Understand and value yourself

If we're looking for long-term success in our relationships then it's vital we understand our own values first. It seems so obvious that knowing yourself is important to create a successful relationship and yet this is often the very thing we overlook. However, the values that sit at the very core of who we are will be the deciding factors in whether we can make a relationship work, and how we go about it.

When our relationships get difficult, it's so easy to look at our partner, lover, husband or wife and blame them. It's far easier to do that than to dig down a little deeper and discover a shared responsibility. It's rare we hear people come out of a broken relationship saying:

'I'm incredibly sad, but to be honest I should have seen it coming. I'm not easy to be around when I'm stressed and I didn't really communicate my needs to my partner. I think if I had been more open and less resentful, we could have been happy. My partner never really had a chance to make it work. My expectations were totally unrealistic and they were never going to meet them.'

Of course, we might look back on a past relationship some years later and realise what we might have done to salvage it, but that's no use to anyone trying to revitalise a current relationship, and not much better to someone on a first date or entering into a new relationship.

Helen is thirty-seven and has been in a relationship for three years. This relationship is honest, open and communicative and Helen has never felt happier. Over the course of this relationship she has learned for the first time what she really values. She talked to me one day about a past relationship:

'My last relationship was completely different. We were together for about two years and I became increasingly unhappy over the final six months. I didn't even want to be in the flat we shared and used to pointlessly drive around at night, dreading going home. It's like I'd been waiting for the relationship to become something else and it never did. I think we were both left feeling incredibly disillusioned and disappointed. Although communication had pretty much broken down, we did finally manage to actually break up. As with most break-ups, it was fairly horrendous – unpleasant emails, demands for money owed, even an invoice for a frying pan. But one email was especially memorable. He wrote to me after all the anger had died down to say, "I'm sorry for taking your joy away." At the time I probably felt like he had, but now when I think of that relationship and particularly of that one phrase, I realise how much I'd expected him to create my happiness. Where had we got to that both he and I believed he'd taken my joy away? No one can take your joy away. No one else is responsible for your own happiness. No one, that is, but you.'

Now Helen understands how to author her own happiness, she is already well on the way to creating a healthy, happy and sustainable relationship. Whether you're in the early stages of dating or years into a relationship, one of the first things to ask yourself is this: how much are you expecting your partner to take care of you? Because once you understand your own values then you can begin to meet your own needs. If you feel frustrated or annoyed that your partner isn't meeting certain needs, ask yourself: Can I meet them myself?

If you can take care of up to ninety per cent of your needs and only expect ten per cent from your partner, then immediately your relationship pressures can be eased. People are often surprised at how much they can meet their own needs and how happy it makes them – and their partner! You'll have so much more energy and willingness to offer each other support when you really need it. So, before you go any further down the path of life, ask yourself who is in control of your happiness. You? Or someone you met along the way?

Understand and value your partner

When scientists asked a study group how they knew they were in love with a partner, the majority of them said 'when they were in a positive mood' around that person.[8] So when we feel good around someone, we're more likely to report feelings of love or being in love.

And when are we in a good mood? When do we feel most positive? It's when our personal values are being understood and acknowledged.

Some people already instinctively understand what their partner values and how to take care of those values. These are the people who celebrate 50 years of uninterrupted happiness on their golden wedding anniversary. That doesn't necessarily mean they never argued, but they probably understood and accepted what was important to each other at the deepest level and then worked to make each other's lives as happy as possible by meeting each other's value needs.

Being aware of your partner's values is an extremely important factor when it comes to relationship success. Not only that, but understanding your partner's values and attitudes, as well as them understanding yours, has also been shown to improve physical health and lower mortality rates.[9] Understanding the importance of values in relationships might not simply be a question of love and happiness, it might also be a question of life and death!

Research by Lisa Neff of the University of Toledo and Benjamin Karney at the University of Florida suggests that 'the accuracy of a spouse's trait knowledge of each other is an important determinant of social support and relationship longevity'[10.] To translate: if our partner knows us as well as we know ourselves, assuming we do know ourselves, then the relationship has a much greater chance of being both long-term and happy.

Why? Because when individuals have more accurate knowledge of their partners then:

1) They are more able to *PREDICT* how their partner might feel or react in a given situation. Having that knowledge about our partner can be very comforting and lead to a more harmonious, day-to-day relationship dynamic.

2) They have an insight into when to offer *SUPPORT* to their partner. Knowing what your partner needs and when not only makes you feel more in control, it increases your partner's perception of how responsive and loving you are. *Being supportive* and *feeling supported* at the right moments will increase overall happiness within the relationship. For example, if you know your partner has just had to give a work colleague bad feedback and you know he really prefers to please people and make them happy, you will know to provide emotional support in that moment or as near to it as possible and delay getting your own needs met for a short while.

3) You can learn to ACCEPT YOUR DIFFERENCES. Even if you disagree with one of your partner's values or beliefs, if you know in advance that you feel differently around certain issues, you won't be upset or disappointed when those issues arise. It won't be a shock. It would be like getting upset because there's bad news on the television. You know there will always be some bad news, and it might not be what you'd prefer, but you know and accept it's the reality.

4) You can anticipate and potentially AVOID any misunderstandings or conflicts. By being fully aware of how your partner feels and of any differences you might have, you can decide to avoid those subjects (e.g. If you're never going to agree about the benefit of acupuncture because you swear by it and he thinks it's nonsense, then agree to disagree - agree it doesn't really matter and stop talking about it[11]).

If you and your partner have matching or similar values, then the relationship can often be easier to manage. So, if you're looking to enter into a new relationship you might want to think about surfacing any potential partner's values before you commit to them long-term.

However, whether couples share the same values or not, the exciting discovery is that if both of you understand what drives each other towards happiness – as well as what drives you up the wall! – then you will be:

- ▸ Less likely to fight
- ▸ More responsive and supportive to one another
- ▸ Far less likely to end the relationship than couples who remain unaware of each other's values or needs.

CHAPTER 2

Stress and Your Values

There are many things that humans value in life. We all vary in how much we value one thing over another and our values can shift and change throughout our lifetime – sometimes over the course of a year, maybe a week or even in one day – and it's what we value that shapes our personality.

We now know enough about neuroscience to know that there's no such thing as a fixed personality based on genes or DNA.[12] As an identical twin I've always known that to be true. It is not simply genes that define who we are and what we value. My twin and I are genetically identical and yet have had some fundamental differences in what we value at different times in our lives.

For all of us, the reality is that it can seem like our personality shifts and changes over our lifetime. That's because our *values* shift and change according to our life conditions and who we're with. Often we or our ex-partners might start dating someone new and both suddenly seem like completely different people.

You only have to glance at online agony pages and blogs to see the tip of this shifting personality iceberg:

Dear Lauren,
My ex is starting to date again less than a week after our break-up. Ours was the first serious relationship for the both of us but the last time I spoke to my ex, she seemed like a completely different person, going to places and doing things she never did with me. I'm shaken up and feel like I'm not only mourning the loss of a relationship, but also of a person I once knew.

Dear LoveBlog,
My ex broke up with me five months ago. I was devastated. It took months for me to stop crying and get my life together. Today I feel completely different and many people that know me look at me like I'm a whole new person. My ex has been trying to contact me, but since I haven't spoken to him in months, I'm beginning to feel that the new me will not be happy with this man any more. Months ago I'd have done anything to have him back in my life, now I'm not sure I want him back or even that I love him. Is this normal?

Yes, it's normal. We shift and change, and that's part of the reason why, even within a relationship, we can be surprised by a partner's decisions or opinions. The person we love can suddenly seem so inconsistent and unreliable. But if we understand that people are fluid and change their outlook according to their values, we can stop being disappointed or unnerved and begin to see what value our partner is expressing at any given time. Once we recognise the motivation underlying what they say and do, we can start to respond in a way that will benefit us both.

This is particularly important when it comes to stress within relationships.

Much is written about stress in relationships – the behavioural factors, the brain chemistry and the ensuing emotions – but when you or your partner get stressed, it can often be far more useful to start looking at what lies underneath the behaviours, emotions, hormonal frustration and external day-to-day factors. Something is driving that stress and that something will invariably be related to our value set.

Rob is an insurance broker. He works incredibly hard, often arriving home after the children have been bathed and fairytaled to sleep. His partner Cath is a caring, empathetic mother who also works full-time.

She noticed that Rob had become increasingly stressed over a period of some weeks. He was often short-tempered and less attentive or affectionate towards her.

Once Cath discovered Rob was approaching feedback and appraisal time, she simply put his behaviour down to work pressure. She tried to make all the right noises and make his life as easy as possible but still Rob's stress seemed to increase.

Cath and I talked about the fact that simply labelling Rob's behaviour as work pressure hadn't proved helpful. As much as she's tried to alleviate his stress, nothing had changed. We talked about what might be driving Rob's stress. What did Rob most value? Cath suggested it might be the need to achieve or be the best in his team, but reassuring him he was the best didn't seem to help. Then Cath mentioned Rob's need to get things right and maintain his position. Together she and I explored the values that were potentially underlying Rob's stress – his need to get things right, his respect for authority and his obsessive attention to detail and preparation. Cath began to understand that reassuring Rob that he was the best and would get a promotion was not going to alleviate his stress.

She started to talk to Rob about recent projects and tasks that he would be talking about in the feedback session with his boss. She helped him get his head clear around all the facts and figures as well as his performance and attitude. She asked Rob how various members of the team responded to him, allowing him to remind himself of how respected he was within the team. With a fresh sense of having followed all the right procedures at every stage, as well as recalling the respect he had earned, Rob was able to reduce his stress level. He felt solid and prepared for the appraisal session and was even able to devote more time to the children.

Our own or our partner's stress can feel overwhelming and, at times, impossible to deal with. Sometimes all it takes is recognising the core values that lie at the heart it.

Stress is a potentially devastating factor in a relationship. If you or your partner suffers from stress, you'll know how challenging it can be for both of you. It often turns into an opportunity to fight each other. What if we can turn it into an opportunity to support and strengthen each other?

Simply understanding that stress is connected to the release of cortisol and a series of hormones doesn't necessarily help us do anything about it. However, once we know what core value has been crossed and is driving the stress, both in ourselves and our partner, we can stop aggravating it and start to alleviate it.

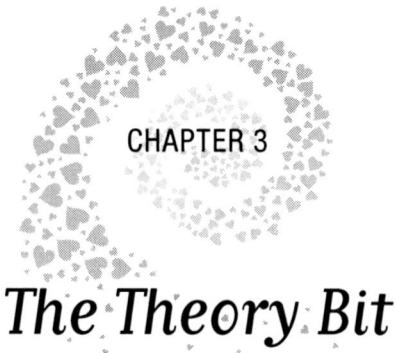

CHAPTER 3

The Theory Bit

So, the next thing we need to know is what these values are that tell us so much about who we are, how we respond to our partner and who we can love over a lifetime? And which ones do you personally value the most?

The theorists (or 'science bit')

There are a number of theorists whose research supports the idea that what we value is a key indicator of how we'll behave. I've looked at several of these theories in the course of my work as a counsellor, communication skills trainer, facilitator, writer and business coach. Here's an outline of four key sources that have inspired this book.

1 The first is the work of Abraham Maslow who developed a theory of human values and drives in the 1940s which he called the Hierarchy of Needs. Maslow's ideas are still applied today for understanding the part motivation plays in personal development. The theory was introduced in his two main books *Motivation and Personality* and *Toward a Psychology of Being*.

Maslow's model proposed that each of us is born with and driven by an innate set of needs. His theory states that through life we seek to satisfy each innate need in turn, starting with the most basic physical needs for survival of the organism itself. Once the basic order needs of food, shelter and safety, together with emotional well-being, are met, we are then free to continue evolving consciously into the higher order needs of self-esteem, creativity and self-actualisation. (See page 257.)

2 The second key source is more recent. This theory suggests that our unique personalities are defined by our drives and values and has been proposed by Dr Steven Reiss, a professor at Ohio State University. After conducting an extensive study into human values involving over 6,000 people, Dr Reiss proposed that all human behaviour is guided by sixteen basic desires that help shape and form our personalities (see page 257).

According to Dr Reiss, it is not solely genetics that shape our personalities but the impact of culture and society that determines what we value. The values we hold then determine how we behave.

3 Dr Reiss's sixteen values map fairly neatly onto another values-based theory – Spiral Dynamics. This theory can help to determine whether the most important relationship of your life is the success story you want it to be. It's time to look at the dynamics of your relationship – the Spiral Dynamics.

Spiral Dynamics is a model of evolving human values. It grew out of the work of an American psychologist and doctor of philosophy – Clare W Graves (1914–1986) – and suggests that human nature is not fixed.

Rather, humans are able to adapt, change and evolve according to their life conditions. As we encounter new and potentially challenging situations, our values may shift enabling us to better respond to the given circumstances. Dr Graves proposed that personality is a continuous process that evolves through time. Rather than having a set personality, human beings move and flow through various stages throughout their lives according to what they're doing, what they need and and who they are with. This constant, fluid and ever-changing process can be imagined as a personal energy that flows up and down a spiral of different values. In other words as we move, shift, change and grow, we can imagine our experience being shaped by the active dynamic of our values shifting up and down the spiral. Hence Spiral Dynamics.

Spiral into Love draws on a version of Dr Graves's original theory created by Dr Don Beck and Christopher Cowan called Spiral Dynamics.

4 The final source of inspiration for the ideas presented in *Spiral into Love* is the work of philosopher and psychologist Ken Wilber. For the past forty years, Wilber has studied human development and presented his ideas in more than a dozen books on psychology and spirituality. His essential aim is to integrate the best theories into one integral 'theory of everything' which could be referred to as a manual for life and death. His work is specifically relevant here as he worked closely with Dr Don Beck, revising and further developing the theory of evolving human values called Spiral Dynamics Integral.

The following descriptions of the value sets outline the key concepts explored by the researchers I've just mentioned. These five value sets are present in all of us and it is by understanding them that we can begin to spiral into love.

CHAPTER 4

The Five Value Sets

We will begin at what is known as the Purple stage of values development.

Purple stage — 'We' orientated

Purple values are about bonding to one's family and tribe. In humankind's distant evolutionary past, survival and security was ensured by safety in numbers. Tribal communities formed with beliefs and rituals to explain and manage the conditions of living in the world. Someone expressing Purple values tends to look after only those very close to them. They seek security and safety but will look to the group or family to provide it. People with strong Purple values won't strike out on their own to make something happen in the world. They will always follow the pack and do what the rest of their tribe does – hence why this value set is referred to as 'We' orientated.

This set of values operates heavily from emotions rather than rational thought. Purple values drive people to make decisions based on their feelings or intuitions rather than on pure reason or logic.

Purple thinking is informed by knowledge that has been filtered down from the immediate family, gang or tribal elders. Decision-making will revolve around accepted customs, superstitions and rituals, unquestioningly honouring laws like 'Don't go out on Friday the thirteenth' or 'Never buy a green car because they are unlucky'. Any new concepts or ideas that don't fit in with the tribe will be rejected.

Bonding with the group is very much where Purple emotions are focused. The same goes for Purple within a partnership.

A couple expressing Purple values will be very close-knit and wary of outsiders who are different from them. These relationships are often all about the immediate family, with couples tending to stay living close to their relatives. Habits, home-making and child-rearing will often mirror the style, customs and rituals of their parents. Behaviour and emotion is driven by loyalty to the family and tribe – regardless of any abuses that may take place behind closed family doors.

Because of this sense of tribal loyalty, reciprocity is a key influencer – you scratch my back and I'll scratch yours – although, as connection and belonging are the principal drivers, Purple will only help out those who are part of their tribe. Trust is highly important within Purple cultures and will be demonstrated through personal sacrifice and investment in people close to them. Purple's mantra might be 'Blood is thicker than water'.

Purple behaviour is imitative. People expressing this value will often copy the behaviours and phrases used by their family, close group of friends, local community, team or organisation. As a result they can be over-sensitive to unfamiliar body language, environments and tone of voice. Physical characteristics and habits shared between family members are seen as a sign of belonging and are greatly valued. Dress sense is influenced by the need to display membership of group loyalty to a brand, e.g. branded T-shirts, football strips and tribal symbols.

Purple's emotions are tied up with ritual and custom and they are quick to interpret meaning in the context of their own belief systems. Purple values usually include magical and superstitious beliefs. A reliance on omens and spells can be a big part of their biological, psychological and social habits. They may refer to powerful supernatural forces, guardian angels or the spirits of their ancestors who watch over the tribe. As dreams, magic and luck are seen as likely causes for events in life, the placebo effect can be a powerful remedy for people expressing Purple.

The healthy expression of Purple is in a well-functioning, loving family or group full of tradition and care.

However, unhealthy emotions are expressed in rampant xenophobia, racism and intolerance of the customs and religions of others. We see Purple values in strong grass-roots family communities as well as in street gangs and organised crime syndicates like the Mafia.

Red stage — 'Me' orientated

Red values are all about strengthening the ego by affirming one's individuality. A person at this stage will often behave assertively. They may also display narcissistic qualities and often seek to dominate others in a quest for power and control, hence Red being referred to as 'ME' orientated.

When Red values are expressed healthily, a person's behaviour can be an energising, creative and heroic force that makes things happen in the world. However, in terms of human evolution, this stage is essentially pre-law and order and can cause a person to show minimum regard for right and wrong.

This behaviour is most often first seen when a toddler reaches the terrible twos. As they can't understand logic, and are unable to see things from another person's perspective, they behave in an egocentric manner. However, plenty of adults still default to this stage. Some of them are highly successful CEOs! The truth is that most of us have Red stage values alive and well and active within us. Some of us may deny or suppress these values but they are in fact essential for survival and, some believe, success in the world. Red behaviour can return at any time in life and is seen in the regressive, moody and aggressive behaviour of rebellious teens, tired and angry parents, offended adults and power-hungry business leaders.

When Red values surface within a couple, the relationship becomes about the absolute power and rule of the dominant partner.

A person expressing Red values demands respect and always comes first, even if it's at the expense of the other person in the relationship. Red partners are great if you like someone very strong and independent who will do what they like, when they like, how they like and where they want to.

But don't expect constant attention or support from a partner at peak Red as they are egocentric and narcissistic in love. Their mantra is, 'Do as I say and leave me alone to do what I want!' On the other hand, however, there won't be many dull moments.

Red's personal power is often expressed in a dominant physicality. In healthy mode, your Red partner will dazzle you with displays of confidence, strength and energy. The healthy expression of this emotional energy manifests in heroic deeds and a strong, dominant leadership when required. The unhealthy emotional expression shows in aggression, intolerance or even random violence. When Red is unhealthy, body language can be aggressive and posturing, deliberately taking up space in an environment and sometimes disregarding the personal space of others. Coming out of tribal Purple, the Red value set is self-serving and seeks emotional independence. This is about ego development and the evolution of a sense of self.

A quick shift from 'normal' feelings and behaviours into sudden rage can be an indication that Red values are energising your or your partner's emotions. The motivating principle of Red is that self-expression takes precedence over everything, regardless of the consequences, as shame and loss of face is unbearable at this stage of development.

'Knowledge is power' could be the motto for Red. Thoughts and concepts are mostly self-centred. Their intellect is in service of self to gain control of persons, places and things and they will reject any thoughts of responsibility or guilt. Mental toughness and thinking that supports instant gratification through quick wins will be their focus. Knowledge is acquired only to support a 'What's in it for me?' attitude.

An individual living Red values will think that learning anything that does not command the respect of others, or doesn't deliver a large reward, is a waste of time.

However, when it comes to Red, the intellect will be entirely the slave of the emotions. Whatever Red feels is what they will express and sudden waves of emotion – be it love or rage – will totally consume them.

When Red's emotions are in full swing, there's no point trying to reason with them – it's like trying to reason with a toddler. When the ego is inflated to that extent, no rational or intellectual argument will get through. Red sees himself or herself as the sole creator of their world and destiny, and will challenge any force or power that claims to be above them.

On the positive side, healthy Red is spiritually independent and autonomous. In early childhood we need to develop a separate ego so we can set healthy boundaries with others and move into adulthood. We could not differentiate as individuals without going through the Red value stage. It is also vital for creativity and confidence.

When Red is unhealthily expressed, the world can be seen to be full of threats. It can cause us to be aggressively defensive, stubborn and unreasonable.

Red can be seen popping up in every walk of life, from the boardroom to the classroom to a night out with the girls.

Blue stage — 'We' orientated

After the self-orientated, powerful, wilful and emotional behaviours of the Red values stage, it is time to create some stability and order. This is when the Blue values emerge to demand obedience to the rules laid down by a higher authority.

A person's values evolve into Blue after having transcended and included Red, so the highly expressed emotions of Red now become restrained and controlled by the obedient energy of the Blue values. This stage of development is essentially about creating order out of chaos.

The central principle of Blue is that one must sacrifice one's own needs now to serve a higher purpose and gain bigger, better rewards later, even if those rewards come after death. It is at this point in human history that we find the beginnings of monotheistic religions where the majority of people were expected to submit to the few who have supposedly been given authority by the higher powers. Judaism, Christianity and Islam are examples of peak Blue religions.

In terms of childhood development, the Blue value set emerges between the ages of seven and eleven. It is at this time that children begin to think logically about life events, but still have difficulty understanding abstract or hypothetical concepts. They need concrete rules and regulations to help them understand the world and their place in it. Adults healthily expressing Blue values look for order and meaning in their everyday lives and often tend to be organised. They believe in a social and moral system in which there are laws and codes laid down that we must all abide by. Hence Blue values being referred to as 'We' orientated.

From a Blue standpoint, those who obey the rules will be rewarded and those who don't should be punished. Blue values see the world in very black and white, right and wrong and non-negotiable terms. Someone expressing Blue is comfortable being told what to do by a person in authority whom they respect. When someone with Blue values finds themselves in a situation where their old belief system no longer serves them, they feel it very strongly. Suddenly the certainty they had in the world has gone, and Blue very much values certainty.

A person embodying Blue values won't bend the rules to accommodate anyone, not even their life partner.

So, while offering a high degree of loyalty, predictability and stability, a relationship with a Blue partner can sometimes be inflexible and pedantic. They will want to get things right and expect you to do the same.

They can have high expectations in terms of what's right and wrong about you in the relationship and their behaviour towards you can be driven by a sense of reward and punishment.

Conforming to the rules, Blue will be expressed in compliant, controlled and restrained physical behaviour. Conservative dress and orderly demeanour might best describe the physical appearance of your peak Blue partner. They will most likely be very comfortable wearing a uniform of some sort.

When emotions are present, they are galvanised around the rules of fairness and judgement. There is an emotional shift from Red's 'express yourself', to Blue's 'sacrifice yourself' in order to preserve the law. Spontaneity must yield to compliance to keep emotions in check. This can manifest as a rigid and dogmatic attitude to life and work, with little emotion. Your Blue partner will probably value judgement over compassion and express limited tolerance or understanding of others who break the rules.

On the positive side, Blue values bring order and structure to any chaotic emotional situations. However, when expressed negatively they will look to find fault rather than building on strengths.

Following the letter of the law is the prime focus of Blue thinking. Blue can be highly logical and rational, but they risk becoming dogmatic and immovable to the extent of insisting people follow a particular set of rules and orders regardless of personal feelings and thoughts. There is only one right way and it must be learned thoroughly and adhered to.

The mind of somebody expressing Blue values is unquestioning of authority and merely focuses on preserving the accuracy of learned knowledge. Always working by the book, obediently following the straight and narrow path, Blue's intellect is disciplined and obsessed with getting things correct. A healthy Blue intellect is accurate, precise and thorough. However, pedantry, stubbornness and closed-mindedness can be the signs of unhealthy Blue thinking.

When healthy, Blue can be a stabilising force that can seem to guide the way towards truth and feel like a source of security and comfort in times of uncertainty. In Abraham Lincoln's words, 'Let's have faith that right makes might; and in that faith let us, to the end, dare to do our duty as we understand it.' Or as Margaret Thatcher said, 'I am in politics because of the conflict between good and evil and I believe that in the end good will triumph.'

In its unhealthy expression there can be a fundamentalist intolerance of alternative worldviews, with an adherence to hierarchical laws, systems or religions.

Orange stage — 'Me' orientated

Transcending the superstitions of Purple, containing and including the egocentricism of Red and challenging Blue's myth-laden, dogmatic rules, the Orange drive is innovative, rational, opportunistic and success-orientated.

People at this stage are entrepreneurial and independent. Hence Orange is referred to as 'Me' orientated. Someone with Orange values loves to compete and especially loves to win. Achievement means everything to Orange. Like Red, they will sacrifice others for their own selfish gain, but unlike Red they are strategic and enterprising.

This stage appears in children at around twelve years old when they develop the ability to understand abstract concepts. At this stage children begin to consider the possible consequences of their actions. They start to develop the capacity to manipulate information, use deductive reasoning and strategically plan.

Orange values are prevalent in the western world. Capitalism thrives on them. It is thinking and behaviour in service of Orange values that has created so much innovation, wealth and opportunity in the world. However, it is also these same values that allowed excess human greed to bring the world economy crashing to its knees. People expressing peak Orange values may be able to predict the consequences of their actions, but if they can get away unscathed, they won't feel guilty if others suffer as a result.

When in love, an Orange partner is often highly inventive and progressive but can sometimes behave in Machiavellian ways. They are driven to succeed at all costs. Orange can be challenging when conflict occurs within a relationship as they may only be concerned with themselves and merely see their partner's emotion as a weakness. On the positive side, the Orange partner wants the best of everything and will work hard to make sure they get it. Life is all about keeping up with the neighbours, exceeding expectations and striving towards constant achievement.

Being so competitive, entrepreneurial and expressive, Orange partners are often highly skilled communicators with a front foot physical attitude. Because they tend to always be looking out for the next opportunity, they often have an underlying physical restlessness. Orange expects both themselves and their partner to always be on top of their game and looking their best. They may even start looking elsewhere for a partner if they feel standards of self-presentation and physical attractiveness are slipping!

A person expressing Orange values physically would most likely have a highly developed self-awareness and the ability to mirror and match the energy levels and body language of others in order to manage communication and gain the advantage. An Orange-inspired dress code would include high fashion and exclusive styles bearing designer labels.

Emotionally, Orange people are proactive and impulsive. They can often be emotionally independent and self-centred, making it difficult to get close to them. They express occasional sympathy but have little genuine empathy. While seeming to need validation and often requesting feedback, they rarely act on any response that does not support their own agenda and self-perception. A person with high Orange energy thrives on a connection with others, but only if you are helping them acquire and achieve success. Ultimately, they will disconnect once you cease to be of use.

Negative Orange emotion includes distrust, ruthlessness, insensitivity or even a lack of emotion. On the plus side, they exhibit self-confidence, are entrepreneurial and innovative, have high levels of personal drive and are often positively contagious. Their daily mantra might be, 'What's the next bright idea?

Thinking from an Orange perspective means looking for the next big thing. Experimenting with current knowledge and concepts, their intelligence drives them towards the discovery and creation of innovations in order to beat the competition and stand at the leading edge.

Seeking to create niches, thoughts are focused on ideas that support autonomy, personal ambition and individualism. The mind in service to Orange enjoys applying itself to risk and change that leads to progress and material gain. Science, knowledge and inquiry are valued over faith, belief and religion. However, unhealthy Orange thinking may ignore vital information, offer up only partial truths and manipulate data in the pursuit of results.

Orange spirituality is often expressed as secular humanism and is centred around mastering the material world and the mechanical laws of nature. Positive Orange wants to make the world a healthier, better-educated and safer place for those that can afford it. If you work hard, the rewards are not in heaven but right here on earth. Unhealthy Orange will disregard or even reject dogmatic religions and mock 'soft and fluffy' new-agers.

Green stage — 'We' orientated

Along the spiral from the more self-serving, materialistic Orange perspective, we move into the sharing and caring Green values stage. This value set is relativistic, communal, sharing, affiliate and consensual – very much about 'we'.

Someone expressing Green will seek unity and authenticity in their lives. They prefer collaborative, cooperative interactions with a focus on ethics and morality. Green thrives on harmony, empathy and love. There is an emphasis on joining together with others across nations and cultures for mutual growth as one big, global family. Everyone is welcome and everyone's opinion is right. This value set embraces diversity and seeks to help others realise their potential.

However it's not all 'green' and fluffy as unhealthy Green pluralism can lead to debilitating levels of political correctness and the inability to lead or make tough but important decisions. Also, people expressing Green values can be so overly trusting and blinkered in their belief that all people are kind and sharing that they can end up being easily exploited by others.

Green relationships are the archetypal touchy feely, warm and cuddly, lovey-dovey experience. A Green partner will seek a close and loving relationship . . . with everyone. Honesty, authenticity and trust are highly valued, and you can expect some serious sharing, caring and long-term communal living. Your Green partner will have an open home policy together with a 'What's mine is yours and vice versa' agenda. There are no proprietorial rights – everything belongs to everyone in the Green house.

Most people expressing this value will be physically inclusive, open and comfortable around others, unless high Orange or Red values start to upset the group. If that happens, someone with Green values may feel nervous or physically distressed. But if all is agreeable, Greens will enjoy the physical presence of others.

They are far more inclined than other value systems to get into close proximity with others and embrace people – be they friends or strangers.

Able to quickly establish a rapport, people in Green will often display a relaxed, informal posture and dress sense. Their clothing is likely to be an eclectic mix of styles, perhaps favouring ethically sourced fabrics or recycled items. Even though Green has experienced all previous values, they may look at Orange and Blue and see high fashion or strict dress code as a waste of time, money and energy. They have a whole new way of thinking now. External physical appearance doesn't matter that much. It's the inner world of self that is important.

For the most part Green will put their focus on people and the environment. Their emotional drivers are all about bonding with and supporting others, selflessness, inclusiveness and sharing. They have high levels of tolerance and, in disputes, being liked and accepted is more important than winning.

Negative expressions of Green include excessive permissiveness, lack of self-assertion and over-emphasising equality. This can lead to an inability to recognise, and intervene in, situations when emotional abuse takes place.

Green believes all knowledge is equal – none being any better than any other, simply different. In this mind-set, the primary driver is for cohesion and acceptance and, therefore, non-linear and lateral thinking is valued above logical and rational thought. Green reaches decisions through reconciliation and consensus, though a down-side might be a lack of discernment in terms of the real value of ideas and information. Everyone and everything is equal and right in Green.

A Green partner will want to accept and embrace all types of spirituality and religions as well as new-age beliefs, whether it's

Christianity, Islam, Judaism, Hinduism, Sikhism, Scientology, paganism or vampirism, or it involves crystals, tarot, wicca, reiki, yoga, drumming, incense or free-form dancing. Anything goes as far as Green is concerned.

Moving through the spiral

As our values develop along the spiral, each transcends and includes the previous value. We may find ourselves at different stages on the spiral at different stages in our lives. At any one time, a certain value set will be more dominant and a shift in values can be brought about through a global or personal crisis, or perhaps through a more long-term period of personal growth.

For example . . .

▸ Shaun Casey was a happy family man expressing dominant Purple values, until the terrorist attacks on the Twin Towers on 9/11. Shaun suddenly shifted along the spiral into Blue and was compelled to join the military and serve his nation in the fight against terror. His values shifted up-spiral overnight – from family and security to nation and honour.

▸ A London-based trader called Jeremy went into a personal crisis after the financial meltdown of 2008. Suddenly seeing only futility and selfishness in his previous job, Jeremy left the city and took up work as a teacher. In the space of a few critical weeks, his values had moved from an Orange value set of personal ambition and material gain up spiral to a Green value set of helping and nurturing others.

▸ We can of course also down-spiral, as the disaster of Hurricane Katrina showed us. Hundreds of families and individuals found themselves thrust from their everyday lives into a situation of chaos and fight for survival. The atrocities that occurred over that time only went to show how quickly our values can shift from being caring towards our neighbour (Green) to self-survival at any cost (Red).

Dr Don Beck has been using the theory of Spiral Dynamics to broker peace across the world including working along side Nelson Mandela in the 1980s. It has been acknowledged by FW De Klerk that Dr Don played a fundamental role in bringing about change and peace in South Africa.[13] Dr Don is currently applying the theory of Spiral Dynamics Integral in the Middle East – working with groups of young Israelis and Palestinians. The theory and practice of Spiral Dynamics is working towards peace between peoples and nations all over the world. Imagine what it could do for your relationship!

CHAPTER 5

The Rainbow Perspective

The next stage . . .

Once we have understood and experienced the values from Purple to Green, there is a whole new perspective we can take that will move our relationships to the next level of understanding. We call this the rainbow perspective.

The rainbow perspective is less about living in service of a set of values, and much more about taking a new perspective that takes into account all the other value sets. In other words this is about recognising your partner's current values and being able to adapt your thinking and behaviour to meet them wherever they are.

The Rainbow Persepective — 'Me' orientated

From here people can see the importance of their partners values, even if they are different from their own. As a result, they now have an objective perspective and are able to spiral along the five value sets from Purple to Green.

Someone operating from the rainbow perspective understands that all the values along the spiral, are valid, but they don't feel the need to get locked into any single one of them. They acknowledge that they need to take different value perspectives depending on where they are, who they're dealing with and what they're trying to achieve.

Whatever kind of relationships we are in, it can be extremely challenging when we're faced with other people holding belief systems and worldviews that differ from our own.

Even the most rational of individuals can suddenly become irrational and angry when someone confronts them with an entirely different outlook or tramples on their values. Our main challenge, of course, is that we are often only able to understand feelings and thoughts based on the perspective of our own values, beliefs and worldview.

When it comes to relationships, this can often make communication between couples who have different values somewhat challenging. But *not* impossible, especially once you take the rainbow perspective.

The reason I decided to write *Spiral into Love* was not only down to the emerging theories and understanding of scientists, sociologists, philosophers and psychologists on love and happiness. It was also down to my personal understanding – and how far that has come!

Having experienced a number of relationships, having been on the search for love and happiness all my adult life, I now understand more than ever what it takes to make even the most challenging of relationships thrive. And what's wonderful is that we can have it all – the fairytale and the reality – if we understand how we can make it happen.

The fact is, people are easier to understand if we take a moment to stop and work out what's driving them. Research has revealed that while most of us can be motivated to take action for financial gain and reward, human beings are even *more* motivated to do something if it has intrinsic value for them[14] – in other words, if something is perceived to be in alignment with our own core values. As people are more inclined to engage with a person, place or thing if they are intrinsically motivated, it is important to understand which values are active within your partner – and indeed yourself – because that's the quickest route to the longest lasting love.

CHAPTER 6

The Gender Issue

Just before we look at how these value systems combine within relationships, I want to very quickly address one important issue – and explain why I won't be addressing it throughout the rest of this book! That issue is how men and women communicate.

A huge amount has been written about whether men and women speak a different language,. But as we reach for another copy of another bestseller telling us another reason why men and women will never understand each other, the fact is we never have the full picture.

When it comes to media journalism and literature on inter-gender communication, the books that sell tend to pit men and women against each other in a battle for the perfect relationship. However, quite often any relevant information in these books that is pulled from research studies will include only isolated elements that demonstrate how some men and some women occasionally interpret language differently. To say men and women speak an entirely different language is over-simplified and inaccurate.

For a more detailed exploration of the wonderful world of how men and women communicate, I refer you to Deborah Cameron's book *The Myth of Mars and Venus*. Cameron's insightful look at some of the broader truths and more in-depth analysis surrounding communication between the genders exposes much of what we believe to be untrue.

That's not to say books expounding the differences between the sexes aren't helpful. There are plenty of useful hints and tips to be had from them and, when it comes to the complexity of human relationships, if anything is genuinely useful then grab it with both hands! Feet too, if necessary! As John Lennon said, 'Whatever gets you through the night'. However, it is also worth being open to a wider truth. A truth that might be very useful indeed.

It's all too easy to make it a blanket rule that men and women communicate in entirely different ways. That simple belief provides a quick answer as to why men and women experience irritations, arguments, conflicts and divorce when it comes to their relationships. But then one might ask: Why do gay couples argue? Why do sisters argue? Brothers? Daughters and mothers? Fathers and sons? Best friends? Flatmates? Our ability to live in close and intimate proximity with someone and effectively communicate with them on a daily basis can't only be about gender.

I live just round the corner from the Arsenal FC stadium in London. I see fans interacting every other weekend during the season. When it comes to a Man U vs Arsenal fixture, male and female Gunners supporters will have more in common, more camaraderie, more mutual understanding and more loyalty than a male Arsenal supporter and another male United supporter. The Purple value set will understand and respect their own tribe before they understand and respect their own gender. Most of our interactions are about values, and much less about gender.

A woman giving birth will have far more likelihood of necessary and easy communication with her male nurse in that moment than with the female hospital administrator who wants only to record dates, times and birth statistics. We are usually more role, context and value driven than we are gender driven.

The truth is, our relationships are about more than simply understanding how to communicate with a member of the opposite sex. Otherwise, why are we not all still with our first boyfriend or girlfriend? If it's only a question of dealing with the gender 'divide' and everything else is equal, then perhaps we would have stuck with the first relationship we had.

If all we need to do is understand how men and women communicate differently then I guess we can all learn to get on with anyone we happen to land in a relationship with. What's more, if relationship difficulties are only about the gender communication divide, presumably gay couples must live in a permanent state of euphoria!

It's easier to blame any differences on different communication styles rather than different opinions or values, but we're better at this cross-gender communication thing than perhaps we care to admit. We all know how to decode phrases that our loved ones say to us. If a wife says to her husband, 'The bathroom shelf needs fixing', he's very clear she means either 'Can you fix the bathroom shelf?' or, 'Can you get someone in to fix the bathroom shelf?' Few men really believe his wife is merely relaying information to him about the current state of the bathroom shelf. In truth, we're all expert decoders. Men know how to decode, 'Did you know it's Valentine's Day next Wednesday?', as much as women can decode, 'It's not you, your bum's tiny, it's the weird cut of the dress.' If a wife says the shelf needs fixing and her husband doesn't understand her, he's probably choosing to avoid the issue because he doesn't want to get out his Black and Decker on a Friday night. That may well be fair enough, but this 'miscommunication' isn't about language difference, it's about a difference in needs, values and desires.

If we want to spiral into a long-lasting life of love, it's time to move on. It's time to really understand the dynamics that inform our relationships and what we can do to bring further happiness and success to our lives. And that's exactly what we're about to do!

So now we understand a little more about how these value systems affect our worldview and day-to-day behaviour, it's time to explore how each of them react to one another when they are in a relationship together. A Purple/Red relationship dynamic for example is very different from an Orange/Green relationship.

But now, in order to assess and learn about your own personal value set, it's time to take the Spiral Profiler questionnaire (see page 259).

You can also get your partner to take the profiler, but don't worry if that's not possible, or you haven't met them yet! As you read through the combinations and consequent dynamics of the value pairings, you will be begin to be able to recognise certain behaviours and speech patterns that tell you where your partner or potential partner may be. Just to remind you, when we look at each spiral pairing, we will explore:

1) **Dating and early romance** – giving you a chance to assess a potential partner right from the word go or, indeed, remember how it was between you and your current partner when you dated.

2) **Long-term and marriage** – an exploration of the current or future dynamic of the relationship will enable you to deal with and lessen any conflict as well as create long-lasting harmony.

3) **Kids and family** – understanding how you and your partner approach parenting will help you consciously choose the impact you want to have on your children.

4) **Friends and social life** – will be having more of an impact on your relationship than you might think. None of us live in isolation.

5) **Money** – because who doesn't argue about this?!

6) **Sex** – taking a look at how we can get our sexual needs met as well as trying to help meet those of our partner based on how we understand each other's values . . . Sex can be the central core along which you can start to spiral into love.

The Spiral Pairings

Now you have a profile of your own values, it's time to look at the value combinations in the spiral pairings. This will show you how your values will impact on your relationship, depending on the value set of your current or potential partner. You will be able to recognise your relationship dynamics and identify the patterns your value systems create in your relationship as well as understand why your particular relationship dynamic plays out the way it does. Afterwards we will take a more in-depth look at the Rainbow Perspective and explore how to manage each partnership towards a deeper and richer experience of love.

While you are reading the following combinations, do keep in mind that the examples drawn for you are couples expressing *one* dominant value set each. This is to help you get a full understanding of the peak phase of each of the values and how they complement or clash in the context of a loving relationship. In reality, while we can live in service of one, dominant set of values, we may express all the five values, at differing levels of intensity, depending on who we are, where we are, what's happening and who we are with.

With that in mind, do take the time to read about all the value pairings, not just the ones relating to your own and your partner's current Spiral Profiler results. As you and your partner shift and change, or as you enter whole new relationships, these other pairings will contain useful information and insights to guide you in the future, as well as help explain past events!

CHAPTER 7

Purple and Purple

BLOOD IS THICKER THAN WATER.

Dating and early romance

When two people with dominant Purple values meet and fall in love it's truly magical. They will both feel that something mysterious has happened and it can only be that there are magical forces of nature at work behind the scenes. These two won't have time for rational explanations about love, based on some scientific laws of attraction to do with some hormone called oxytocin. No, this love can't be written in a neuroscience book. This love is written in the stars. It wasn't the biological laws of human attraction that brought them together, it was the secret, magnetic laws of nature. It was the intention of the universe. It was fate, destiny and a sprinkling of magical fairy dust. Their guardian angel Seraphiel probably had a hand in it too.

Before a couple in Purple initially go out together, the first thing they will probably discuss is their star signs. Depending on their age, they will then either take out Mark Husson's *Lovescopes* or a battered copy of Linda Goodman's *Love Signs* to check whether they are astrologically compatible. Once they've verified that Aries and Cancer can successfully interlock their ram horns and crab claws into a fulfilling, long-term zodiac relationship, they'll agree to date. Until someone in Purple knows whether their new partner's Venus is rising, nothing that rhymes with Venus is going anywhere.

Two Purple lovers will attach all kinds of weird and wonderful meanings to their new-found love. This will make them feel very special. They have, after all, been brought together by some kind of very special magical force. They will love to spend their first few days together looking back over the possible moments when they nearly but didn't quite meet, places they've both been but at different times and strange coincidences that didn't, might have or oh-so-nearly-did bring them together. They will marvel at the enchanted powers of unknown spirits who simply must have known that these two lovers needed to be brought together – it was meant to be.

'*You know, the night we met, I very nearly decided to not go out,*' Penny Purple exclaims.

'*Yes, and I remember I nearly went to an entirely different pub,*' Purple Paul replies.

'*But, something was telling me to go out, like I was meant to go . . .*'

'*I know. It was like . . .*' And just before she can finish her sentence, Paul joins her in a destiny-filled chant of unison: '*We were meant to be together.*'

Ahh, they sigh. It's good to know you have a guardian angel to guide you through life.

For our magical Purple lovers, the heady days of early romancing will be filled with significance and meaning. They will lavish tokens and gifts on each other to symbolise their unique and special love. A daisy bestowed on a picnic together will be carefully pressed in between the pages of *Harry Potter* or *Spells for the Twenty-first Century* and kept forever. Wallets, purses and dressing tables will soon fill up with photos, poems, charms, trinkets and amulets – mystical and priceless tokens of this magical union.

People in Purple are sometimes very good at hiding their deep-rooted superstitions under a thin veil of logic or science, but listen carefully for those tell-tell phrases about the red sky at night, touching wood, coincidences and destiny – and if you're both doing it then you know you're entering into a dominant Purple/Purple relationship.

But magic and superstition aren't the only powerful forces that bind these two together. When two lovers in Purple find each other, they both understand the importance of those close to them. Most spiral value pairings have a certain order of doing things when it comes to dating. They'll initially date for a while, see if they like each other enough and then decide to introduce their new partner to their parents and immediate family. Purple on Purple, however, do the dating thing in reverse. They will immediately introduce each other to the parents and extended family, check the level of approval and *then* decide whether or not to continue dating.

Purple embodies the archetypal family values. Family comes first. The family's approval of a partner makes for a better relationship. Blood is thicker than water, and this relationship will go nowhere until both sides of the family bless the pairing. Luckily both share the same values so both will want to belong to each other's tribe.

Both Paul and Penny Purple will be happy to sit for hours on end with Penny's great aunt Jess or Paul's cousin Viki, staring at endless family photos of countless family members through the ages. They both know the importance of respect for and investment in the family unit. If the family approves, the signs are good. So, after a toss of the rune stones, one last glance into the crystal ball and a visit to Mystic Mary for a final laying of the tarot cards, these two may very well decide they were meant to be together forever.

Long-term and marriage

Purple adores a wedding. A wedding brings together the family, the close (and often old) friends and all those ancient rituals and superstitions that Purple simply loves. Whether it's a druid ceremony at Stonehenge, a big fat gypsy wedding or a good, old knees up down the local pub, a Purple wedding will have all the trappings of ritual, luck and traditions passed down through the family – something old, something new, something borrowed and something blue. With a generous smattering of plastic silver horseshoes for good luck.

Even if this wedding takes place in an official building like a church, synagogue or town hall, it will be more about the ritual than the religion. There'll be no peeking at the bride the night before the wedding because this value code is all about superstitions, omens and signs of bad luck. Everything is given a meaning. If it rains on their wedding day it will definitely mean something more than a little too much precipitation has gathered in the atmosphere. It could well be a sign that their marriage is doomed to failure before it has even begun. Until, that is, they're reminded it rained on Uncle Ted and Aunt Judith's wedding day and they had four healthy children and not one day's unhappiness in forty-five years of marriage. Sometimes rain can be lucky. Especially in June, in a leap year, during a full moon and when the solar system is aligned with the Sagittarius dwarf stream. Phew.

Luck features heavily at the Purple stage. Lucky that they get on so well. Lucky that they like the same kind of holidays. Lucky they both like the same kind of films. Lucky that they met. How lucky they will feel in those early days of marriage. They both value a tight-knit family group and they'll both love this new sense of belonging to someone.

Penny Purple really values marriage. *'I didn't think it would feel differently actually being married, but it does. I actually feel different. I feel whole, complete. I feel like I'm now part of my own unit, like this is what I've been waiting to feel my entire life. I can't really explain it. I just feel like it all suddenly makes sense.'*

Along with their trusted circle of friends they've known since childhood, this couple is very likely set for life. Once they decide to commit long-term, they will already have everything they need. They aren't looking to meet new people or explore the world. They have their family, friends and one or two holiday destinations they'll go to for the rest of their lives – as a family.

Every relationship is unique and each relationship is about what's important to those involved. What's important to two people living in Purple is that they both value security and familiarity. They're both a bit wary of new people, places and things and will gather evidence to support these feelings.

'Look at Kate and Tim down the road. They suddenly booked that adventure holiday to Thailand last year and look where they both ended up – Kate in a two dollar a night beach hut with a dose of dysentery and Tim in some dodgy bar catching ping pong balls out of a lady boy's bottom. Kate's just filed for divorce. New isn't always good.'

Purple people don't talk about 'I', they talk about 'we'. Keeping their partner happy and maintaining a solid home life are priorities for them both. These two won't hesitate in making sacrifices for the sake of the other and either would give their last crust of bread to their partner rather than scoff it themselves. Together they will build themselves a stable, loving and protected home life. The focus will very much be on the home, the relationship and the family. They'll spend their evenings decorating the house, their bank holidays at Ikea and their weekends popping to see the in-laws. There is potentially a great deal of agreement between these two. From kitchen colour schemes to taste in fashion, these two will usually agree, or work hard to agree and make most decisions together. In time, after consulting their horoscopes and intuitions, the Purple couple will be ready to fulfil their ultimate destiny together. They're now ready to have children.

Kids and family

There's nothing more important to a Purple couple than family and children. This is the reason they exist. To bring children into the world and continue the family name and tribal ways is the very meaning of life. Purple values are connected to deep and ancient emotions. If a couple has any trouble conceiving a child, Purple emotions will often rise forcefully in them both.

Even if a couple needs to go through more scientific routes of IVF, they may stay in this highly emotional value set until they have been able to conceive. If they are unable to conceive, this powerful and deep-rooted value may drive them to sublimate their need for a family by having cats or dogs or nurturing life in some other way. If they don't have their own children, Purple individuals make absolutely wonderful aunts, uncles and godparents – so wonderful that they can become a fundamental part of their nieces, nephews or godchildren's lives.

But if and when a little one arrives, this newborn will be inundated with family visitors within hours of coming into the world. Grandmas, grandads, cousins, aunts, uncles, nieces and nephews will all be jostling at the hospital bedside to get a glimpse of the latest addition to their tribe. If these Purple relations could get away with it, they'd have all been in the birthing room – with the video camera for posterity. When the new little Purple baby finally arrives, they will be welcomed into their new world with an overwhelming amount of family love.

Even though this couple are now both parents in their own right, they won't necessarily establish themselves as the new heads of their own mini family tribe. When it comes to raising a family, a Purple couple can often struggle with parental leadership. They're used to deferring to their own tribal elders in the form of their parents or grandparents and the responsibility of being a role model to children can be a shock to new Purple parents. Their children can therefore often find themselves buffeted between the familiar cries of 'Listen to your father' and 'Go and ask your mother' before they shrug their shoulders and look for grandma. Grandma always knows best – just like Great Grandma Purple did before her.

That's the thing about being born into a Purple family – you're part of a long line of tradition. Another link in the genetic Purple chain. You won't necessarily be allowed your own identity. You may not be seen as a unique individual that's arrived in the world to make your mark. You're more likely to be seen as the reincarnation of one of your ancestors.

The whole family will be looking out for signs of exactly which one you're like. You don't need to find your own identity – because one familiar facial expression in front of Grandma and she'll soon tell you exactly who you are.

'Ooh that look on your face. You're just like your Great Grandmother Betty. She used to get that look in her eye, just like you. So stubborn. She had this weird habit of pulling on her earlobe to communicate with the dead. You're just like her.'

When all is said and done, a Purple couple will put their children before everything else. Absolutely everything. Whether their children are in the right or the wrong, whether their children break the law or hurt someone else, these Purple parents will always side with and support their children. Nothing comes between Purple and their children. Purple parents are not interested in reasoning with their children's school teachers over low grades or disruptive behaviour. Purple parents won't hear another parent's side to a dispute between their respective children. As far as Purple parents are concerned, the teacher needs to work harder and the rival parent should have taught their child to fight their own battles. It will never be the fault of Purple's child. Purple and their family unit will always stick together no matter what.

On the plus side, this of course makes for an incredibly supportive and loving foundation. Purple children will always have a very deep sense of belonging.

For a Purple couple, having children together is the ultimate bonding experience. The more roots they lay down together, the safer and more secure they will feel about the future. Purple's children are in many ways their social security and protection in old age. Where some value pairings can feel hemmed in or restricted by the bonds of parenthood, Purple adores this sense of belonging and togetherness. A Purple couple is never happier than knowing they and their children are bound to each other for the rest of their lives.

Friends and social life

It's very important to a couple expressing Purple values that they like and accept each other's friends. It will be extremely difficult for this partnership if they don't. Acceptance is of primary importance for both of them and neither is very good at managing or juggling difficult, tension-filled dynamics in their social circle. Everyone needs to get on and be on the same side. So both Purples will do their utmost to find a way to integrate and gain each other's approval of their tight-knit social lives. Once each has been accepted into the other's circle, their friends will provide a huge amount of support through the challenges and tricky times that any couple must face.

However, if one set of friends doesn't like their Purple friend's new partner, it can be problematic. These friends will tell Penny Purple exactly how awful her partner is and why she shouldn't be with them. This will create a huge conflict in Penny. It's almost impossible for someone with Purple values to divide loyalties and split their inner circle of trust. If this couple doesn't get on with each other's friends, it will potentially create a great deal of conflict within the relationship which can only go one of two ways – resolution and acceptance or division and separation. This couple will need to work hard to make sure the important people in each other's lives are accepted and integrated into one whole unit.

A Purple social life will be mostly limited to family and a small number of trusted friends within a very local community. Far from being claustrophobic, this close-knit, safe and trustworthy clan suits this couple just fine. They like it that way and have no desire to expand their horizons. This can make them appear unfriendly to outsiders, but until you prove trustworthy, that's just what they are – unapologetically wary. No one will successfully achieve a close relationship with a couple living Purple values unless they prove themselves over the long haul. Usually, the only way to be a part of Purple's tight circle is if you went to school with them, grew up with them, married them or gave birth to them. Protection of the clan is all, which means being careful who is allowed in. Anyone outside of this select group will always remain on the outside looking in. A casual acquaintance perhaps, but never a close friend.

So, peak Purple values won't allow Penny and Paul to stray too far when they socialise and they will usually be found in the same pubs, clubs and family homes on the same nights of every week. They like routine and familiarity. When they go down the local pub, the landlady won't have to ask what they want to drink, she already knows: the usual.

Money

This matching pair shouldn't have too much trouble when it comes to money. Purple values don't support big spending and are very risk averse. As for new business ventures . . . What? Partner up with a business colleague and take out a large bank loan to invest in an uncertain start up? There are way too many things wrong with that sentence for anyone living this value set to even contemplate it. A business colleague? Someone outside the family? Forget it. A bank loan? Banks can't be trusted. An uncertain start up? Why risk it when the family business has been running successfully for over fifty years?

Purple people will often go into business with a family member or work for the already established family business. They like to keep cash circulating within the tribe and Purple and Sons will make sure that money stays in the family. So bank loans will be avoided if at all possible. Our Purple couple are much more likely to go to their parents or grandparents for a loan than they are to their bank manager. Their relatives won't throw them out of the house if they default on their loan. That security suits Purple perfectly.

A Purple pairing is very likely to pool their resources. As more and more modern couples keep their finances separate, Purple values are all about the unit, not the individual. Both are happy to intertwine completely in each other's lives – emotionally, physically, domestically and financially. They don't value separation at any level. They will very much want to trust each other and sharing their finances is another symbol of this trust. It's not even a question of one helping the other out if the other doesn't have much money – any money belongs to the family unit. Neither of them is prone to fight for possession of something over their partner. Their relationship and the trust between them are far more important than anything else.

Purple values won't necessarily drive people to become millionaires – unless Daddy already is one – but that's okay. They don't need a lot. They're less likely to spend than make do and mend. There'll always be hand-me-downs and cast offs from sisters, brothers and cousins so they will never go without. Somehow the Purple family will always have enough.

Sex

Purple values are about belonging, relating and bonding, and the bedroom is where this couple can really show each other how they feel, all with the help of some well-placed candles, a couple of wind-chimes and maybe the odd sex spell or two. Purple loves a bit of ritual when it comes to sex and will often take time to prepare the scene for the magic that's about to come.

Purples tend to be very thoughtful, generous lovers when they put their mind to it. Together, these two can find a very deep connection. Sex represents more than just the physical to this couple. It represents their bond and commitment to one another. When these two have sex they can truly become one unit with no boundaries to divide them. A couple in Purple finds great peace and reassurance in feeling absorbed into each other. Sex is the perfect symbolic act of oneness for these two. Caring, sharing and fiercely loyal, these Purple lovers simply love to be together. Unlike many couples, they can even laugh about the day's events, the kids, the in-laws, the botched DIY in the bathroom and still find each other sexy.

However, they do need a bit of privacy. The thing to watch out for when it comes to sex is the rest of the family. The Purple household is so open that kids and relatives will come and go as they please with little concern for anyone's privacy. Any minute Grandad Jim might walk in to find Penny and Paul going full throttle and casually ask if they've seen his screwdriver. Children may suddenly burst in demanding a lift down the shopping centre or the mother-in-law will walk through the front door asking if she can borrow the ironing board. It's the rest of the family that can make it hard for this couple to put important time aside for themselves and their love life, but they should. They need to nurture each other, so that together they can renew the energy and strength they need to nurture the rest of their brood.

CHAPTER 8

Purple and *Red*

RELATIONS AND THE REBEL.

Dating and early romance

How can I put this? If you are living dominant Purple values, and you're about to start dating a person whose centre of self is in Red, then you'll need to watch out! I don't mean to give people with Red values a hard time, but no one is ever going to be more important to someone with Red values than they are to themselves. That's the bald truth of it. Even they would admit it. And that's fine. Nothing to feel guilty about – not that Red would waste their time with something so pointless as guilt. I just think lovers with dominant Purple values should know what they're getting into with Red.

Purple values are all about 'us', 'we' and 'the family'. Which couldn't be further from how a person living Red sees the world. So, Purple, just be sure you go into this relationship with your eyes open rather than wake up out of the romantic haze three years and one child on. People with strong Red values really should come with a health warning. Not that Purple will necessarily take any notice.

'I don't get it,' Purple Penny will say, *'I'm having so much fun. Richard Red is so charismatic and exciting. He doesn't need a health warning. I understand you might need a health warning on something like alcohol, because, you know, it's highly addictive and it can do you serious damage in the long term . . .'*

But that's just the point. A person living Red values can be highly addictive and, if not properly handled, could do damage to Purple's more sensitive and emotional nature in the long term. As the neuroscientific research from Chapter 1 revealed, feelings of love are connected to the same part of the brain that deals with addiction. Going out with a person living Red is a bit like going out for a fun-packed night of margaritas, tequila shots and crazed salsa dancing. It feels amazing at the time, almost intoxicating, but there's usually a stinking hangover the following morning.

But forewarned is forearmed. If Purple Penny goes into this relationship with her eyes open, life could get very exciting. In the short term a person predominantly at the Purple values stage could well have a fabulous time dating someone expressing Red. When an extravert person with dominant Red values is on form, they can be an all consuming and highly contagious presence – fun-loving, carefree, creative and spontaneous, they can draw you into their highly energetic field.

Even a more introverted person expressing Red can be an intense and powerful partner – just the kind of strong presence Purple people often look for in a partner. As for the Reds, they will love the attention that a Purple partner is happy to give them. Purple values don't usually motivate people towards the limelight, so they are happy to sit back and let Red take centre stage.

This usually suits both parties, and for that reason the Red and Purple combination can make ideal dating partners. Richard Red can call the shots and dictate where they go and when. He will also be able to cancel dates and let Purple Penny down without too much repercussion. Penny initially won't want to make a fuss.

But at some point Penny will want Richard to come and meet the family. This might be the moment Richard makes a swift exit. For someone in Red, family usually represents commitment, ties and expectations, none of which Red values are drawn to.

If they do decide to meet the parents, they may well make a very good first impression. People manifesting behaviours motivated by Red values have every chance of winning over Purple parents – if they want to! If Richard Red is in a good mood on that all-important first family visit, everyone will be taken in by his self-assured charm and charisma – and Purple Penny seems so happy.

'Ahh, those two seem so good together,' warbles Grandma Purple over the lemon drizzle cake, *'and Richard seems to fit right in with us.'*

But Grandma P needs to look a little closer. Richard Red isn't paying any attention to that family photo album she's trying to show him. Richard couldn't care less that Great Aunty Reenie has successfully come through her fifth hip operation and is utterly disinterested in Grandma P's acting career on the amateur stage in 'Annie get Your Gun' for the Padstow Players all those years ago. In fact, for the last half hour Richard Red has been doing a performance of his own. It's entitled, 'Me, Myself and I' – a highly entertaining monologue in three acts spread over a lifetime.

But when Purple people become intoxicated by the Red energy, they can sometimes ignore these signs – particularly when caught up in the maelstrom of confusing emotions that early dating brings.

Red people will initially flirt, excite and say whatever necessary to impress and win Purple's affections. Purple Penny will marvel at the risks Richard Red takes to express his love and desire. He seems to want her so much. This is the real deal. Penny feels she's found her provider and protector but . . . once Richard has won her, the battle may well be over. Purple Penny needs to be careful; once Richard has won the prize, his Red values may drive him to seek out the next challenge. Like bored toddlers, people at the Red values stage are always looking for a new game to play. An early relationship with a person driven by such a high level of egocentricism will nearly always end very abruptly.

The best thing Purple Penny can do is keep a bit of her heart for herself, because just when everything seems to be going swimmingly between her and Richard, one morning she may wake up and find her Red hot lover has gone. No warning. No forwarding address. Not so much as a Post-it note.

But Purple Penny shouldn't be too sad. She's probably had the best that Richard Red could offer. With his dominant Red values, he is unlikely to fulfil her need for stability, familiarity and group loyalty. So perhaps leaving a relationship with a Red person as a fun, if somewhat turbulent, memory is for the best.

Now Penny can go and find someone who can give her the love and security she really needs while Richard can go and enjoy his next romantic, action adventure. However, Reds might want to bear in mind there may well come a day when they too will want to find someone with whom they can feel safe. Romantic whirlwinds can get exhausting – even for the most Red of values.

Long-term and marriage

What if Richard Red was finally ready to settle down after all? Well, maybe not *settle* but certainly set up a life with his family-orientated Purple lover. For her part, Penny has decided to risk her happiness on a partner living in service of peak Red values. Even though Richard's egocentricism will ensure he will always be the star of the show, Penny has understood how to make it work and draw on his energy to serve her own needs, but she'll need to stay strong and keep her eyes open. Then all will be well on this exciting adventure they've just signed up for!

One thing that can be said about a long-term relationship with a partner in Red – you won't ever be bored. Red values can manifest some extremely impulsive and highly whimsical behaviour. Their plans, not to mention their moods, may change dramatically from moment to moment.

The truth is, though, that a Purple partner wouldn't mind a bit of boredom sometimes. As we have discovered, Purple values are about security, safety, routine and family. Red values are about independence, status, power and themselves. Penny wants to be loved and protected.

Richard wants to be wild and impulsive. Penny needs close proximity and bonding. Richard needs personal space and total freedom.

Penny will want to set up home near those she loves and fall into a routine with someone who will care for her, but Richard doesn't relish routine and won't let family ties bind him. On top of which, Red likes to be in charge. If Richard wants to move away from the family area, that's what these two will do. Penny needs to find a way to make sure her own needs are met in this relationship as much as possible.

A little advice for all you Purple values people: being in a relationship with a Red partner is the perfect example of when you need to check with yourself that you are creating as much of your own happiness as possible. The more you can make sure your own values are honoured, the easier this pairing will be – by meeting your own value needs, you will place considerably less unrealistic expectations on your Red partner. Otherwise everyone loses. Purple needs will be left unmet, you will end up disappointed with Red and your Red partner will end up furious that you feel disappointed with them.

Purple will need to look at their Red values partner as just that – a partner. Not someone who is responsible for Purple's own life, security and well-being. Red values will create an exciting dynamic in this relationship, but if Purple wants a stay-at-home, solid, reliable, family-orientated person then they will probably be disappointed – and Red hates to feel like they are a disappointment.

As with any partner, and particularly a Red partner, the key to making this union a success is to look at what Red brings to the relationship as opposed to what they lack. If your Red lover (male or female) feels they aren't meeting someone's expectations, they'll be gone in a heartbeat – off to find someone who appreciates them. Red might not put their Purple partner first much of the time – Richard Red might even forget Purple Penny's birthday, but he will definitely live life to the full doing what he wants, when he wants and however he wants to do it. If Purple Penny is prepared to be strong and take care of herself to a great extent, the ride with Richard could be a lot of fun.

Back to family matters. If Penny places her emotional needs and desire for family time on Richard, this relationship could become very frustrating for both of them. Richard needs space – mentally and physically. He may well want to be left alone when Purple Penny insists they go to yet another family barbecue. If she lets his need for independence get to her, she may end up feeling neglected. If she keeps insisting that he should be more present, supportive and involved with friends and family, Richard will feel totally hemmed in.

What Penny must avoid doing at all costs is telling Richard he should be 'more like the fantastic, caring, kind, considerate partners that her friends and relations all have'. Those kind of words are the very worst Red rag to a very volatile Red bull. Be they male or female, the last thing a person with a Red centre can tolerate hearing is that someone is better, more adequate, more successful, more *anything* than them. If reminders of inadequacies become a pattern here, the Red partner will eventually detach from the relationship entirely. A Purple partner will need to do all they can to keep the Red ego safe and healthy.

In this paring, Richard needs to go easy on Penny. Purple values can be extremely sensitive to direct one-to-one conflict. If Richard needs some space, and if he doesn't want to spend the weekend helping her decorate the living room, there are ways to communicate that to Penny without shattering her world. Richard would do well to find ways to make Penny feel loved, and try to make it clear he needs space for his own well-being and therefore the well-being of the relationship. If possible, he needs to communicate to her that he wants to be the best he can be for both of them, but that he must be allowed to be himself.

Penny's Purpleness is more likely to make her respond to a need for support and collaboration than a blunt rejection.

If a person at the Red stage is capable of making any compromise at all, they might let their Purple lover down with a smile and a cuddle rather than a short, sharp snap. Otherwise, this pairing can end up being a match made in hell for both parties.

The challenge for two people with Purple and Red values in a long-term relationship is that they see the world in completely polar opposite ways. While Purple values sit very firmly in the 'We' position, Red values couldn't be more firmly in the 'I' position. As these two look ahead down the aisle of life and wonder where it will lead, there are two very different minds at work. Purple Penny might be thinking,

'We'll go together', but Richard Red is very much an 'Ego alone'. For Penny, life is a journey to be taken together in a bonded family unit of love and trust. For Richard, it's a one-person mission that will take him wherever he needs to go, regardless of anyone else.

Richard might well buy a house with Penny, take a vow of marriage with her, and even agree to father children. All of those things smack of total commitment, right? Maybe for Penny they do, but for Richard all those things are simply actions, happenings, incidentals and events along the way down his own unique path of life.

That's not to say Richard doesn't love Penny very much. It's just that his Red values version of love is conditional on him feeling happy, free and independent. Ironically, the more independent Penny can ensure Richard feels, the more likely he is to do the things she wants him to do and the more likely it is Penny will feel more secure. Purple Penny simply needs to be clever and covert about how she goes about communicating her own needs, and she must always remember there needs to be something in it for Richard.

People living Red values are most at ease around compliant admirers, so anyone in a relationship with Red needs to hold their own and make sure they don't tip over into becoming a sychophantic slave. Unfortunately, a large proportion of abusive relationships are based on the dynamic of this value pairing, but a little Red ego stroking will ensure a happy household.

As anyone who has experienced a Red partner will know (or will quickly learn), there's just no point trying to fight a partner energised by a Red centre of self. In any argument, Red values will drive a need to win at all costs. Red will fight to the death to save face and avoid humiliation. They'll never take the blame and never admit they were wrong about anything. In fact they'll project all the blame onto others. In the extreme, this value set leads to narcissism (excessive self-love or vanity), and at its worst, psychopathology (self-centred pathological deviation from normal behaviour).

As I said, a relationship between Purple and Red holds many challenges. However, the relationship can succeed if both parties are aware of the other's needs. If they can both look at the positives they each bring to the partnership and are able to discuss possible compromises, they will be able to energise and hold each other in a dynamic, mutually beneficial relationship. In reality, most compromises will be down to Purple. 'Compromise' is not a word a person operating at Red really computes. If you are a Purple people-pleaser then be prepared to make big, generous, one-sided compromises for a life with your Red hot lover.

But when in a relationship with Richard Red, Purple Penny actually has something very strong and very important to help her along this all-consuming path: Penny's strong family network will be invaluable to her throughout their life together. It is within the warm familiarity of the family that Penny can go to recharge. It is here that she can escape to fill up on all the loving, caring, sharing and sense of belonging that she needs.

So, all you Purples, if you really love your Red hot lover and want the relationship to last then give them all the space they need. Make as few demands on them as possible and place all your emotional and practical needs onto your close-knit family circle. They'll always be there for you, even when it doesn't feel like your Red partner is. Be warned though: Red values can cause your loved one to easily get jealous of the close relationships you have with your family members and try to prise you away from them. Hold firm and hold strong. You'll need your family if you're to make it through this partnership.

Purple values are never going to be able to change Red values and it would be a big mistake to think they will. All Purple can do is roll with the punches – and I sincerely hope they're not real ones.

Kids and family

So Richard and Penny have decided to have children. As we know, Red values are about living life in fast-forward and if there's one thing kids do to life, it's slam on the breaks. No more gallivanting or lazing around whenever you like. There are other little people to consider now, and Richard isn't necessarily going to like that very much.

Purple Penny may have initially looked at Richard's strength and independence and thought what great qualities they'd be when it comes to parenting children. *'Richard is so strong, so fiercely protective of me. I love how proud and determined he is. Think what an amazing father he'll become when all that strength is focused on our children.'*

It all looked very appealing in theory. Richard might like the idea of children as trophies of his own fertility – a little brood of Mini-Mes that others will admire – while Penny is convinced that once her rather self-centred partner has kids, he will melt and fall into parenthood, just as she can't wait to do.

The first few days after Penny gives birth will usually be fine, as long as there is no postnatal depression and she can keep telling Richard how thankful she is, how amazing he is and what marvellous genes he has given their child – all back slapping, Champagne and general cries of congratulations. But once the cameras have stopped flashing, Richard could quickly lose interest. As Penny revels in the most important bonding experience of her life, Richard realises he has just created his very own competitor for Penny's attention. What was he thinking? Taking responsibility for anyone, including babies, children, the sick and the needy, really isn't a Red values thing.

So, Penny may very quickly find herself in the role of single parent. Richard may suddenly become disturbed by the sight of stretch marks on Penny's once tight abdomen. He may even become overwhelmed by a need to escape the crying, the sleepless nights and the endless dirty nappies that baby-rearing involves. But not to worry – Penny, meanwhile, is overwhelmed with love for this little creature who can't survive without her. Penny has been waiting her whole life to have her own family and now she does, everything is wonderful in the world. Purple Penny's need to love, care and nurture now has a very clear focus. She will do everything she can to take care of this new addition to the tribe. On top of which, she will probably have siblings and cousins who will help out and possibly even parents who will move in.

Richard might not be a big fan of having the in-laws intruding in his space, but as he's also not a big fan of baby-changing and domestic chores, he might just suck it up. At least it gives Penny a bit more free time – time she can now spend turning her attention back onto attention-hungry Richard.

The key to the continuing success of this relationship depends upon Penny finding enough energy to stay partly focused on Richard. It's a lot to ask with a new baby, but this period of time is crucial. Penny needs to do all she can to keep Richard engaged and attached to her during this tiring period. A superhuman effort at this point will pay huge dividends for this partnership in the future.

In the meantime, Penny mustn't be surprised if the childish screams of 'I want it, it's mine, give it back' coming from the next room turn out to be Richard screaming at their two-year-old over who has possession of the TV remote. Richard Red will very much find his emotional match in his own two-year-old. There is an easy way for Penny to manage all of this – she simply needs to stop thinking of Richard as a grown up or co-parent and start thinking of him as another one of her toddlers or teenagers. Once she gives Richard just as much attention, just as much leeway and just as little responsibility as the children, everyone will get along fine.

In fact, of all the value systems, Purple has the best shot at making a family unit with Red function very well. People with dominant Purple values love to parent, love to provide and are happy with a little, or even a lot, of self-sacrifice. In the same way that those qualities are essential as a parent, they're equally essential when it comes to partnering someone with strong Red values. Better to tolerate Red's unpredictable behaviour and keep the family together, Purple mothers or fathers will reason. Otherwise Red might leave and Purple would be left alone, the family in ruins. Even the thought of that is unbearable to Purple. The breakdown of the family unit is a nightmare Purple will do almost anything to avoid.

Even though Richard won't always be on hand for day-to-day to parenting, nappy changing and homework duties, rest assured, if anyone ever threatens his brood they better watch out. A person living Red values isn't at a stage where they can easily control their emotions. If Penny or the children ever face potential danger, Red Richard will come down hard on the perpetrators. This is where Richard's Red values suddenly surface the behaviours that Purple Penny hoped for. When behaviours motivated by Red line up with Purple needs, they bring an extremely forceful energy to the party. With Richard on

Penny's side, both of them with the same goal in sight, these two both have one hell of a powerful team-mate.

When it comes to their children, Penny wants their brood protected from harm more than anything and Richard will make sure that happens. If the children of this pairing are ever bullied or threatened, it will only happen once. As soon as the school bullies find out little George's dad is a fierce Red warrior, they'll soon back off. And for Penny Purple that's a big point scorer and benefit of having a partner with Red values. The protection of the family is paramount. No one messes with the honour of Red's genetic line and gets away with it. When life turns into an action thriller movie, Red energy rises and comes to the rescue.

Most of the time, however, this couple, like everyone else, will live a relatively ordinary, everyday life where Red is more egoic than heroic!

Friends and social life

It's quite simple really. Purple Penny will see her close friends and family on a regular basis. Richard Red will turn up if and when he feels like it. When he does feel like it, Richard will be the life and soul of any party. That's the basic pattern of the Red and Purple social life. Purple people need other people around them. If they can't be with friends or family in person they'll be phoning, Skyping or texting them. They need to feel connected as much as possible. They need to belong and love being part of a group.

People with strong Red values don't need anyone and they certainly don't want to be part of a group. They're happy to be the central focus of the group's attention for a while but only when it suits them. One too many cries of 'Tell us that joke again', 'Sing that song', 'Tell that story', 'Make us laugh, go on you're hilarious' – and that old Red response will rise up and cause the classic fight or flight behaviours. They may suddenly withdraw, sulk or throw a tantrum. A Red warrior is no one's performing monkey. Neither are they too bothered about social niceties.

But hey, on the up side, if Richard does come to Penny's brother Tony's fiftieth bash, she will know it's because he wanted to be there.

At least you know where you are with Red. They won't hide their true feelings from anyone at anytime. No one ever has to worry that someone with Red values is doing anything they don't want to do – they'll soon let you know. When they've had enough, they'll quickly tell you that they're leaving, assertively making their position nice and clear. Red won't leave room for ambiguity. They'll simply the leave the room.

Money

As with most things in their lives, Purple Penny and Richard Red think very differently when it comes to money. Penny is more interested in security than spending and will mainly spend on others within her tribe. Richard is more interested in spending than security and will mainly spend on himself.

If Richard has money, he may spend it on whatever takes his fancy. It's not that his values make him materialistic in the way that Orange is, but he does seek instant gratification. Penny will be driven nuts as she plans for the family holiday or the kids' education only to come home and find Richard has suddenly bought himself anything from a Porsche to a pony. Spending can be whimsical for people hijacked by Red emotional energy. If Richard hasn't got the money, he'll find a way of getting it, even if it means squeezing it out of Penny's gullible and malleable family members.

'It's for a TV for the kids,' he'll tell Grandad Purple. *'They will insist on the latest in visual technology and customer interface.'*

'Goodness, three-year-olds are advanced these days,' thinks Grandad, as he unknowingly hands over a wad of cash to appease Richard's latest whim.

If Penny finds out she'll be furious. Richard has once again taken advantage of and trampled all over her most important values – the family. But she will probably keep quiet.

When it comes to Richard and money, she's learnt to pick her battles – and not pick very many at that. It's just not worth the days of sulking or shouting. She gets enough of that with the other kids. Anyway, if Penny's Purple values are healthy and active, she'll have a tidy stash of cash somewhere Richard will never find. Someone's got to think about the future.

All that being said, money is often the first area where someone in peak Red might begin to shift to Blue. A person motivated by Red values may demonstrate all the usual Red behaviours except when it comes to cash. Although it can seem like an anomaly, saving and being careful with cash is in fact very common with individuals at the Red stage. It is usually a sign that the person has begun to value a sense of future security knowing that their own future security also means their own survival.

Richard being more careful with cash would be a welcome shift for Penny as it would put this couple's values around money in much closer alignment. Either way Richard will want control over the finances – remember, money is all tied up with power and emotion. A Red value set will drive a need to be in charge. If Penny wants any say in money matters, she'll need to make sure she has her own income or find clever ways to stash some cash, though she need never really panic – her close family network will never let her go without.

Sex

While sex and love are all part of the bonding experience for Penny, for Richard sex and love are two very different things. Unsurprisingly, when it comes to sex, he will tend to focus on his own sensations and getting his own needs met. Penny is also focused on Richard's needs and will do all she can to bring him maximum pleasure in the bedroom. Penny is not demanding of Richard when it comes to sex and he likes it that way. With his inflated sense of self and need for instant gratification, he likes to have sex the way he wants it, whenever he wants it.

However, if Richard feels Penny is denying him sex or rejecting him in any way, he will take it deeply personally and possibly become irritable and aggressive towards her. Red values are very connected to the physical self and if hormones need releasing, they need releasing! For a few days after having sex, Red energy will still be dominant in Richard and possibly even aggressive, but it won't now be directed at

Penny. This energy is most active in the archetypal, alpha male who often feels powerful after sex and on some very deep level wants the world to feel how powerful they are.

Needless to say, Richard is an alpha male and is confident and autonomous in the bedroom. Initially, that dominance can be very sexy to Penny. All she needs now is a little romance and sex with Richard will be perfect, but romance takes up far too much time for Richard. Although Penny would ideally like love making to be sensual and magical, he may mock her mood lighting and scented candles and suddenly she won't feel quite as generous any more. Richard seemed so strong and sexy, but it's a short trip from confidence, autonomy and personal power to aggressiveness, intimidation and abuse.

Unless Penny remains robust and open and Richard remains engaged and excited, this sexual partnership can become fragile, particularly after they have had kids. Once children are on the scene, Penny has the family unit she needs but Richard is no longer getting the attention he craves. Penny must be careful to never ever let him feel sexually rejected. Underneath Richard's Red bravado lies a deep sensitivity when it comes to sex and being desired. A big ego can also be a delicate ego. Sexual rejection or indifference strikes at the very core of his being. If he feels rejected, the consequences will be huge – expect screaming and shouting or weeks of sulky detachment. Either way, be very clear: Red needs attention.

If Penny wants to avoid Richard going elsewhere to get that attention, she'll need to keep making him feel powerful, desired and sexy. When Richard feels consistently wanted and admired there may even begin to be a little space for the odd candle and a little more foreplay.

If Penny can remember to stroke Richard's ego at all the right times then he could well be stroking her in all the right places. Then whether she calls it sensual and romantic love making or he calls it raw, sexual lust – it won't matter. It'll be mind-blowing for both of them.

CHAPTER 9

Purple and Blue

IN-LAWS AND STRICT LAWS.

Dating and early romance

You never knew there were very strict rules to love, right? Well, you've clearly never dated someone living in service of Blue values. Dating a true Blue lover, you'll learn a whole heap of new stuff about love. There are set date nights, clear etiquette around calling or texting the other person back, standards about who should pay for dinner, time frames when parents should be introduced and a definite three-date rule around first having sex. Phew! There's so much to learn.

Dating a person who expresses Blue is more about correct procedure than impulsive spontaneity. That's not to say Blue values can't inspire romantic behaviour – on the contrary – but it will be romance according to the book, not sudden, rash gestures of love. People expressing Blue like to get things right.

When a Blue values person comes into Purple's life, they don't so much crash into it as make an appointment and show up on time.

People motivated by Blue values don't tend to sweep new lovers off their feet and embark on a fling of wild abandon. They're far more likely to ask nicely and pop a date in the diary for two weeks' time to take you for a drink. Blue values are all about rules, regulations and delayed gratification. No passion or emotion is going to interfere with any commitments Blue already has scheduled over the next fortnight.

Also, do note this first date is a drink, not dinner. You don't have dinner until the second date at the earliest. That would be sending out all the wrong messages, and Blue hates sending out the wrong messages. Anyway, what if you don't get on? You'd both have to wade through three painful courses, coffee and small talk knowing you were never going to repeat the experience. That would be so dishonest, and Blue can't abide dishonesty. Plus, it's not like you could leave a dinner date early just because it wasn't going well. You don't leave a date stranded and alone, however incompatible the two of you might be. That would just be rude. Blue will not tolerate rudeness; people should be treated with care and respect – which Purple people will love!

If you have strong Purple values, then kind, caring and considerate Blue behaviour has the capacity to make you feel more secure, more special and more utterly cherished than you've ever felt in your life. A romantic partner expressing Blue values is driven to be in control and take care of the situation. For the best of everyone, not just themselves. This isn't like Red who needs to control for their own personal power. Someone with a Blue value set controls in order to do the best and right thing for all concerned. A Purple partner will adore the strong guiding hand that a person living in accordance with Blue can offer. A romantic partner expressing Purple values loves to be taken care of. Perfect!

So far, Purple and Blue values are proving to be a gorgeous match, oozing with thoughtfulness, kindness and consideration. This is down to the fact that, in terms of the spirals, both Blue and Purple values are centred in the 'We' position. Therefore both of them value collaboration, assessing the needs of those around them and spending time with other people. Unlike Red, Blue and Purple people are very comfortable being part of a group. These two are not natural loners and they totally understand the other's need to spend time with friends and family. Early days of dating, therefore, won't necessarily be an isolated affair. This couple won't disappear into some kind of romantic isolation tank for the first few weeks.

Let's take Simon (predominantly driven by Blue) and Kate (serving Purple) for instance. They used to work together and have known each other for some time. They have always got on very well and what's more have always been highly attracted to each other.

Because they were work colleagues, Simon thought it inappropriate for them to take their friendship any further, but recently Kate has moved to a new office in another region. So, after a few drinks at her leaving party they decided to begin seeing each other.

Though they have begun dating, Simon has commitments, friends and obligations and so not much will be changing in his world. However, Kate is constantly updating friends and family on exactly where this new relationship stands. Every tiny detail of the relationship will be shared with Kate's close-knit group. She won't really feel she's experiencing anything real and meaningful unless the people she cares about are sharing it with her. Kate doesn't like keeping secrets from her loved ones.

Simon's Blue values can drive him to be a little more reserved, certainly on the more personal details – no one needs that kind of information! He would be shocked to know just how many people in Kate's world have a great deal of very intimate information about him. Apparently, everyone in Kate's world does need that kind of information! Of course, Kate's local world can often be a little smaller than Simon's wide Blue kingdom. Not to mention a little different in outlook and beliefs.

Simon feels he has so much to teach Kate – about how the world really works, how it is ordered around higher principles outside of the family or tribe, and how things could be improved even further if everyone would adhere to the rules that he abides by. Kate has never really thought about society in this way. As far as she is concerned, as long as the people she loves are healthy and prospering, that's all she needs to know.

As they begin to consider each other as potential life partners, Simon may soon be disturbed by Kate's Purple attitude. He may feel that she needs to think a little more responsibly about society and the nation they live in.

Simon and Kate may not quite see eye to eye when it comes to the fundamental questions around what's important in life and how the world operates, but it might not matter.

Kate's Purple values offer Simon a very unique kind of partnership. Someone that he can love and cherish and build a life with? Yes, but also someone he can teach, shape and organise, and that's pretty much every box ticked as far as a person living at peak Blue is concerned.

As for a person at peak Purple, if they've fallen in love with Blue and Blue then takes charge and sorts them out, it can feel like the safety and security Purple has longed for has at last arrived. They will be dying to take Blue home to meet their parents. They will of course have to wait until Blue feels an appropriate amount of time has passed and the relationship is solid enough. After all, Simon Blue would hate to meet Kate Purple's parents and then break off the relationship only days or weeks later. It would be so messy and disruptive, and Blue deplores messy and disruptive.

So the date of parental meetings will be written or typed neatly into the diary that Simon carries everywhere with him and the appropriate location and clothing selected for the event.

'Oh, we can just pop round unannounced,' Kate will say. *'And wear anything you like. No one will care.'*

But Simon *will* care. What if he wears the wrong thing and feels completely out of place? Simon hates to feel out of place.

'Don't worry,' says Kate as she leaps out of the car on the appointed day and races up the driveway to bear hug the whole extended family who have gathered to meet Simon.

'Mum, Dad, this is Simon. We're going to get married. But not yet though. Simon insists we only set the date when we've saved enough money for a deposit on a house. And Simon says we're going to have three children. Yes, three. And we're going to be safe and secure and happy for the rest of our lives. Isn't he wonderful, Mum? Clever, successful, steady, kind – and so organised. We've got so much to tell you. Simon has everything planned for our future.'

Simon loves a plan.

Long-term and marriage

This partnership can be a match made in heaven – or the astral plane– depending on which partner we're talking to. Although Simon may well insist there are one or two, or maybe a couple of hundred, rules to abide by in order to keep this heaven on earth together. But OMG – or OMGA (oh my guardian angel) – will it be worth it. Blue values have so much to offer.

In terms of real earthly success and achievement, this can be a very welcome leap forward for Kate. She might not always love the non-negotiable way Simon goes about things, but there's no denying that his flow chart systems are highly motivated towards building a solid future for them both. Kate always hoped for love and security and tended to put all her faith in fate. Now Simon is here, everything seems to be progressing in an orderly way. Maybe he was the very fate she had been waiting for.

Together these two lovers will very probably create a good life for themselves, often surrounded by friends, love, warmth and gradual promotion or advancement. Simon will put their success down to his considered forethought. By getting the finances in order, they have been able to save towards a bigger house and nicer holidays – plus, with the five-year career plan in place, his work-life has gone from strength to strength. While Simon is putting all this success down to careful planning, Kate will more likely put it down to the fact that Simon is Sagittarius and didn't buy that green Mondeo. But whatever, whether it's down to spells or spreadsheets, everything's going really well for Kate and Simon.

Simon likes the new, bigger house. It's efficient and well ordered, which makes far more sense than Kate's first choice of a romantic tumbledown cottage strewn with artefacts and subsidence.

The holidays are thoroughly researched and well co-ordinated by Simon, which makes far more sense than Kate's choice of the same destination her family always go to – familiar maybe, but poor on amenities, sight-seeing or expert recommendations.

Simon really doesn't like to do things without expert guidance or a logical process. Kate might prefer to do things in her own weird and wonderful way, which might not always be logical, but Simon likes a clear, rational system. It's far better to have all the holiday documents filed in a clearly marked folder six months in advance, and even better to have every possible household and personal document filed in a clearly marked folder. Which, if you live with a Blue Partner, you will. If you don't, it will drive them insane.

Along with the structure Simon brings to Kate's physical world, he may also bring a sense of hierarchy and higher purpose to Kate's more tribal, magical way of thinking. A structured mythic, Blue religion like Christianity, Judaism or Islam may well play a strong part in Simon's life. Kate is a reiki practitioner prone to superstitious thinking. She doesn't adhere to a religious doctrine. For this partnership to feel like a complete union for Simon, he would prefer Kate to convert to his specific belief system – and not just something similar. For Simon Blue, there is no approximation of the rules. There are the rules as he understands them and that's that. No negotiations. Rules were not made to be broken, they were made in order to be strictly adhered to.

If Kate doesn't conform, Simon may quickly lose respect, or, at best, spiritually separate himself from Kate. Kate Purple hates separation from her loved ones so the temptation to take on Simon's thinking and park her own will be very strong.

Spiritually, Blue values are often monotheistic, serving and respecting a single deity, with little time for magic and superstition. If Simon catches his Purple Partner touching wood or waving a crystal, he will come down heavily with mockery or criticism making Kate feel small and stupid.

Simon believes in skills and powers that are sanctioned from above, often accompanied by a wall-mounted certificate. He adores certificates and his study and the downstairs loo will be plastered with them. Simon is always quick to remind Kate of the value of authorised certification, and that you can't get a certificate in crystal waving.

'Yes, you can!' Kate will say. 'My aunt Susan is certified in crystal therapy and tarot reading.'

'Who certified her?' Simon will ask.

'Her friend Phyllida. She's a professor in magical arts.'

'A professor? Don't be ridiculous! You can't be a professor in magical arts. What's her name – Phyllida Dumbledore?' Simon will reply. *'Magic doesn't exist. It's pure delusion and imagination.'*

Kate is confused – why is tarot card reading any more delusional than the religious beliefs Simon adheres to? It really feels like there's one set of rules for him and none of the other rules count.

But for the sake of love, Kate will learn to keep her need for horoscopes and counting magpies to herself. She will hide her copy of *The Secret* in a bottom drawer and carefully stow away any lucky charms. Her guilty magic pleasures must remain a secret from Simon, but deep in her heart, Kate still holds on to her own truth. Simon might believe he got that pay rise because he'd put in extra hours and over-delivered on a new important project, but Kate will secretly know it has nothing to do with hard work. It was because of that shooting star last week. She knew it was a good omen.

Even though they have their differences, remember both these partners are in the 'We' position so selfishness and ego won't necessarily be a problem.

They'll both do all they can to accommodate the other. As long as Simon is allowed to keep making the rules and as long as Kate doesn't break too many of them, all will be well in this garden of Purple and Blue flowers.

However, if Kate refuses to adhere to the rules, Simon can become highly discombobulated. He isn't trying to hurt anyone with his rules – quite the opposite; he's trying to help. The rules are there to make the family safe and happy. But for Kate, the family being happy is the only rule. Happy family comes first, rules second – if at all. Simon might like to remember that the more rules he creates, the more likely it is that some of them will be broken. That's just the law of probability, and Blue likes a law!

Kids and family

When it comes to parenting, it could well be the rules that cause these two to face challenging times.

Both Simon and Kate place a great deal of importance on the family. They both want the best for their children and will devote a great deal of their time and energy to parenting to the best of their abilities. Perfect. Everyone agrees, right?

Not necessarily. As much as these two feel strongly about parenting, they feel strongly in different ways. While they both want the best for their kids, Kate will be mystified by some of Simon's ideas when it comes to educating and rearing their offspring. For Kate, the kids come first. No question. Whatever happens, whatever they do. Whatever challenges come their way, those kids and their welfare come first. You protect your own over and above anything else.

A Purple father or mother sees their brood as their own little gang which will do whatever it needs to do in order to protect itself and its members, but a mother or father in Blue doesn't see things like that at all. No gang is above the law of the land.

If anybody does wrong within the family, then they must learn their lesson and pay the price. The same goes for Purple! They might be Blue's partner, but if they cross the line of the law then Blue will no longer be able to protect them.

 **Don't think you can get away with not paying a parking ticket, Purple. Not because the council will be on to you, but because your Blue partner will!**

Purple needs to be aware that, in the nicest possible way, their Blue partner is somewhat policing them from within. Blue won't break the law to protect their partner, their family or even themselves. On the contrary. They'll feel it's their duty to let the authorities know if one of their brood has done wrong.

If this couple's child steals sweets from the local shop, Kate will want to protect their little one and keep it quiet. However, as much as she protests, Simon will immediately be marching their little one down to the shop, telling them if they don't say sorry and take the sweets back, the big, nasty policeman will come and take them to jail. It would have been a Blue values parent that handed in their teenage kid to the police after they'd been caught on CCTV participating in the London riots in August 2011.

Blue values people admire any system that lays out clear guidelines of right and wrong, good and evil, and punishing the bad and rewarding the good. A consistent code to live by and everything in its place will very much appeal to Blue's values. But if Blue's order and rules seem to turn against the family, Purple will suffer a deep personal crisis around their values.

So Kate and Simon need to watch out for these potentially conflicting areas. In times of difficulty, crisis or change, Simon will tend towards pragmatic, practical thinking. Kate, on the other hand, will lean heavily towards her emotions. When the kids grow up and move away Kate will be bereft, but there's no point turning to Simon for sympathy.

As Kate stands in the doorway, sadly waving goodbye to her last Purple chick, he'll simply say, *'You're being ridiculous. What did you think was going to happen? Of course the children need to leave home. That's how child-rearing works! It's the order of things. Come on, let's clear out one of their bedrooms. I thought we could build a library for my books.'*

Friends and social life

Overall, Simon and Kate are pretty compatible. They certainly both value social interaction. They both appreciate family and friends. They both understand the need to make time for other people and listen to their needs. They are both thoughtful and, to a greater or lesser extent, are able to be selfless and supportive when necessary.

There are, however, one or two areas that can end up creating conflict. Again it all comes down to Simon's acute sense of right and wrong versus Kate's sense of family loyalty.

If this couple are in company and get into some kind of discussion, debate or argument, Kate and her Purple values will call upon Simon to show loyalty to her and her family. But of course, Simon won't necessarily take Kate's side – Simon will take the 'right' side. If that means taking a stance against Kate or her family, so be it. This adherence to higher codes of conduct tramples on Kate's need for utter loyalty to the tribe. Consequently, she may be deeply hurt at what feels like an act of betrayal.

If this deep Blue sense of right and wrong is triggered in Simon, he won't be able to hide it, leaving Kate bemused as to why he refuses to do things that she considers important. Why won't he come and visit cousins Gary and Fran? They haven't seen them in ages.

'I've already told you,' says Simon, *'I'll never spend another moment in those people's company.'*

'But they're family!' Kate will plead.

'There is no way I will be seen in that house again. For a start, I'm sure Gary's been dodging his taxes. I definitely heard something about rolls of cash on top of the wardrobe.'

'He's not a tax dodger. That's just where he keeps the family savings. You know my family never trusts banks,' Kate replies.

'Whatever. They're a bad influence. Gary has a criminal record, Fran's definitely had a coke habit and their kids are feral.'

'So he dealt a little pot at college. Fran was a model – they all do coke – and the kids are just . . . very creative.'

But Kate can call it what she likes. For Simon, the law is the law and decent behaviour comes in very few flavours, none of which are 'criminal', 'vandal' or 'try to get away with it if you can'.

However, all the time the line of the law or the demarcation of decency remains uncrossed, a person expressing Blue values will be comfortable and relaxed around most people. They will in fact be far more open to meeting new people than someone at the Purple stage.

While a Purple partner may find the idea of meeting new people daunting, with a Blue partner leading the way, they are in the safest of hands. Blue won't take Purple somewhere unfamiliar and then run off and abandon them like some social butterfly in the way a Red or an Orange partner might. Blue is a solid, thoughtful and reliable security blanket for Purple as they enter into alien arenas. Blue creates an unthreatening opportunity for Purple to begin to expand their social horizons, always making sure their Purple partner is comfortable, safe and knows Blue is right there by their side.

Money

In this partnership Simon will almost certainly control the family purse strings, and very organised purse strings they will be. Kate will most probably respect Simon's need to sacrifice now and save for later and together these two can create a great deal of financial security. With Simon's steady planning and foresight, this pairing has a very good chance of gradually moving up the property and investment ladder. Kate may still put it all down to luck and Simon down to the ten-year plan, but however they think they got there, each will feel very comfortable knowing they have a secure future. Both of them would much rather have security than luxury goods or last-minute romantic cruises. Not that they won't have those things, but never if they can't afford it. Simon would rather starve than rack up crazy credit card bills.

'It's crazy credit card spending that got our society into this mess in the first place,' Simon will tell Kate, *'and now we all need to take responsibility to rebuild it.'*

'Absolutely,' Kate will agree, *'whatever you say.'*

As long as the house is secure, the bills are paid, the children are happy and no one goes without, then Kate is happy to let Simon handle things – be it family money or the global financial crisis.

Sex

A combination of Blue and Purple values fuelling a love making session can head in one of two directions. It can be a very sensual, almost ritualistic experience, or equally it can become a little perfunctory and practical. This sexual pairing can tip either way.

These two need to be careful they remain open to the gifts each of them brings to the bedroom, otherwise sex risks becoming simply functional. Particularly after it has served its function of providing them with children.

When they're trying for a family, female Blue will know exactly when they need to have sex in order to conceive. She will have spreadsheets, timetables and thermometers to tell them exact ovulating hours and record precise body temperature fluctuations. A person living by Blue knows you don't leave anything to chance, but even so, they'll still have their differences about what to do with that information depending on when and where they receive it. If they're in the Tesco car park when ovulation peaks, both male or female Purple will be more than happy to go for it up against the trolley shelter. But, as we know, Blue lives by the rules and sex in public places is definitely a no-no.

Sex with an organised, rule bound, risk-averse partner sounds like it's unlikely to be wild. However, the bedroom can be the very place that a Blue lover finally releases their controlled emotions and really lets rip!

Both Purple and Blue appreciate ritual, though admittedly for very different reasons. Purple is drawn to the magic and spirituality of ritual, while Blue appreciates ritualistic order and repetition. Still, given a few candles and a sexy sequence of events from foreplay to exhaustion, these two can find an unspoken sexual practice that will bring out the primal lover in both of them. A lover with an aura of Blue authority gets Purple's wild side racing and, in response, their Purple innocence, vulnerability and openness will drive didactic Blue insane! In fact, Blue might just find an intimate space where they can finally let go of all their shoulds and should-nots. If someone with Blue drives is prepared to take the plunge, then sex with a Purple lover will offer them a wonderful release valve from the stresses and strains of every day life. It's tiring always having to stick to the rules! Sometimes, you just need to swing from the chandeliers.

These two express very different value systems, but if Blue and Purple can find a way to worship at the altar of each other during sex then their love making has the potential to be incredibly magical. Sorry, Blue – did I say 'magical'? I meant magnetic!

CHAPTER 10

Purple and Orange

BEHIND EVERY GREAT MAN AND WOMAN...

Dating and early romance

Now here's an interesting mix. On the face of it, one might wonder how these two could ever get on. Purple values create a drive to keep things the same while Orange values embrace constant change. Purple motivates us to look inwards towards family and unity while Orange compels us to look outwards for new opportunity. Purple folk worship at the door of tradition while Orange people are bashing down the door of ambition. Completely different, it appears. So what happens when people expressing these two value systems fall in love?

Lets take the case of Mark (Purple) and Olivia (Orange). For a start, traditional gender attitudes and roles can appear to be reversed as a person's values become apparent in their feelings, thoughts and behaviours. So in this couple's case, one thing that's almost guaranteed is that at the moment these two met, it was Olivia who approached Mark and not vice versa.

Olivia would have gone out that night, as ever on the look out for new people and experiences, while Mark was probably there passing the time quite happily with his closest friends or family.

Olivia might have initially appeared a bit over assertive to Mark whose bulls**t-meter would have gone onto high alert as soon as she started talking. But for all Olivia's self-aggrandising and flirty attitude, Mark couldn't resist this smart, assertive, person in front of him.

Olivia might be full of herself, but she's also full of ideas and promises, not to mention a fair few compliments. So Mark's heart was soon beating in triple time, and for all the right reasons. Mark adored Olivia's confidence and somehow she knew just the right things to say to win him over.

To be fair, Olivia knows just the right things to say to win *anyone* over. That's why she's so successful. She is an expert at listening carefully to what people say in order to assess the quickest and most effective ways to influence them. She's a strategist. She knows that mirroring someone's body language and speech patterns can create instant rapport. Some might call it manipulation, but right now, in his deep Purple haze, Mark is calling it profound and magical intuition. This was clearly meant to be.

Olivia will be quite literally speaking Mark's language. This is Olivia's first manoeuvre, matching his linguistic style in order to develop rapport and put him at ease. In other words, getting into Mark's inner Purple sanctum. Next stop, Mark's heart. Unless of course she is only interested in some short-term, light entertainment.

Orange values are all about ambition, acquisition and achieving success everywhere and anywhere. Dating desirable people is no exception. Any prospective date can expect lots of fabulous evenings out and a wealth of even more fabulous gifts because this is how people living Orange values express their feelings. The more time and money Orange invests in a relationship, the more they will be emotionally invested. The gift of a Louis Vuitton handbag, means there's some big Orange love in the room.

As Olivia and Mark sit at their window-side table in the Oxo Tower on their first date, she will most likely be boasting about her social network and how knowing all the right people can secure the best table in one of the best restaurants in one of the best capital cities in the world.

Mark on the other hand will be staring out into the night knowing this was all meant to be.

It's too much of a coincidence that Mark's mother used Oxo cubes to make the Sunday gravy and now here he is in the *Oxo* Tower sitting across from this amazing woman. Purple values never ignore a sign. Just as well there are some fortune cookies handed out at the end of their meal.

Your heart will always make itself known through your words, Mark reads as he looks over at a fidgeting Olivia.

'Ahh, yes,' Mark thinks as she's about to speak. *'It looks like Olivia might be about to make her feelings known through her words right now.'*

'I'm just popping to the loo,' she says.

'Hmm, what does that mean?' thinks Mark. *'It must be a sign.'*

It could of course be a sign that Olivia is off to text, call or even meet someone else. Remember, Orange values are about acquisition and achievement and in these early uncertain days of dating, Olivia's fortune cookie might well read, *Why settle for the one lover when you can spread your bets with four?*

So how can Mark be sure Olivia is serious about him? Well, knowing that a person with Orange values is in the 'I, Me and Mine' position and will be absolutely focused on getting what they want, one of the best ways to secure Olivia's interest is to deny her just that. If Mark suddenly acts disinterested towards her, then she may well suddenly sit up and pay a lot more attention. In fact, there's not much else Mark could do to be *more* attractive to Olivia's Orange-driven values. After all Olivia loves a challenge and Mark could be a very new kind of thrill. It's important to note that this strategy won't work with the other 'I, Me and Mine' position of the Red value set. Red wants to be wanted. Full stop. No games, no psychological strategies and definitely no emotional trickery.

Mark will likely have a secure network of family and friends around him. At this point, he really doesn't *need* Olivia – emotionally, romantically or financially. He may, however, *want* her. Therefore, he can use this lack of need to his advantage – it will make him appear confident and so help him secure Olivia's affections. Olivia will be well schooled in dealing with competition and extroversion when it comes to the dating game, but a secure, disinterested date can be very exciting territory for her.

A great example of the Orange and Purple values combination is Richard Branson and his wife Joan Templeman. Part of the reason Branson bought the Caribbean island of Necker was to woo Joan. The island is today worth a cool £60 million. Branson is as Orange as they come in his pursuit of new businesses and Joan has fulfilled her Purple values by building a family and bearing him three children. According to the *Guardian* newspaper a few years ago, they live in 'a fluid, slightly shabby mix of home and office, with Branson sitting on the sofa, fielding phone calls, while Joan potters in the kitchen next-door'.

That's a peak Orange and Purple values success story, but it's important to remember that Richard Branson had many other girlfriends before he met Joan. There's no guarantee a Purple/Orange relationship will go long-term. In fact, aside from the usual factors like attractiveness and sense of humour, the long-term success of the Purple/Orange relationship really depends on one thing: timing.

If a person living Purple is ready to fly the nest, and Orange is feeling their next achievement should be family and children, then these two might well take a one-way trip down the yellow brick road to their very own fairytale. But if the stars or, more importantly, the body clocks aren't aligned, then this relationship is headed down a one-way cul-de-sac towards Break-Up Alley.

The thing is, even though this couple might have a great time dating, if male or female Orange isn't at a time in their life when they're ready to settle down – as much as Orange can ever settle down – then this relationship will be doomed to flingdom.

That's not to say these two won't have a lot of fun in the kingdom of fling, but if Olivia Orange isn't ready to build a castle there then Mark Purple may well end up broken-hearted back at the family's gingerbread cottage.

Long-term and marriage

So let's assume that these two did get their timing right and have decided they're ready to settle down. Olivia may still not be ready to settle in one place. Mark might not initially like to keep moving home, but if there's one thing people with Purple values excel at it's creating a 'home is where the heart is' environment wherever they are. Mark can create a home environment in no time, anywhere from a camping site in Snowdonia to a six-star hotel in Dubai. He's learned to. It keeps him safe and happy.

As the months turn into years, Purple and Orange values can be a really fabulous mix. If a person has healthy Orange values it will be because they have been through Purple, Red and Blue and really understand the importance of all three.

Orange and Purple can truly complement each other. Mark won't mind if Olivia bends or breaks a few rules if it means Mark's needs are met, and if bending a few rules means Olivia wins the upper hand then she is happy too. Neither of these two are sticklers for correct procedure. Whatever gets the job done and benefits them both is fine as far as this couple is concerned. All will be well as long as each are allowed to express their values within the relationship – in Mark's case, family interests; in Olivia's case, business interests.

Many an Orange-driven entrepreneur has a husband or wife with Purple values standing beside them who work hard to maintain a fun, safe home life and refuge from Orange's globe trotting and deal-making. However, one important challenge Mark may have to face is how to keep his challenge-seeking partner engaged and interested in him.

Olivia might initially love that she has a reliable and comforting partner to come home to, but she still needs the thrill of the chase. If Mark doesn't keep this relationship fizzing, he might just see it fizzle out. Unless he energises this relationship on a regular basis, he may soon find Olivia is 'working late' or 'travelling overseas' a little too often in the name of 'networking' to further her career, or indeed her self-esteem. Because, sometimes, underneath many an Orange's need to acquire material wealth is a great big confidence void. It can be useful to remember that both Orange and Red, being 'I' positions are predominantly 'ego' positions and as much as the ego can show itself to be strong and powerful, underneath it can be extremely vulnerable.

A clever and intuitive person – as so many Purple people are – will feed their Orange partner's ego, as well as their stomach. Making Olivia feel successful and daring is the key to keeping this relationship strong, but when things are not going so well for her, sympathetic Mark needs to be careful what words he chooses to support her. Whereas Mark will find comfort in more spiritual, emotional and intuitive support, Olivia needs rational and logical words of advice.

When it comes to problem solving, this couple will first need to solve the problem of their very different approaches and beliefs about how the world works.

'Why don't you relax more, darling?' Mark offers. *'What will be will be. You can't shape the future. All you can do is send your hopes out into the universe and let fate do its work. Anyway, I've got a strong feeling that you're destined for success.'*

'Are you joking or are you nuts?' Olivia retorts.

Mark thinks back to his fortune cookie at the Oxo Tower. *Your heart will always make itself known through your words.* He is crushed. *'Did she really mean that?'* he thinks. *'Can she really love me? Was what I said really so terrible?'*

Mark has just learned to never again speak of fate or destiny to his rational, Orange partner.

He must comfort her in a different way. Mark is beginning to realise there are very few people who truly understand about the magic in the universe. No wonder there is so much stress and war.

But don't worry, all you magic loving Purples out there – when your cosmic chemistry blog becomes an overnight internet sensation, your Orange lover will be right by your side with every venture capitalist and social networking expert in line behind them.

Orange values might be about rationalism and materialism, but there's nothing irrational about a new multi-million pound dot com venture. When it comes to building another successful business, what's wrong with a little alchemy between colleagues?

A person motivated by peak Orange values would likely sell their grandmother to make a few quid. After all, if she can bake exceedingly good cakes, she'll be a great asset for producing passive income. But they mustn't ever reveal that capital-raising business strategy to their Purple-loving partner; for Purple, selling family members is about as evil as it gets. For Orange a set of solid business values combined with a commercial insight into family values is about as good as it gets. Understanding family spending habits is big business.

Kids and family

If this pairing produces children, their values and drivers will really shift up a gear. Suddenly Mark has everything he ever dreamed of and is totally motivated to protect and care for their little brood. Olivia, however, is desperate to get back to work. They've agreed Mark will be house husband so Olivia suddenly has twice, three, four, five times the reason to keep on earning and achieving.

Once children are in the mix, Mark may begin to see less of Olivia. This is partly because she will be out doing more deals to be able to afford more Xboxes, puppies and trips to Center Parcs, but also partly because the honeymoon phase of dinners and fine wines just turned into a chaotic party of breast milk, regurgitated pureed fruit and poopy nappies. This is not necessarily a party Olivia will want to be at for too long. She'll probably be back online when the kids are talking, eating properly and acting more like cute parental accessories than little human chimps.

Mark will wallow in his new-found little family, but Olivia may not necessarily feel the same. He might be fully satisfied now, but she'll still hanker after the good things in life. From Mark's perspective, the gift of children is the greatest gift of all, but Olivia may begin to become disappointed in the gifts she continually receives from Mark.

Materialistic Orange values will equate how much a partner loves them according to the gifts they buy them and as Olivia tears open another birthday gift, she may seriously question whether Mark really loves her, or even knows her. When it comes to birthday gifts, as much as Olivia may love the children, she really wanted a new iPad, not another framed photo of the children with burger grease running down their chins at Granny Shirley's annual 'bring your own barbecue' shindig. At least Mark can upload all the family photos he wants on the latest MacBook Air that Olivia bought him last Christmas. All she can do now is upload that one hideous photo onto the mantelpiece to collect dust. Great. And did he have to get the kids to make the photo surround? At what point did Mark think that twig frame glued with lentils, sweetcorn and broccoli would match the Jasper Conran shelving unit?

As their children grow up Olivia will be encouraging them to break out and explore the world while Mark will be reassuring them that they have everything they need right here at home. This will be a trying time for Olivia and Mark. Through their own experience of life, they will both feel they are right. Mark knows it's right that their child gets a secure job with a local company and Olivia knows it's right to take that internship in Thailand. Mark values safety, Olivia values new experiences.

But if they can both agree it's ideal to help their child to make their own best decision then this couple can give their children the best of both worlds – opportunity and possibility along with security and support. That's one very strong combination when it comes to launching children into the big wide world.

Friends and social life

In terms of their social life, Mark will immediately want to introduce Olivia to his friends and family, but unless his family is related to the Royals, the Rothschilds or Bill Gates, she might not be too interested.

'Why spend all day Sunday at your parents' bungalow in Byfleet when we could be brunching and networking with my work chums in Shoreditch?' she protests.

A person with peak Orange values has a clear filter system when it comes to friends and acquaintances. In the past, when Olivia was seducing Mark, she may have given more time to his family interests but only because, at the time, they fell into one of Orange's two networking categories – useful or very useful. On the upside, she may well root out a well-connected or wealthy long lost cousin of Mark's during one of her late night Google-fests trawling the net for opportunities. She may then re-introduce them to the fold. If there's one thing Olivia understands, it's how to create and optimise new networking opportunities.

As far as making new friends is concerned, Mark will feel extremely torn between wanting to please Olivia and wanting to continue spending time with his oldest and truest friends. Family and friends are a lifeline to Mark as much as success and achievement are life's blood for Olivia. This is an area where these two really need to communicate to make it work.

A note to all the Purple people in the house: you may have realised by now that lovers with Orange values will respond well to a good bout of negotiation. So, rather than getting frustrated when they won't come to nephew William's wedding, learn to negotiate. Work out what a given situation is worth from an Orange perspective, then sit them down and lay your cards on the table.

'I am looking for one family wedding, including ceremony, reception and cake cutting, returning home ten p.m. at the latest. I'll drive. In return, I am offering one business dinner with boss and wife plus attendance at the annual company slap on the back gala award ceremony at overpriced badly carpeted hotel on the M40. Will participate in obligatory table magic. Will not drive. Do we have a deal?'

Sometimes you might not want your Purple heart to make itself known through your words. Orange values won't respond to the language of fortune cookies. Sometimes, to get what you need, you might want to get down to the nitty gritty words of hard negotiating! It's a language anyone expressing Orange values understands perfectly, mainly because they invented it.

Money

The single most important factor for Purple people is that their partner is emotionally involved, but someone holding Orange values will often put money first.

However, if you are a person driven by peak Orange values, it's worth bearing in mind that the love of money and success is not entirely repulsive to the Purple tribe. They will love the fact that they have someone successfully providing for the family. Even better, they won't judge you if you lose it all, just as long as you don't gamble with members of the family or sell their heirlooms.

If you're the Purple half of this partnership then just be careful. Enjoy the spoils when they're brought home to you, but if the odds start to go against you, try not to rely on tarot, the zodiac or the National Lottery to help you. Alternatively, squirrel some money away in a secret savings account and tell yourself it would be 'bad luck' to ever touch it. Hopefully you may never need to – only if your Orange lover totally screws up, and then, from your perspective, that would constitute 'bad luck' anyway.

It's worth remembering that people with an Orange worldview have arrived there as a result of their personal evolution along the values spiral. As this is a process of experiencing and including previous values, they will have been intimately familiar with the Purple perspective. So, although they are usually incredibly rational, if times get truly desperate and they mess up big time, Purple might find that Orange suddenly seem to share their more poetic world view. After all, when it comes to losing money, it couldn't be anything to do with Orange's strategic thinking or business acumen, could it?! All of a sudden Orange, rational thinking may fly out of the window.

'I just got unlucky,' Orange may say.

'But I didn't think you believed in luck!' Purple may reply smugly.

But Orange isn't listening. They've down-spiralled and are desperately searching through Jonathan Cainer's zodiac column for a sign their fortunes might turn.

This couple may be able to see their way over many of the marital bumps life throws at them – Olivia not always being there for another school nativity play, Mark letting the kids use the Bang and Olufsen speakers as frisbees – but if times get tough and money gets short, trying to blend and integrate Purple and Orange values can get very tough indeed.

Mark won't really mind if there's extra money or not, but he will mind if the family is not united and happy. However, if Olivia starts to lag in her pursuit of wealth or achievement, she may begin to feel like a failure.

Mark may not understand why Olivia is so stressed about material wealth. So what if they lose everything? They'll downsize. Mark is a handy man, an expert at making do.

'As long as we're all together, it doesn't matter. We could live with my parents. We could live in a tent for all I care. In fact, I was just reading about a man who built a hobbit hut in a forest in Wales for only £3,000. It had fairy lights and everything. We could go and live in a hobbit hut,' Mark says reassuringly.

But it will matter to Olivia. She will care deeply that neighbours and colleagues see her as a failure. She won't want to live in a tent – not unless it's a silk one located on a luxury Bedouin holiday retreat. She really doesn't want to live in a hobbit hut, and she definitely won't be moving in with Mark's Purple parents! Living on charity? In community with others?! That will cross every one of her Orange values.

'Live with your parents? Absolutely not. No, no, never and no. I'd rather live in the hobbit hut. In fact, I'd rather be a hobbit.'

Whereas for Mark, living with his parents isn't even a compromise. Family charity? That's what life is all about.

Even if these two do fall on difficult times, even if they do end up living with Mark's parents, Olivia's Orange entrepreneurial spirit will always lead her to find new opportunities and solutions.

'Now we've moved in with your parents, I'm thinking of remortgaging their house to raise some capital,' she says.

'What will that mean?' asks Mark. *'Could they lose everything too?'*

'Yes, but I think it's worth the risk,' she smiles.

'Are you joking or are you nuts?' says Mark, his heart truly making itself known through his words.

Every sinew in Mark's body tenses as his value boundaries are crossed. Suddenly he shifts up-spiral from loving Purple to raging Red warlord in a flash and Olivia has just learned to never again speak of using Mark's family for financial gain.

Sex

When a couple holding these two values combine, it can be a truly healthy and satisfying embrace. Purple passion offers an ease and a sensuality in the bedroom. Orange originality is risky, curious and hungry for new ideas. Purple lovers can be deeply in touch with raw, pagan sexuality, while Orange explorers have the courage and sexual ambition to go ever further. In the bedroom these two can definitely set off the fireworks their vibrant colours promise. As with fireworks, the sky really is the limit.

So that's the healthy version, but sex between these two can also have its challenges. If Purple Mark doesn't stay in touch with his own deep physical need for connection, he could quickly get caught up in the tables and chairs of everyday work-life conflicts. School runs and supermarket shopping lists will never be sexy to Olivia. If Mark then allows the banalities of everyday life to swamp him, there is a danger that the sex will become safe, unadventurous and quick.

Sex is a basic, physical and visceral urge, very tied up with ego. At the peak Orange stage, Olivia's ego is very much expressed through her worldly success. So if she isn't experiencing success in her everyday world of life and work she may begin to feel less sexy.

Unlike a lover submerged in narcissistic Red values who can detach the ego from the world around them and find sexual satisfaction whenever, wherever and from whoever they so desire, Olivia's Orange drives mean her self-esteem is very tied up with her daily, materialistic achievements.

In short, if Olivia's business or creative projects are going down hill, so is her libido. If a business deal has gone sour or she's been made redundant, it will be hard for her to assert her basic sexual drives. A person motivated by peak Orange values who finds themselves on social benefits doesn't benefit anyone in the bedroom.

If Mark and Olivia ever faced this scenario, it would be doubly frustrating for him as not only does he value the basic physical release of sex but, more, he values emotional commitment, regardless of external factors.

For example, perhaps Olivia's just heard from her broker that she's lost big time playing the stocks and shares. Mark attempts physical contact.

'Don't touch me. I'm not in the mood. I've lost everything!' she recoils.

'You're being ridiculous, Olivia. I love you. I don't care about the bank balance, the bonus or the stock exchange. We have the kids, we have each other. Money can't buy us love.'

Mark might, however, want to look back through the diary to compare and contrast the performance of their sex life against the performance of Olivia's bank balance, the Dow Jones and the FTSE 100. Money might very well be buying them love.

CHAPTER 11

Purple and Green

FAMILY AND FRIENDS OF THE EARTH.

Dating and early romance

When a family-orientated person with Purple values meets a potential partner holding pluralistic and inclusive Green values, they will feel they have met someone who loves and accepts not only them, but all their family.

This combination represents the coming together of the love for both the local family and the global family of the planet on which we all live. This can make these two lovers feel extremely powerful together, and powerful is not necessarily a feeling either are used to experiencing from the perspective of their Purple and Green worldviews.

A fundamental difference between the *Spiral into Love* approach and all other theories of why people fall and stay in love is the focus on values. People with aligned values can overcome many differences, including gender, race, ethnicity, sexuality and religion.

Sean (Purple) was born into a Romany Gypsy family. After centuries of persecution, Gypsies are the archetypal Purple tribe, suspicious of outsiders and protective of the Romany customs and traditions. If you leave or betray the traveller tribe, you could be outcast forever. Sean grew up in a tight-knit claustrophobic community and extended family. Caravans and travelling, living from day to day and hand to mouth, was his lot. He hardly ever went to school and rarely mixed with non-Gypsies.

The culture was traditional. Men were macho alpha males and women, though strong and wilful, were subservient and always obeyed the men. However, Sean knew he could never fully belong because he was gay – a secret he couldn't reveal to his family, particularly his father. Despite all this, Sean has a regular job working for an insurance company.

Anthony (Green) was born to bohemian middle-class parents. His mother, an ex dancer, is now a poet and his father is a music teacher at a major public school. Growing up in the heart of the Lincolnshire countryside and a small flat in London, Anthony's early life was unremarkable in its normality. A more perfect and free childhood you could not have wished for. As an only child, Anthony was showered with love by his parents who ensured he experienced an eclectic education. Frequently travelling abroad and staying in ashrams and communes from Iowa to India, Anthony had friends all over the world. He truly was a global citizen. Anthony is now a geography teacher at a modern secondary school.

When they met, Sean and Anthony quickly found a very deep, spiritual connection. Individuals in both Purple and Green are very much led by their emotions. So Sean and Anthony didn't ask many questions around the tangible or practical areas of each other's lives.

Information about what jobs they do, where they live, their history or where they stand politically did not even come up at first. The flow of feelings between them was so strong that they were lost in the beauty and wonder of human love and connection rather than worrying about the practicalities of long-term compatibility. Why worry about that when their deepest intuitions, emotions and desires are sending nothing but positive signals? It feels right, so it must be right. In terms of their respective Purple and Green values, Anthony and Sean are incredibly 'people orientated'. So much so that any potential differences between them could easily get hidden beneath the need to please and appease. Initially, these two look absolutely perfect for each other.

Anthony loves how much Sean cares about his family and those close to him. He can relate strongly to this caring and sharing quality. As a person who lives by Green values, he patiently sits for hours listening to Sean happily recount endless stories about his Romany roots and travellers' tales.

Anthony knew he would have to meet the whole of Sean's clan within the first few weeks but obviously as Sean's friend, not as his lover. Anthony knows that family gatherings are Sean's make or break in this new relationship. Sweet old Grandpa Harry is in fact the tribal chief deciding whether Anthony will be accepted into the clan or be cast into the wilderness. Anthony will be fine with this arrangement and do whatever it takes to make Sean happy. He understands how central the family unit is and how important tradition is to Sean. Anyway, everything will settle down when they eventually come out and start cohabitating, or even get married and set up home together. Then they'll start to carve out their own new life . . . right?

Long-term and marriage

Wrong. As they get to know each other more, Anthony quickly realises that Sean has absolutely no desire to tell his family he is gay and even less of a desire to start any kind of new life. Even with the challenge of being gay in a culture and community that will never accept him if they knew the truth about his sexuality, Sean still isn't interested in leaving the tribe or meeting new people. All he wants is to be around his family and close friends – that's what makes him happy. Even in the times it makes him unhappy, it's still all he wants. He's learned from hearing about the bitter experiences of other gay youngsters rejected by their family and outcast from the traveller community. Our deepest values will almost always win out.

So if Anthony is serious about a relationship with Sean, it will come with Purple baggage, but the deceit, routine and ritual may become a little frustrating for Anthony.

Apart from having to keep the full extent of their relationship a secret, Anthony may tire of going to the same pub every Friday night, drinking with the same people who talk about the same things. There's a world out there to explore. But, not wanting to upset Sean, Anthony will most likely bury any feelings of unrest.

Purple and Green couples need to be more careful than many other spiral pairings that they are truly aware of each other's values and needs. These two can fall into the trap of thinking they value exactly the same things – and on the surface it can look that way. Their friends and family will only strengthen this belief, because to everyone else too this couple looks so perfect from the outside. Purple and Green are often the combination that make up a large number of shock divorces – the break-ups that no one saw coming that rock other people's understanding of the world. These two seem so similar, so right for each other. In many ways they are, but there are big differences – differences that they both need to be aware of sooner rather than later.

It's important to realise that a person authentically expressing peak Green values will have come through the Purple, Red, Blue and Orange value systems. Some of the values from these earlier stages of development will have been integrated into Green's personality as their life conditions changed. However, they will probably be feeling that this new Green stage is now the 'right' and only way for them to live, over and above any previous stage of life they have experienced. A person expressing pluralistic Green finds Red values too egotistical, Blue values too conservative, and Orange values overly selfish and soulless. Therefore, the life mission of a person motivated by Green values may well be to help people at these earlier stages of development to see the Green light.

Green loves helping people develop, evolve and reach their full potential, so they can sometimes forget that not everyone is on a mission of self-actualisation! Some people are happy right where they are.

This essentially means that a person in Green may look back at the drives and behaviours of the other values with a certain amount of disdain.

As much as Anthony claims to accept everyone as they are and not judge others, once the haze of initial attraction clears, Sean's tribal values may appear very narrow-minded to Anthony. For Anthony, there are always new people to meet and learn from, books to read, courses and retreats to attend, and a planet to save. Isn't Sean interested in doing it all with him? No, I'm afraid he isn't. This is where these two value systems must face their differences. While for Sean his small, family community represents his whole world, for Anthony his whole world is just that – the whole world.

Green values drive a person to feel a part of the planet and connected to everyone who lives in it. Purple values see people outside their tribe as alien, irrelevant and potentially threatening. *'Why does Anthony need new friends?'* Sean will wonder. They already have friends. But for Anthony to be happy, Sean must let him go and explore a little. It will be worth it. Anthony will come home from a course, a trip or a new social event rejuvenated and revelling in his new found communion with newly met people, newly discovered information or a newly experienced spiritual awareness.

Anthony is totally accepting of Sean's superstitions and magical beliefs. Now Sean must try to accept Anthony's search for his own personal and spiritual understanding. As Anthony embraces Sean's need for the traditional family way of doing things, Sean might try to be open to Anthony's mission to find the good, true and beautiful qualities in everything and everyone.

Sean might be happy cooking his favourite shepherd's pie based on his grandmother's recipe for the rest of his life, but sometimes Anthony fancies a bit of Thai, maybe some Moroccan or even perhaps a taste of Katangan curry. Variety is the spice of life for Anthony. He understands he only has one life on this planet and he wants to experience it all, as long as it doesn't leave too much of a carbon footprint.

His values implore him to not only want to explore the planet, but also to save it.

Sean couldn't care less if the planet sank into a cess pit of filth – as long as his family, his tribe and his race was saved. Anthony has higher ideals, but Sean is simply being honest. Anthony might struggle slightly with Sean's views around equality and openness to others, but equally he will do all he can to accept the truth of how Sean feels.

This can often be the difficulty for someone with strong Green values. They want to accept everyone's point of view, but when that point of view doesn't take everyone's needs into consideration, it can be challenging for them. This is the Big Green Trap – everyone is right, everyone is equal, I shouldn't feel upset when someone holds selfish or thoughtless values . . . but somehow I still do.

If you have identified yourself as a person living peak Green values, remember you're still human – and sometimes you'll have not very nice thoughts. You have a set of values based around equality and acceptance, and anyone who doesn't agree with that . . . er, doesn't seem to belong? Isn't accepted? You could even say they're wrong. It feels like a moral cul-de-sac, doesn't it? But try to relax. Someone still at peak Purple can teach you a lot about allowing yourself to accept your darker side, which can be a relief to your highly demanding Green value set.

In a Purple/Green relationship, Green needs to understand that they're on their own with their egalitarian and ecological values. So rather than Green keeping on at their Purple partner about separating the plastics and the paper, they might just want to dig the recycling out of the rubbish bin themselves. It'll save both them and their Purple partner the continuous arguments. It's important to pick your battles. Sometimes you don't need to fight, you just need to do the thing you want done yourself. Anyway, Green surely isn't trying to change anyone, are they? Everyone's already equal and right, right?

Kids and family

Lucky are the children born into a Purple and Green values-based partnership. A more family-orientated, inclusive and nurturing world you could not hope to be born into. These are parents who will selflessly adore their children and shower them in a daily dose of Purple and Green love. By giving Purple some children to add to the family and tribe, Green has made them the happiest person alive. By giving Green their own personal experience of Mother Nature at work, Purple has done exactly the same.

A couple that combines Purple and Green values will bring their children up in an environment filled with siblings, grandparents, cousins and oodles of love. They will teach their children to love and care for each other and so continue the support network that has been so vital in Purple's own life, and possibly Green's as well.

The only conflict for these two comes in their attitude to the outside world. The Purple parent will want the best for their own children above any others, whereas their Green partner will want the best for everyone – even at a cost to their own brood. In the face of teenage competition, threat or bullying, Green values will drive a parent to encourage their children to turn the other cheek, while Purple values will encourage their children to give that other cheek a good slap. For the Green parent bringing up their children, it's sometimes worth spiralling down to their Blue values in order to establish some agreed rules or guidelines.

Overall though, the bond these two will experience over their children will be very powerful. Both value systems sit clearly in the 'We' position and both will do all they can to ensure their offspring's' happiness, even at their own expense. In fact, for the Purple/Green pairing, this is something to watch out for. So focused are they on their children, that their own needs can very often be thrust to one side.

While some couples may be fine with that, it's worth Purple and Green checking in with themselves every now and then and asking a couple of questions:

1) Am I taking care of my own individual needs?
2) Are my partner and I nurturing our own relationship as well as our relationship with the children?

Purple and Green parents would do well to keep nurturing the unity and magic of their own relationship, as well as taking care of children, domestics or the planet. Both are highly emotional and often sensitive souls. Purple and Green must try to look after each other. They have something very precious in their possession and would do well to value and take care of this relationship. As much as Purple cares about those close to them and as much as Green cares about the entire human race, these two must also both care about an important part of both those things: their love for one another.

Friends and social life

The first thing to know upon meeting and dating a person who is expressing Purple values is that they come with some luggage. Whether they are eighteen or eighty, it's not enough to simply love them alone. No, it's more a case of love me, love my tribe – their tribe being their family and close friends. If Purple's tribe doesn't accept Purple's partner then this relationship has a limited chance of long-term success, if indeed any chance at all.

Emotionally, Anthony and Sean are similar, but socially they have opposing attitudes. However, Anthony will do what ever it takes, even if it means sometimes sacrificing his own needs, to make Sean feel loved, safe, secure and accepted. Green Anthony is very adept at understanding people's sensitivities and needs.

If he can carefully and selectively introduce new people to Sean then he may be able to gently ease new individuals into Sean's precious inner sanctum. By widening their social circle bit by bit, Anthony's need for expanding friendship and love can be satisfied and Sean can remain safe and secure in a group that doesn't allow strangers in from the outside. At least, that's how it feels to Sean because Anthony is quietly letting them in from the inside.

Money

For this couple, money is rarely a priority. There are far more important things to focus on, like being near the family and doing good work for a worthy cause.

Sean, for example, is unlikely to take a promotion that means lots of foreign travel or relocating, even if there's a vast sum of money on the table. As for Anthony, he certainly won't give up teaching to make a fast buck in the city, trading in blood diamonds. That's not to say these two won't have money, but they won't go after it at the cost of their family or the environment, which may limit them somewhat if they live in a predominantly Orange society.

If a couple living in service of Green and Purple values live in an expensive city like Tokyo, Moscow, Geneva, London or New York, they can become frustrated at the expense of daily living.[15] When they look around them, it seems that the only people who seem to be able to live comfortably in these environments are in peak Orange and focused only on getting as much for themselves as possible, regardless of others. A person at the Green values stage has just recently shifted up and out of Orange and feels almost the opposite of this value set, while someone in Purple will rarely be driven to look very far for any new opportunities and might not even see them if any turned up.

The Purple and Green couple's most likely way of making money is to team up with others. These two make fabulous collaborators and networkers. Anthony loves meeting new people and Sean is excellent at loyally representing and selling his own brand and team. These two can be invaluable in a small or large organisation, working alongside an Orange colleague who is happy to do the hard negotiating or a Red business partner who loves the kill of closing the deal.

When it comes to money, Anthony might sometimes become concerned if Sean spends too much, particularly if it's on another, unnecessary, plastic, non-biodegradable product. Sean, on the other hand, might get annoyed that Anthony keeps throwing ten-pound notes into charity buckets and homeless hats, not to mention giving their debit card details to charity muggers on the street. Sean would never trust his bank account details to a young charity worker; Sean barely trusts his bank details to his own bank manager. Anthony, on the other hand, can be naively trusting with his money, particularly when it comes to charity requests. Sean doesn't get it; everyone knows charity begins at home.

But overall these two will be fine with money. Big cars and wealth are not the answer to this pair's contentment. As long as the family is healthy and happy and Green can still afford to buy the odd self-discovery or self-help book and attend the occasional retreat then these two will have all that money can never buy: inner peace and emotional security.

Sex

For a couple sharing Green and Purple values, making love will be a connected, loving and generous experience, because that's what these two value most. Both will love the aromatherapy candles, dangling crystals and Celtic ambient moods CD that Purple likes to have in the background of any love making session. The Green values of inclusivity, adaptability and flexibility will possibly add some smoking incense and a couple of mini Buddhas into the mix. This sex just got totally spiritual and a bit of spiritual in the bedroom suits these two just fine. On the Purple side, it will feel pagan, magical and a little naughty. In the Green corner, it feels deep and connected to the oneness beyond the physical of the two bodies in the room. This isn't just two people having sex; this is humankind uniting through these two individual bodies. However they choose to translate the experience, they'll both have a good time.

What's more, a Green lover may suddenly find himself or herself in the slightly unfamiliar territory of being the dominant partner. Paired with a partner expressing Red, Orange and even Blue, someone expressing Green values will usually be the more submissive partner, but with Purple, it's time for Green to take the reins.

Purple will be happy to find a position that works and stick with it. It's up to Green to cajole Purple into something a little more adventurous.

But be brave, Green. Enjoy a little mystery, even a touch of sexual Cluedo. Delve back down to those Red values you left behind and have almost entirely rejected. Let the sexual magic and mystery unfurl. It might just be that you, in the bedroom, with lover Purple and the incense burner, are just right combination to reclaim that Red physical fire. Turn up that New Age Vibes CD and take your Purple lover to an ancient time of wild, magical and uninhibited raw sex. They'll absolutely love it.

CHAPTER 12

Red and Red

ME, MYSELF AND I.

Dating and early romance

When two people with egocentric, Red values get together, the relationship can be full of great passion but also great pain. Red values promote unadulterated self-assertion, so when peak Red energy is present in both partners, any sense of control goes out of the window. As we discovered in Chapter 5, Red values motivate a person to be independent and autonomous. As children we need to develop a separate ego so that we can set healthy boundaries with others and confidently move into adulthood. We would not be able to establish our individuality and sense of self without going through the Red value stage. But when Red is unhealthily expressed, the world can be seen to be full of threats and can cause a person to be aggressively defensive, stubborn and unreasonable.

Whether these two Red-hot lovers are loving or loathing, it really is no holds barred. That's what happens when there are no grown-ups in charge. When it comes to a Red on Red love affair, think two toddlers in adults clothing. There's no getting around it – this pairing will be stormy. This is the classic tempestuous relationship dynamic that fills so many agony columns.

Dear Rhonda,
I love him but we fight all the time. It frightens me because it can get so out of hand. Should I leave him?
Stormy from Clapham

Dear Jane,
My girlfriend and I are screaming and shouting at each other more and more often. I'm scared it will get physical. I love her, but sometimes I think I actually hate her. Is this normal?
Horny from Stockport
P.S.: The sex is amazing.

Importantly, two lovers expressing high Red values must absolutely find each other attractive from the get go. These are not two people who are motivated to patiently work on a relationship so as to gradually build attraction, connection and common ground. If he or she doesn't wasn't to tear off your clothes on the first meeting and take you right there and then, forget it. It's never going to happen.

Research suggests that speed-dating events are an ideal place for egocentric Red people to find a new Red partner. A key study revealed that kindness and intelligence are the top qualities people generally look for in a partner – except for people who go to speed dating events. At a speed dating evening, it's all about how physically attractive you are, and Red is absolutely grounded in the physical self. It's all about finding a magnetic, trophy partner.

Early dating for narcissistic, status-hungry Red will involve lots of sex and public posturing. These two will very much want to show off this new relationship.

'Look at us!' they each think as they place themselves up at the well-lit neon bar in full view of the entire restaurant. *Aren't we gorgeous? I'm gorgeous. My new partner is gorgeous. I know you're looking at them thinking how much you wish you had them for a partner. But you don't.*

I do. Because I'm gorgeous and powerful and this gorgeous new partner of mine only proves that even more. I love my new Red partner. Mainly because they make me love me even more. Yes, look again. Keep looking. Aren't we gorgeous?'

But when people living and breathing this value set clash in a battle for dominance, this relationship goes from gorgeous to grim overnight. And then back again.

A double Red relationship soon becomes an endless round of wildly damaging and destructive break-ups followed by wildly passionate and powerful make-ups. You can't live with them, but the attraction is almost unbearable. You can't live without them, but you probably should.

So what makes someone manifesting Red behaviour so attractive to other people driven by Red values? Simple. They get each other.

'This person isn't afraid to talk my language. In fact, they're a lot like me, and I love me. I love to see me reflected back in someone else. It makes me feel even more powerful than I already am. But they won't beat me. My Red is stronger than theirs. As much as I love them, I will never let them dominate me.'

Reds don't always recognise themselves as Red! They're too busy 'being' Red and being right! With two people thinking in this way (consciously or unconsciously), this dynamic is exciting but totally exhausting. It's unlikely either can sustain a full-blown double Red dynamic for too long. It's just not humanly possible. Or is it?

Long-term and marriage

So miracle of miracles – or madness of all madness – these two individuals, with all their Red rising moods, have decided they're in it for the long haul. The most important thing they can do, right from the very beginning, is work out how they're going to structure their lives. Oh, and make sure their home has plenty of mirrors.

When one or both partners express healthy Red values, they will naturally seek independence from everyone – including each other. It's nothing personal; it's just how their values drive their behaviour.

That might not seem like an ideal basis for a unified partnership, but that's only if we go by conventional rules – which these two don't.

The key to their success will be in creating a more unconventional set-up, with lots of personal space and freedom. These two might spend weeks or months apart, socialise separately and never quite know where the other one is. If they have the means, they may even do a Helena Bonham Carter and Tim Burton and live apart within the same house, which will work wonderfully for them – independence *and* a relationship! Red didn't know such an ideal was even possible. What's more, it means they can plaster their own living quarters with mirrors, self-portraits and reminders of their own greatness without having to compete with their partner.

Competition is best avoided in a double Red values relationship. Both will always need to win, which is a problem when they are competing against each other. Laid-back Green might see a way for everyone to win, Orange might weigh up the odds and seek the best strategy for the most profitable outcome, Blue might arbitrate a fair solution, Purple might retreat to their tribe for agreed consensus, but for Red there's only ever one winner – even if it means fighting to the death. When you've got two people prepared to fight to the death, it's not pretty.

Red understands that 'the world is a jungle where only the strongest and fittest survive'. Each will choose the game they play and make sure they win, regardless of who else is playing in the same arena. The benefit of two people with peak Red values being together is that they both understand each other's hard-wired hard-drives. They are able to leave each other alone to pursue whatever feels good for them, partly because they're so wrapped up in their own needs.

These two can live like passing ships in the night and still potentially maintain a healthy partnership, providing they acknowledge and respect each other's right to be free.

If they can stay emotionally healthy and not fall into the jealousy trap, these two might just let each other breathe and express who they really are, without making each other feel guilty or hemmed in.

At their most healthy, Red partners won't feel they are living in the shadow of one another. Whatever they do, even if they screw up, these two understand and respect the need to act on impulse and indulge in risky, self-serving behaviours. People living Red are tired of being judged by others and feeling like the world is against them, but with a matching partner it can suddenly feel different. They may very well not feel judged any more.

However, as much as they might avoid judging people, they'll still love to boss others about. Control is very important to this value set, so these lovers need to get clever when it comes to controlling the relationship. The way for them to negotiate this Red squared pairing is for each partner to learn to tacitly set boundaries through behaviours, rather than explicitly dictating rules. As tempted as they both might be to lay down the law, unspoken agreements will serve them much better. It's important to each of them that they can both feel like they're the one in control. As long as they can each delude themselves that they're the one in charge, they'll be happy, and perhaps even a little smug.

But, when the Red on Red relationship goes bad, there's nothing worse.

As much as people expressing Red values can unite against the world around them, when it comes to their own private relationship, they'll face a number of challenges. To start with, these two are both prone to unhealthy expressions of narcissism, so deep intimacy and lasting fidelity may be a problem, as will deciding who controls the TV remote. Also, a person with a Red centre of self will hate to feel vulnerable, so these two will always have their defences up and be ready to stage a pre-emptive attack – even with each other. Once they attack, they don't care who hears, as anyone who lives in an apartment block with a Red couple can verify.

Hell genuinely hath no fury like a Red partner scorned. What's worse, Red and Red both know exactly what buttons to push when it comes to winding up their partner. They know only too well the four things that will hurt their partner more than anything:

1) Being embarrassed in public
2) Being disrespected
3) Being made to feel stupid and ashamed

4) Being made to feel jealous.

If any of these four big Red buttons are pushed, this relationship has the potential to go nuclear. When a couple starts mutually pressing on these triggers, it's nothing short of catastrophic. The heady cocktail of early attraction will soon turn into an endless round of narcissistic-driven jealousy and possessiveness, coupled with thoughtless, aggressive and selfish behaviours. This combination then becomes an emotional Molotov cocktail – not something anyone can to sip for too long without getting third-degree burns.

In a highly emotional state, a person hijacked by the emotions of Red values would rather lose everything, including the partner and even children that they love, than back down and say they're sorry. There's nose-cutting and face-spiting galore when Red and Red get caught up in conflict. We see plenty of examples of unhealthy Red relationships that end quickly in a blaze of alimony and acrimony. We see far fewer sustainable Red pairings.

This archetypal Red on Red relationship was epitomised by Richard Burton and Elizabeth Taylor. They were powerfully attracted to one another and married, then fought violently and divorced, only to be irresistibly drawn back together and even remarry again. But just like their starring roles as Anthony and Cleopatra, this combination rarely ends well, unless they both find themselves held in a long-term, mutual suspension of attraction – with each appreciating how lucky their partner is to have them, and how lucky they are to have their partner.

But whether it holds up or breaks up, this couple will have had a lot of fabulous times on the way. Fabulous times are important to Red values because, as they know, you only get one life; might as well do what the hell you like with it.

And they will.

Kids and family

Firstly: Whaaat and why?

Secondly: Get a nanny, get an au pair, get the in-laws, get the neighbour, collar a stranger off the street. Anyone. Just get help. Oh, and while you're at it, get a TV crew to make a reality show about the minutiae of your family life. This is Katie Price meets *The Osbournes* meets *Surviving Gazza*. You might as well cash in.

Seriously though, it's very trying having kids, as those with them well know. If peak Red values are dominant in this household, having demanding children in the mix will take the word 'trying' to a whole new level. Red warriors are the least able to set aside their own feelings for others, including their own children. Unless one or both of this pair is able to surface more Purple or Blue values then parenting is going to be extremely troublesome for them.

If a Red parent can't make their children feel cared for and nurtured, it may result in issues for their offspring in later life. When Red on Red parent together, the children may need somewhere and someone to go to for support. The children will need a strong family network or close friends who are prepared to step in and help their parents. But whether the Red parents have external support or not, when the teenage years hit – run for cover. This household will be in Rouge overload.

The Red value set is naturally expressed through adolescence, but two Red parents won't tend to make any allowances for this – they'll simply go head to head with this new perceived threat under their roof. This is when kids storm off, run away and, at worst, break off communication from their parents. Having children can often trigger hormones in the parent, such as oxytocin, that will shift someone's value set into Purple, Blue or Green, but if it remains in Red, these parents need to give each other and their children lots of space.

Playing lots of sport together can be a good idea for the Red family. The more this unit can put their energy into something physical like a shared sporting activity, the less emotional energy and frustration they will have to take out on each other. Though of course they will all be very competitive, so even if little Millie *is* only five, Daddy and Mummy won't give her any concessions when it comes to that family bike race. It's dog eat dog remember, and Millie has to learn that no one, not even her parents, will pretend to let you win in the game of life.

Friends and social life

If this partnership works, it means both parties have been able to find a ton of mutual respect for each other. However, there probably won't be very much left over for anyone else.

So here's my advice to all you Reds in the house: don't expect your Red partner to like or even tolerate your friends. It's probably better if you keep your social lives somewhat separate, anyway. In truth, neither of you particularly needs a lot of friends and there are very few people you would trust to be close to you. Those few close friends you do have will have to be content to mainly be an admiring audience for you.

If one looks at Red's close social circle it's unlikely there's anyone else in that group who frequently expresses a dominant Red value set.

It wouldn't be sustainable. The dynamic would create far too much unwanted competition and Red would have quickly, and fairly ruthlessly, expunged any other threatening competitors from the group. There's only room for one leader in all areas of Red's world.

Here's the question for the Red hot lovers amongst us: why ask your new Red values partner to be part of a group that has been specifically sculpted and honed to only need one Red member – you? Is there really any room for sharing the space around you? Let's say you do bring your Red partner in – how are you feeling when they begin to steal the limelight? What do you do when they start interrupting you and completing your sentences or correcting your facts? What will you do if they're funnier than you? Have better stories than you? Are more likeable than you? Start to get invitations without you? Have you really thought this through? You've created your very own piece of social theatre and cast yourself in the leading role – why would you willingly bring someone else in to audition to play the part of your replacement? You might be better off being a solo act, which you've always really known.

A person firmly ensconced at the Red stage doesn't tend to rely on anyone but themselves. They understand the limitations of friendships. They also understand there is a cap on how much they themselves will invest in a friendship, so neither of these two will want friendships that require much maintenance. They need to know they have people that they can pick up whenever it suits them, and put down for the same reasons.

They won't want any pressure and will avoid needy people like the plague. They definitely will have no time for weakness. Most people driven by Red values would find it incredibly hard to empathise with or help a friend with ongoing emotional issues. Remember, they believe it's a jungle out there and only the fittest survive. If you can't pull yourself together and get on with it then you're not cut out for this world, and you're certainly not cut out for a friendship with them.

Rebellious Red can be as spontaneous in their friendships as much as they can be spontaneous in the rest of their life. So, if a friend crosses them or ceases to be of any value, someone expressing Red is capable of cutting them off irrevocably.

A Red on Red partnership will make it clear to each other when a certain friend needs to be cut loose.

Just ignore their calls,' Roan Red will advise. *'They're a loser. So what if he can't find another job and his wife has left him. It's been three months. What if we all whinged like that? The human race would be extinct.'*

'You're right,' Rebecca Red replies. *'I'm exhausted with him. He's no fun any more. What are you doing tonight?'*

'I'm seeing some friends.'

'Maybe I'll come with you.'

'No. This is my thing. You're not invited.'

Having said all that, occasionally these two are able to become a kind of social double act, in which case it might well be a lot of fun. This couple could be the talk of the town for two reasons: either because they're so entertaining together that everyone is drawn into their social halo, or because they break into a fight and have a screaming break-up in the middle of the restaurant every time you go out with them. Either way, it will be entertaining for those around them.

In the long-term, though, these two might be better off having fixed evenings in a week where they see their own friends and come back to each other – egos refreshed, stroked and adored. That's when Red values are expressed at their healthiest and happiest.

Money

Money can be a real source of tension between two people living self-serving Red values. Not because of the way it's organised or even what it's spent on, it's just that Red needs to be in control. Joint bank accounts are definitely not a good idea. The psychological structure of a person at the Red stage has a lot of emotion tied up with money and anything tied up with Red emotions is an extremely volatile area.

Just like their living quarters, this Red partnership should ideally keep finances separate. Red partnerships need to find ways to reduce potential conflict and there's just way too much potential conflict over money. Money isn't just money, and neither is it simply an enabler. Unlike people living Orange values, those living Red values don't crave big houses and fabulous cars as material possessions that have intrinsic value or beauty in themselves. Neither is money simply about enabling them to enjoy new experiences. If they can afford nice things and new experiences they may well buy them – but only to further advertise their own personal power and status. No, money is a lot more than that: it's life and death.

Both these individuals fear self-annihilation more than anything. The primary driver for these Red lovers is survival of both their physical selves and their own ego. The ego must survive at all costs, even if that cost is to others, including their partner. They both understand that, in the current economic system, money means survival.

On the positive side, this does mean that a couple holding dominant Red values will always make sure they have enough money. Whatever it takes, they won't go without. This tends to make them quite hard in business and money matters. It's every man and woman for themselves out there in the world. Red will do whatever it takes to get as much reward and respect as they feel they deserve.

Someone at peak Red is often very clear about how much they will or won't pay for something.

Once they've decided, they won't budge. Unlike strategic Orange who has learned to negotiate, Red will make their decision based on nothing more than how they feel and what they will or won't accept. Women or men expressing Red values won't easily be influenced by external factors such as market forces or a competitor's negotiating tactics. A person motivated by the Red value set can often do very well in a deal such as house buying – simply by holding firm. They may have to walk away of course, but equally they can squeeze a deal out of the situation that others would never have even dared consider possible. At the same time though, because they have no patience, they may end up paying through the nose for something that, had they waited, they could have got much cheaper. Impulsive Red can end up crashing and burning when it comes to money. Like every other area of their life – money can mean volatility, unpredictability, but also sometimes a great deal of fun and fortune.

Sex

Red on Red action equals 'movie sex'. Think raunchy electric guitars, thrashing power chords and wah wah pedals over a pumping bass. That's the soundtrack under these two lovers as they roll around sweaty and entangled in white silk sheets – panting, hungry, animalistic and barely able to get enough satisfaction. These two are totally and utterly about the physical, so let's be very clear about this: if sex between two Red partners isn't instantly totally and utterly bloody amazing, this relationship is over. Done. Gone. Cold. Dead, dead, deadety dead in the water. There will be no visits to a sex therapist or Relate for these two. If it's not firing on all cylinders from day one then they'll go and find someone else to relate to.

So that's the early days of Red on Red's sex life, but where does it go from there? This couple will need to work hard to maintain a strong and healthy sex life. They'll probably set the bar very high at the beginning and, unless they're extremely committed, the only way is down.

Sexual satisfaction and instant gratification are important, but more than that, it has to be the right kind of sex.

Red values mean a lot of sexual energy. Both these lovers need plenty of attention. If either partner is tired or disinterested, the other won't take it lightly. Red isn't someone who empathises or understands their partner's moods or needs. They are driven by a set of values that only understands their own needs, and if they need sex, they need sex.

Not only that, but they also want to be desired by their lover. Male or female, they won't want to have to keep demanding sex from their partner. That won't do their ego any good at all. They want their partner to lust after them, adore them, hunger for them. If their partner doesn't see their value and desirability, Red will feel angry and frustrated.

So, in this coupling, both parties will have to do both the wanting and the needing, and that's why it takes so much more effort for this sexual relationship to flourish long term. They must allow for no let up, no time off. Once either of them feels the other isn't bothered, the rot will begin to set in, and then it will become challenging. A Red partner will find it hard to come back to their lover from a few months apart on a sexual sabbatical. The flame will have died and both will expect the other to rekindle it.

Sex is a hugely important element in this combination and, as such, the bedroom can be a place where many issues and conflicts are resolved. Because Red values are fundamentally bound up with the physical and emotional dimensions of human expression, the quickest way for this couple to get back on track is to have a good session in the bedroom. Once they feel sexy and powerful again, they may well forget what they were even arguing about. Until the next time. Which probably won't be too far away.

Exhausting, right? That's why a Red partner will often prefer to detach emotion and love from sex.

It might hold less meaning as far as some of the other value systems are concerned but for Red, sex for sex's sake is just fine, if not ideal. In the words of Woody Allen, *'Sex without love is a meaningless experience, but as far as meaningless experiences go, it's pretty damn good.'*

CHAPTER 13

Red and Blue

LAW-MAKER AND RULE-BREAKER.

Dating and early romance

If you're predominantly expressing Blue values and you fall head over heels for someone expressing peak Red then your wonderful world of order and rules is about to erupt, explode and generally be tested to the max. If, on the other hand, you're predominantly expressing a Red value set and you fall for someone expressing peak Blue then your wonderful, self-serving world of freedom, independence and spontaneity is about to be curtailed, controlled and squeezed to within an inch of its life.

Blue needs safety and security while Red values are all about personal power and spontaneity. Blue seeks reason and purpose. Red wants excitement and action. Blue strives for obedience and meaning. Red craves mystery and adventure. Blue values enforce regulation and direction. Red values spit in the face of authority.

These two couldn't be more different. So, do opposites really attract? Yes, they do. After all, there's no dark without light, wrong without right, lose without win or yang without yin – and there's no Blue without Red. When these two opposite value systems come together, they can be incredibly creative. Blue and Red values embody the fundamental creative forces of the universe – order out of chaos. When these two first meet, it's either going to be cosmic chemistry or the worst date in history. One thing that's guaranteed is that they will drive each other crazy. It just depends whether it's for all the right reasons or all the wrong ones.

Jack (Red) and Tanya (Blue) work in the same organisation. Jack is in marketing and Tanya is in accounts. Let's follow their journey as they go from first date to first child.

These two have been teasing and flirting with each other around the office for a while now – the tension between them is palpable. Tanya trying to impose a colour-coded filing system onto Jack's paperwork chaos, and Jack drawing colour-coded male genitalia onto Tanya's strict washing-up rota. She is highly disapproving, needless to say, yet somehow can't say no when Jack tells her the two of them will be going out for a drink together on Friday. As Tanya regains her self-composure and reluctantly rearranges her diary, she tries to make rational sense out of the uncomfortable emotional and physical desire she feels towards him.

'Hey, it might not be too bad. Anyway, he just needs a bit of guidance, a bit of order in his life and I'm just the person for the job,' she thinks.

Unfortunately, Jack has already decided Tanya needs a bit of loosening up – and he's just the person for that job.

So, it's Jack and Tanya's night out on the town. He has taken her to a restaurant of his choosing and now sits in front of her, self-assured, confident, oozing self-possession and defiance. Tanya is pleased that she decided to wear her gorgeous new LBD – this place is pretty showy. Jeans and boots really wouldn't have cut it. Both of them are thinking this could turn into quite a good evening.

Jack is pushing his way through the crowd to the front of the bar, joking loudly with people around him as he does so. Most people accommodate or tolerate him, but one man gets annoyed and pushes Jack firmly back. Suddenly, Jack turns on him. The funny banter disappears in an instant only to be replaced by an icy stare and a sharp threat. The two men bark at each other before a bouncer steps in and calms them down. The man backs off and Jack steps forward to get served – first.

Tanya has witnessed the scene. Her heart is beating heavily – and it's not because Jack looks so hot. Tanya can see people looking towards Jack and whispering. Some of the restaurant staff even looked concerned. She's wondering if people know she's with him. Maybe the two of them are about to be publicly humiliated and thrown out onto the rainy streets of a very busy Covent Garden. Will someone call the police? Will Tanya's face be all over the internet tomorrow? She can just see the headline now. *Accountant in Restaurant Unrest!* Tanya doesn't like social ripples of any kind – she has a professional reputation to uphold. But Jack couldn't give a stuff. He doesn't need to adhere to society's rules of good or polite behaviour. In fact, quite the opposite – society needs to adhere to his. Tanya wonders if this date wasn't such a great idea. Jack sits back down, smiling his cheeky smile, his dark eyes penetrating Tanya's soul and, despite everything, Tanya is mesmerised by him. She can see he might be selfish, dangerous and unpredictable, but he also presents an irresistible challenge. Like an undisciplined soldier, he just needs a firm captain. She can see that this character clearly needs some Blue values in his life.

'*I will tame you,*' she thinks.

But Jack has his own plans. '*I will corrupt you,*' he plots.

'*Tame you.*'

'*Corrupt you.*'

'*Tame you.*'

'*Corrupt you.*'

There's a battle ahead for these two, but when it comes to keeping Red values in line, Tanya Blue may just have the discipline and patience to do it.

Long-term and marriage

In order to succeed, this partnership relies on the universal, cosmic principles of Time and Space. Tanya will want to organise their time with lists and schedules and timetables and Jack will want lots and lots of space. Tanya loves a to-do list and her bedside table, desk drawer and fridge magnets will be brimming over with them. There's nothing she loves more than crossing items off a list denoting all the things she's done – the little tick next to a chore well done is its own little reward, and Tanya loves a reward.

But Jack hates lists – on so many levels. Lists make him feel limited to only the items that are on them. There's no room for spontaneity. Jack feels hemmed in by lists. Lists just stop him doing other fun stuff. What's worse is that lists make Jack feel guilty and resentful. They sit there, suspended on the fridge, reminding him what they haven't managed to do because he is clearly useless and inadequate. There's nothing good or rewarding about lists as far as Jack is concerned. He feels the same about hindsight – nothing good about that either. It only reminds him that he could have done something better but that now it's too late. But Tanya loves hindsight as much as she loves lists. *'Hindsight gives you the chance to learn from your mistakes and do better next time.'*

These two have fundamental differences in their value set. If this relationship is to find any peaceful ground, the Blue partner must try to disassociate themselves a little from Red's way of doing things; the solution isn't always about sorting Red out and bringing Red into line. Blue needs to learn that leaving Red alone is often the most effective way to bring order to the chaos, but there are different ways of giving Red space. When these two fight and Red rises into an emotional tirade, Blue is often tempted to suggest Red calms down and that they talk later, but that's not the kind of space Red needs. Red will hate being told to calm down, grow up or come to their senses by Blue. Blue has once again mistaken time for space.

Red doesn't take kindly to Blue imposing rational thinking time. Red needs space to vent their Red energised emotions. Sometimes the most helpful way to manage Red in conflict is to emotionally hold them while they kick off. If their partner gets caught up in the fight, it will only go to confirm to Red that the world is unsafe, unsteady and unreliable. Whereas if they can shout and scream while their partner remains strong and calm, Red will feel safe, secure and accepted. Blue might want to give Red some thinking time alone in the naughty corner, but the only time Red needs is emotional airtime.

A quick Red alert to prevent all you Blues getting the blues. Even if the clutter on your Red partner's side of the bed or in their study drives you insane, you might be better off closing the door or closing your eyes to the mess. If you start having a go at them about sorting and clearing and organising, you'll be opening a whole can of worms that will spread their way through the woodwork of your relationship until it rots it to the core. Reds won't be told. So don't get into a habit of telling.

'You should', 'you need to', 'you have to' and 'you must' are all phrases that will take a chisel to Red's love for Blue and chip away at it until there's nothing left.

When these two enter into a long-term commitment, they need to be careful that they don't get stuck playing out the roles of parent and child, or teacher and pupil. This rebel and disciplinarian role-play could easily become a habitual pattern of behaviour between them.

Before this Blue/Red relationship, Jack had been used to doing exactly what he wanted, when he wanted. Though this impulsivity and spontaneous way of life suits him, it didn't necessarily mean he could get a solid financial or social footing in life. Although strong Red values are all about looking out for the self, they aren't at all about working within the system. This means that people living Red values can suddenly find themselves in adulthood without some of the social structures that could benefit them – pensions, savings, mortgages, healthcare, etc.

Anything that requires long-term planning and delayed gratification has probably not grabbed Jack's attention throughout his life. He's lived for instant gratification and while that was fine in his teens and even his early twenties, he may find himself hitting his thirties suddenly worried about the future.

The Baby Boomers are a classic generation overflowing with a strong centre of self at the Red stage, often hiding behind Green values. They grew up under the constant threat of nuclear war and global destruction, and consequently many of them lived for the here and now with no thought to growing old. Many of them didn't think they'd make it past the seemingly pensionable age of thirty. Like a teenager, Red will often grab the moment with no thought to the consequences, thinking, *'Hell, why not? I could be dead tomorrow.'*

But very much alive, and now with Tanya in his life, Jack has a real shot at long-term security and stability. If he hooks up with Tanya, an extrovert with very strong Blue values then this new stability will be enforced quickly and rigorously with no room for negotiation. Tanya will want to tell Jack exactly how life is going to be, what the weekly schedule looks like and how many nights a week it's reasonable for him to go out without her. Needless to say, while offering stability, this approach will potentially push Jack to rebel. He simply hates being told what to do, think or feel.

However, if Tanya is somewhat calmer and can take a more patient and tolerant approach, she and Jack could benefit considerably. Blue values offer something very unique – the chance to focus and channel all that Red energy and really make things happen. Red energy can be quite scattergun, directed at whatever comes their way. They can flit from idea to idea, project to project, and go from love to hate in a matter of seconds. Red values are extremely emotionally driven, so may not always complete a task or reach a goal if they don't feel like it. If a business venture gets too boring or difficult, Jack can easily walk away – just like he can, and has, from a boring or difficult relationship.

But Tanya loves planning organising, strategizing - and all the bits that Jack considers boring. She can remain interested in something even though the reward may be weeks, months or even years away, but sometimes she can lack the emotional energy or passion that Red values can bring to really drive an idea forward. Together, these two can be a very exciting force of focused passion and commitment.

As long as Tanya can learn to be clever and keep her attempts at tight control under the radar, all will be fine. Jack needs to still believe he is in control. Tanya needs to think of herself as the secret PA, the stealth commander, the invisible leader. If Jack believes that without him Tanya will be nothing then together this Red and Blue combination could really be something. This relationship is the classic secret leader dynamic:

'My husband always thinks he makes the decisions but I'm the one wearing the trousers.'

'I let my wife think she's in charge but I'm the one steering this ship.'

What can be wonderful about this relationship is that both parties think they're in charge. Both believe the other would be lost without them. As long as they never – I mean *never* – explicitly state that thought, they may just happily delude themselves and each other to their dying days.

Kids and family

So Tanya and Jack have made it to the long-term commitment stage and decided to have children. Or rather, Tanya has planned conception and birth around various commitments like the house move, the couple's financial situation or the family holiday. Jack on the other hand simply believes he was the one who suddenly decided to have kids.

Different paths, admittedly, but with only one destination: parenthood.

An individual living in service of Blue values is totally ready to become a parent. Before the first child is born, Tanya will have read everything from Doctor Spock to Gina Ford – via the *Pregnancy Bible* – and already worked out which secondary school the child will go to and what might predictably be on the GCSE syllabus for that year. She may even have started reading *Othello* and French Key Stage 3 to the unborn foetus. It's never too early to start planning.

In fact, Tanya can be highly tempted to micro manage her children's career paths, sometimes with detrimental effects. There are many instances of individuals who, during childhood, were forced by pushy parents to have piano lessons, or receive extra maths tutoring, who then rebelled and took the opposite path.

What Jack and Tanya will share when it comes to their parenting values is a keen sense of reward and punishment. Both value honour and status, albeit in different ways, and will want the very best for their children. With Tanya's sense of social honour, she will make sure little

Milo and Gemma get into the best school in the catchment area and with Jack's sense of personal honour, he will make sure no one bullies them in the playground.

But there's no getting away from the fact that while Tanya will take the role of parent very seriously, Jack could, and probably will easily, slip into being one of the children. While having a partner with a childish temperament is trying for anyone in a co-parenting relationship, Blue values are the best equipped to handle it. Tanya will simply continue to lay down the law and just include Jack in amongst the children, even if that means sending him to sit on the naughty step!

Tanya needs to watch out though, because there are two crucial times when the children may well identify more with their Red parent than with the one expressing Blue.

When the children are demanding toddlers, Tanya will be working overtime to discipline them through this difficult stage. Jack, however, just wants a quiet life and will give the kids whatever they want to shut them up and leave him alone. He may suddenly become the favourite parent, happy to raid mummy's secret sweetie stash or buy forbidden toys with small, choke risk pieces.

Then, when the children hit adolescence, their Red-motivated parent totally understands their sudden volatile emotional mood swings. Together, Jack and the children may sometimes form a formidable little gang, united against Tanya's authority. This can be a lonely time for a Blue parent, but hold fast and the children will nearly always come through. They may rebel or even run away but they will come back, partly because their Red parent, with all their crazy, self-centred energy, has made them feel more normal than most teenagers ever get to feel.

A quick word with all the Blue mummies and daddies with Red partners. You may not realise it, but your partner may possibly have a big hand in giving your children the best chance at developing a healthy ego and being fully rounded, self-accepting adults. Red values can show their children how to accept the good and the bad they feel inside them, whereas, if you're honest, if you are holding Blue values, you'll often want to deny or

suppress the bad, darker aspects of yourself and those you love. If ever you can thank your brave Red warrior for the good they do when it comes to parenting, don't think it will go unheard. They'll simply love being thanked and appreciated. An occasional word of thanks and some well-placed words of appreciation and respect can be part of your secret undercover toolkit to keeping this relationship healthy and happy.

Friends and social life

In this partnership, the person expressing peak Blue values will often have a close and trusted network of people around them.

Loyalty will be extremely important in Tanya's friendships, but Jack doesn't have much time for loyalty, even for Tanya's sake. He will respond to her friends very honestly. If he doesn't like them, or if he doesn't agree with them, then he will say so in no uncertain terms, making no concessions to Tanya's feelings. She finds this behaviour very hard to understand. If Tanya is ever in a bad mood or takes against someone in company, she will most likely control her feelings and act like all is fine for the sake of those gathered. But Jack doesn't do 'nice social pretences'; he is authentically himself in every single moment, regardless of the offence that might cause.

Tanya may well find herself having to explain or apologise on Jack's behalf after he has upset one of their friends. There's no point asking Jack to apologise because sorry is not a word that comes easily to someone with dominant Red values. In fact, it doesn't come at all. If she waits for Jack to apologise, she'll be waiting forever, and when it comes to feeling bad and needing to resolve her guilt, Tanya can't wait forever. Feelings of guilt peak at the Blue values stage and will be a huge part of Tanya's life. She will be in a state of anxiety over any conflict or embarrassment between her friend and her Red partner, and no amount of late-night list-making will make her feel better. She needs to confront the person or at least write an email or send a text and sort it out. That's the right thing to do and Tanya will always try to do the right thing.

All is not lost, however, in the social world of Tanya and Jack. What they definitely share is a love of status and position. So these two will come together and mutually shine at any event that might hoist them up another rung on the ladder of social power and persuasion. Whether it's the local Rotary Club or one of Jack's business dinners, they will both be charm personified as they revel in the status of sitting at the top table, lording it over the minions.

Money

As we've seen, Blue values can be a real benefit to Red when it comes to making more money and increasing future security. Together these two will gradually and steadily creep up the economic ladder.

But Tanya needs to stay alert: Jack may well be a constant threat to her carefully architectured financial plan. Jack isn't interested in waiting ten years to buy the big five-bedroomed house with en suite dressing room and second reception. He wants it now. Surely with all Tanya's networks and connections at the bank they could wangle a bigger mortgage. But Tanya hates risk. She wants to be sure they have the money before they spend it. Jack will spend what he wants when he wants. However, there's no need to warn Tanya that she will need to keep a tight grip on the finances, she just will. Control over the money in this partnership might be the one battle that Jack will never win.

It could be tricky for Tanya, though, if she expects Jack to join her in saving for the future. She may feel he has agreed to save a certain amount of money over the next three years and then pool their money to put down a deposit on a house, but when that time comes, she shouldn't be surprised if Jack turns up in a brand new top of the range sports car with not a penny left for the house deposit. It was such a powerful, sexy car, he just couldn't resist.

Sex

Of all the value systems, Blue can sometimes overlook physical attractiveness in their partner in favour of other qualities such as decency, kindness and loyalty. That's not to say Blue doesn't need to fancy their partner, but there may be more to fancying them than simply a beautiful face or body. Red, however, is totally entangled in the physical and emotional dimensions of being human.

Red must want to tear their partner's clothes off and, just as importantly, their partner must to want to tear Red's clothes off right back.

This is where our Blue and Red couple Tanya and Jack might have difficulties in the bedroom. Tanya can be a little more restrained when it comes to sex. There's a time and a place, and possibly even a reasonable number of times a week, for sex. This is way too frustrating for Jack. Firstly because he may end up feeling denied the sex that he wants, and secondly because Tanya doesn't appear to want him desperately, passionately, every single second of every day. Tanya needs to be aware of Jack's large but fragile ego when it comes to sex. Underneath all the primal needs of his physical and sexual energy can sit a very delicate sense of self that can't (or won't) tolerate the feeling of being rejected.

If Jack makes advances on Tanya and she rolls over and goes to sleep, he will be furious. However unreasonable Tanya might find this fury, she'll need to be prepared manage it. If Tanya wants to maintain a healthy sex life with Jack, she'll need to take care to make him feel wanted and safe while at the same time keeping her own wants and integrity in tact.

The bedroom can be a tricky area for these two. Tanya wants to be honest and tell Jack that she's tired, but that honesty will be too harsh for someone embodying Red values. *'Tired or not, surely she should still desire me. I'm irresistible . . . aren't I?'* Jack will think to himself as he lays in a petulant curl on his side of the bed, marinating in testosterone.

This sexual union takes a bit of work because, fundamentally, people expressing peak Blue and Red values see sex as having quite different purposes or roles.

Tanya sees sex as a functional, physical act for two people who love each other to enjoy. There are also unspoken codes and rules around it involving trust and caretaking and kindness and understanding and perhaps predictability. She only wants sex once any disagreements have been resolved and the lists have all been ticked.

Jack views sex as a physical act in its own right. It doesn't have to be connected to any other conditions – not even love. Where Tanya wants to talk and talk to resolve any arguments, Jack knows that if they just have sex it will all be sorted out. Having sex on a row will be an incredible challenge to someone in Blue. It will feel so wrong, even violating, but it doesn't feel that way from the Red values perspective.

This isn't about gender, it's about what we value as important. When it comes to sex between someone with Blue values and someone in Red, both partners may potentially find each other challenging and difficult to understand. For example, if they're on their way out to a party and Jack suddenly gets horny, Tanya will very likely refuse to have sex and say they can do it later when they get back, thinking, *'If we start all that up now, we'll be late.'* Tanya's Blue values make her believe that's fair, but fair or unfair, she has just guaranteed herself one very moody partner, for what may well prove to be a very unpleasant evening. Tanya will need to keep reminding herself that, when it comes to sex, she's got herself a moody, adolescent toy boy.

And what if the sex goes cold? When it comes to infidelity within a partnership or marriage, the Blue values partner is the least likely to stray. Red drives are possibly the most likely, but being unfaithful to a Blue partner is the worst thing they could do to them. However, if Jack is unfaithful it doesn't mean either of these two will finish the relationship. Jack can be a real dog in the manger. Even if he doesn't want Tanya any more, he definitely won't want anyone else to have her. As for Tanya, she made those vows to Jack and will do anything not to break them. A vow is more than just words to Blue values – it's life itself.

So yes, this relationship can be challenging, but it can also be mutually powerful and exciting.

 **Now you know the pitfalls, Mr or Ms Blue, you can work out and plan exactly how to keep this union on track. In fact, you've probably already made a list, haven't you?**

CHAPTER 14

Red and Orange

ACTION AND AMBITION.

Dating and early romance

When Red and Orange values combine it can become electrifying for both of them. A person at healthy, peak Orange will have evolved through Purple, Red and Blue values and had life experiences at each of the previous stages. Though they will still have Red values active within their psyche, they will have tempered and matured. There could be a great deal of empathy and respect between these two.

Let's meet Red Sonia, the warrior princess, and William of Orange, our latest couple wanting to spiral into love. Although Sonia shows up with her full Red armour of dominance and confidence, all guns blazing, it's William who can make or break these first few dates. He will get the size of Sonia instantly. William has been there, done that, bought every Red T-shirt and now, at Orange, sold them all for a profit. William knows exactly how to work this new date and can get

Red Sonia wound up, fired up or sexed up instantly, depending on how he feels about her.

As ever, with the Orange and Red hot colours, the temperature of attraction or repulsion will run high. However, this time, unbeknownst to Sonia, it will probably be Orange values calling all the shots. Sonia will need her full warrior princess armour on for this one.

The coming together of Red and Orange is not necessarily a romantic pairing, though it could be a very sexy one. These two individuals are both very much wrapped up in themselves.

If they are attracted to each other on the first date and decide to continue seeing each other, it will be because they can see a lot of value in the relationship for themselves. Both will be looking for a partner that feeds their ego, bank balance, creativity or self-esteem. Neither will waste their time on a loser. If these two click, this relationship will be highly charged as well as highly productive. If they don't, however, neither will hold back in making it clear this isn't going to work and walk away, wine half drunk and steak half eaten. Men and women living at full Red and Orange don't charity date.

When it comes to playing the dating game, these values will drive the two players to play hardball. Both sets of values are concerned with personal status. Their reputation is extremely important to them. For Red Sonia, her reputation is based on her sense of personal power. For William of Orange, it will be based on social position and material wealth. One of the first things William will be looking out for on a date is whether a person is wealthy, famous, educated, successful or sexy enough to even be considered a potential partner. If he does feel Sonia has enough of these attributes to make the dating grade then she could soon enjoy wallowing in the personal power that William has accredited her. The Red and Orange relationship works best when it is mutually beneficial.

William will want to name the location for the initial date but Sonia will have her own ideas. So it might take these two a few text message exchanges to decide where to go. William will probably win out by using both his charm and his highly developed negotiation skills. Remember, a person motivated by Orange values can be very strategic and persuasive when it comes to getting their own way.

These two may well go for a meal on their first date – unlike Blue, they don't hold to dating rules – but whether it's a drink or dinner, if William has got his way it will be at the latest venue that only opened last week and very few people have even heard of.

Sonia may be surprised to find herself eating in a disused and renovated sewer, being reassured by William that it's the height of cool.

'*It's genius isn't it? I mean they can't lose,*' William will enthuse. '*Even if they get a reviewer saying the food tastes like sh*t – that's still brilliant PR. Shall we try the floating sausages?*'

The conversation will flow easily between these two. Neither are wallflowers when it comes to promoting their talents and sharing their stories of personal success. Somehow these two can manage to spend an entire evening looking like they're in conversation when in fact all they do is talk about themselves. Sonia is extremely skilled at bulldozing a conversation and talking about her favourite subject – herself – while William is an expert at manipulating a conversation in order to talk about his own favourite subject – himself. These two are highly competitive when it comes to being the centre of attention, but they will also enjoy and feed off each other's energy. We join them on their first date at William's hip private member's club – Milk and Money.

'*You're going to love this place – amazing service, full of celebs and great food!*' he says as they approach the entrance of the restaurant.

'*I used to be a chef. I'm an amazing cook,*' Sonia replies.

William is greeted by the maître d' and they are ushered to a waiting table.

'*Wow, that's interesting because I'm just investing in a new chain of Thai restaurants,*' William says as he continues to sniff out an opportunity. '*In fact, I was one of the co-founders of Jamie Oliver's restaurants.*'

Sonia turns to face him and makes sure to lock him in direct eye contact before she barks back, '*Jamie Oliver can't cook. He used to ask me for advice.*'

William casually sits down at the table, unfazed by her energy. Without looking at her he picks up the menu, which he begins to scan, looking for the chef's specials.

'Oh, so you worked together? I know Jamie really well. Great guy,' he says.

Sonia sits down opposite him, places two fingers on top of his menu, slowly and firmly pushing it down. Their eyes meet and again she holds his gaze with fiery intensity. 'He's an idiot. Couldn't cook his way out of a paper bag. You should taste my cooking.'

Her front foot attitude excites him. He gently places the menu on the table. His voice softens as he begins to explore the possibilities. 'I'd love to. How's your Thai? We might be looking for a head chef. A rivalry with Jamie would be perfect. Think of the marketing opportunities.'

Unaware of the subtle shift in his demeanour, Sonia continues in the same tone. 'Come to mine and I'll cook you a pad Thai that will make your pants fall down.'

William decides this challenge is worth the effort. Matching her tone, suggestive of throwing down a diamond-studded gauntlet, he says, 'If your pad Thai can make underwear fall off, we really are in business. Let's go to mine. I've just had an eight gas hob deluxe range installed – cost me ten grand and I can't even cook.'

'Let's do it!' she replies.

They up sticks, abandoning the table, and head out into the night in search of a taxi. As William watches Sonia confidently stand in the road hailing passing traffic, cab or not, he thinks, 'I like her. Someone with drive and energy who needs my know-how to make both our dreams come true.'

As they jump into one of Hackney's finest carriages, she thinks, 'I like him, but I'll get what I want, with or without him.'

William will recognise and acknowledge Sonia's Red confidence and strong sense of self while she will marvel at his assured optimism and creative approach to life. These two will have fun winning each other over. William's Orange values will seduce Sonia with acknowledgement of her potential and by dangling the promise of opportunities for success. His seize-the-day attitude and refusal to get bogged down by rules and regulations, together with insights on how to win by using cunning strategies, will all appeal to her.

Flirtily strutting around each other in a narcissistic tango, this pair will swirl into an up close and personal dance of mutual appreciation.

As they settle down in the back of the cab he leans into her and asks, *'Has anyone told you how powerful you are?'*

'Yes!' she answers. *'But I never tire of hearing it.'*

That's how Red and Orange values spiral into love!

Long-term and marriage

When these two decide they'll be together long-term, the dynamic between them still needs to remain go, go, go. When Red and Orange values are active and dominant, there needs to be plenty of doing! These two are not cut out for endless quiet evenings in front of *Emmerdale*, unless William is producing it and Sonia is starring in it. These two are all about status, and status can't be found in the comfort of your own home, unless it's a fabulous showcase home and they have a constant stream of guests and TV crews round to appreciate and admire it.

Orange values will drive a need to be making things happen – businesses, creative projects, deals, scams, innovations, renovations, transformations, public relations, takeovers, make-overs – all successful and stressful.

Red values will drive a need to feel seen and loved, adored, never bored, admired, desired, commended and splendid, appreciated, validated, celebrated and self-inflated – all me-orientated and ego-related.

As may already be clear, compromise is not something that features in a Red and Orange relationship. If these two disagree, which they often will, the best they can hope for is to beg to differ. In reality, they both may well like the fact that their partner doesn't back down. Orange and Red aren't particularly interested in wallflowers, and quickly lose respect for low status, non-competitive people. So although they won't necessarily like being disagreed with, they will both hold a healthy respect for someone who states their opinion and stands their ground. If a very solid love and respect unites these two then they should be able to withstand the numerous disagreements they will almost certainly have.

William will reassure Sonia that conflict is an important part of the creative process. There's no renewal and innovation in a relationship without a good bout of screaming and shouting. These two may even positively flourish from conflict. Unlike a Red on Red relationship that can spiral out of control when it comes to conflict, Orange values bring to this pairing the ability to manage their heightened emotions back into some kind of rational state. Orange is able to objectify themselves and their behaviour within a situation, whereas Red remains fully emotionally immersed and entangled. An Orange value set contains Red's sense of personal power coupled with Blue's understanding of rules and order, so Orange-driven William knows how to use his intellect to affect Sonia's Red-fuelled emotions. In other words William will be able to nudge Sonia to think about alternatives, but from her own Red perspective.

Orange is well placed to tap into and manage Red emotions and behaviour in this way and yet still leave both parties with a sense of control as well as freedom. The combination of Red and Orange values contains so much energy and mutual understanding that, with a healthy amount of tension, this relationship can really go on smouldering until the end.

However, there are definitely some monumental challenges that will require a great deal of ongoing work. They both need to keep things ultra exciting to maintain the other's attention, as both are highly demanding partners. As soon as this relationship ceases to be of use to either of them, they will turn their attention elsewhere, with little sense of remorse. Neither will waste their time or energy feeling guilty. There are more important things to be getting on with – like satisfying their own desires.

Neither of these two will be motivated towards helping, supporting or nursing an ailing partner. This relationship is definitely not for better for worse, for richer for poorer, in sickness and in health. This relationship is only for better, for richer and in health. If one of these two becomes ill or depressed they will probably find themselves very much on their own. Orange and Red values do not make for natural carers.

Neither of them wants to struggle through hard times unless there's something really big in it for them. This can be a pretty fair weather relationship, which is fine if they are successful enough to afford plenty of holidays in the sun; otherwise the grey and stormy reality of the ordinary trials of life might put an end to this summer loving.

Kids and family

Anyone for happy families? It's a 'No, thanks' from the Orange and Red corner.

The dominant Red and Orange values combination does not lead to a life of traditional family values. People driven by these individualistic energies tend not to spend a lot of time around family units. Christmas and the occasional birthday are usually about the limit. Their own birthday occasions might be more enjoyable for Red and Orange, of course. There'll be lots of gifts for Orange and lots of attention and camera flashing for Red, but even then, if the gifts are rubbish or the attention lacking, both may cease bothering to show up at all.

Family members expressing Orange and Red values can often create a dynamic of complex feelings within family units. They can appear dominant then withdrawn, over-bearing then unavailable. Other family members may complain that their behaviour is inconsistent and unreliable, but that's how it is. People living values at the Red and Orange stage will never reliably step into line with the family dynamic. They will express themselves when and how they want.

Of course, they can also be a great deal of fun. You can't have the highs without the lows. You can't have their highly energised charisma one minute and then expect them to sit quietly and listen to someone else the next. It's true that they can seem either fully present or fully absent, but if anyone starts to make them feel guilty about their behaviour when they are simply being who they are, they may well seek to be as far away from the stultifying and judgemental gaze of parents and siblings as possible. That might mean retreating to an upstairs study for the day, or maybe even moving overseas to start entirely new lives.

When it comes to having their own children, these two face a lot of challenges, as William and Sonia are about to discover. Red values can be very childlike, so the company of children for Sonia is a hindrance at best and a competitive irritant at worse. As for William, he may feel children are accessories, but just like a Mulberry briefcase or an Armani suit, he wants to decide when he takes them out to show them off. But children are a permanent fixture.

William might initially love buying the latest Bugaboo for his cute little angel and proudly parading up and down the high street on a Saturday afternoon looking every inch the successful, twenty-first century Dad. Sonia might be happy to join them for a while to soak up the adoration garnered by their new little Mini-Me, but babies don't stay mute, transportable accessories for long.

By the time their little darlings grow up to have their own opinions, Sonia and William's values will have been stretched and tested to the max.

Plenty of Orange and Red sparks will have flown – both between them as a couple and between them and their children. This is unlikely to be a calm, equality driven, democratic family unit. 'Sharing' was never in Sonia and William's vocabulary and it's unlikely to be a word their children will often hear. William may have a little more emotional control than Sonia, but this whole family is all about me, my and mine. As Sonia and William watch their young children Katie and Dylan fight over a toy, they won't be able to help themselves become emotionally involved.

Katie (five years old): *That's my puzzle. No, Dylan, get off.*
Dylan (three years old): *Mine, it's mine. Mummeeeeeey!*
Sonia: *Actually, I bought it, so it's mine.*
Dylan: *Waaaah. Want puzzle. Mine. Daddeeeey.*
Katie: *Daddeeey. Tell Dylan it's my puzzle.*
William: *No.*
Katie: *Why?*
William: *Because, in actual fact, I paid for it, so it's mine.*
Sonia: *No, you didn't.*
William: *Yes, I did!*
Sonia: *You didn't.*
William: *I can assure you, I did!*

Sonia: *Didn't.*
William: *Did!*
Sonia: *Didn't!*
William: *Did soooo!*
Katie: *Mummy and Daddy are fighting. On the naughty step
– both of you!*

Possessions and boundaries will be a big part of this family's life together. Everyone will have to learn exactly what they can and can't touch and what rooms they can and can't go in. Think commune. Then think the complete opposite.

However, if this couple can afford child-minders or even a live-in nanny then everything should be fairly smooth – no surprise there! Red Sonia will be happier now she can be self-absorbed again and William will be free to pursue success while admiring his brood from afar, like a curious art collection. If however, like the majority of folk, Sonia and William need to get down and dirty with child-rearing in the raw, there may be trouble ahead. Sonia will not be happy about sharing the spotlight with a demanding child and will have better things to do with her time than stand around talking nonsense at loud, sticky-fingered, runny-nosed mother and toddler groups. Even if the mother and toddler group is the exclusive, celebrity-filled nursery that William had to fight tooth and nail to get little Katie into. It is Orange values that will motivate people to put their children's names down for schools before they're even born. Or, if private school isn't an option, they'll be working out which catchment area to move to or who to make friends with long before other parents have begun to consider such issues. Orange seeks the best and won't rest till it's theirs.

As those who have spent any time around young children will know, they need a lot of care and attention, constantly craving your time and focus in the early years and your strength, wisdom and patience later on.

Red values will not represent anywhere near the levels of maturity, tolerance and selflessness to meet the ever present demands of infants and toddlers. Neither will Orange's innovative and strategic mind necessarily pay a great deal of attention to a child's emotional needs.

When it comes to the cornerstone child-rearing qualities of patience and understanding, Sonia and William may be seriously lacking. However, they more than make up for it in the qualities of independence, self-survival and personal dominance – qualities that this pair know from experience are more important than any others if you're to survive in this often cruel and competitive world.

Friends and social life

Here is a potentially sticky area for these two. William Orange will like having an active social life full of acquaintances that can act as an audience for his displays of wealth, success and stories of triumph, but he is also interested in anyone who has information or connections that can serve him – whether he likes them personally or not. Sonia, on the other hand, will be less keen to have others around, and definitely less tolerant of anyone she doesn't like. Either way, in company, a Red and Orange couple will compete for attention in the same environment. William, ever the strategist, will find ingenious and creative ways to hog most of it. This will create tension in Little 'Red Rising' Hood, and stormy discussions may well erupt on the way home from any social event.

Inviting friends over is fine, but whose friends shall they be? Neither of them will want to sit in the company of the other's friends passively watching their partner entertain and dominate the proceedings. However, if they can find a way to co-operate, these two can make their social life work for them both.

William likes symbols of success and Sonia likes to be admired.

So if she can in some way become his social trophy, both social egos can be satisfied. It might be that Sonia is a beautiful trophy partner, or has a talent that William has nurtured. In this scenario, she gets to show off, but he also benefits from the attention and accolades of having 'discovered' and 'created' her. William may well like to be a puppet master and Sonia will likely enjoy performing. William will enjoy orchestrating the social proceedings and Sonia will revel in taking the limelight. If they are able to find a way to operate like this, the two of them can form a great team.

Think Frankenstein and his monster. Frankenstein gets the title of the book but the monster dominates the story. However, just like Frankenstein, it can all start so well, but when this social pact goes wrong, it goes horribly wrong. Damaged Red or Orange egos are one thing. Publicly damaged Red and Orange egos take the need for vengeance to a whole new level. These two need to avoid competing, or inadvertently putting each other down in public, at all costs.

Sometimes socialising is more than simply fun for people at the Orange values stage. Sometimes it's business and they can't afford for those occasions to go wrong. Like every other part of their relationship, William's Orange values will drive the need to covertly control Sonia's impact on his social and business circle of friends.

He knows he mustn't make her feel either offended or excluded. Sonia must believe she is welcome to any or all of William's social functions and the only reason she doesn't join him on an evening out is because she chose not to. But, as William knows, there are ways to get Sonia to autonomously 'choose' exactly what he wants her to choose.

If he doesn't want her to come to an event, the invitation offer might go something like this:

'By the way, we've been invited to Eve and John's for dinner and I want you there with me. I need to close a deal with John. I know you can't stand him but I think it would be good if you could put that aside and make the effort to support me. Just be there. You don't have to speak much. The evening will be about business, anyway. In fact, you could sit next to Eve all evening and listen to her talk about her children. You know how she loves to talk to you about her kids . . . What? You won't come? Definitely not? Oh, well that's a shame.'

However, if William does want Sonia to come, the offer might go something more like:

'By the way, we've been invited to Eve and John's for dinner but I'm sure you won't want to come. I know they adore you and love to hear your stories, but, as you say, they really like a drink and Eve always cooks twenty desserts and expects you to try them all. Oh and John's just had that ridiculous new Jacuzzi fitted in the garden that he wants you to try out. He says it was made for you. I'm only going because I need to talk to

John about closing that deal . . . Oh, you really want to come? All right, darling, whatever you want. I'll drive.'

Money

When money is plentiful between these two, they're like a couple of kids and the world is their toyshop. It's girls and boys with toys, indulging themselves in every up-to-date high end product, accessory and gadget available. These two are wilful and whimsical when it comes to spending. They might spend thousands of pounds having the house redecorated in the latest Farrow and Ball tones, but if either of them suddenly decides they've changed their mind and they should have gone with the Duck Egg Blue rather than the Pigeon Toe Pink then they'll simply have the whole house redone. Sod the expense.

If they both like the same things, they will get a great deal of satisfaction out of spending money and having material possessions. William may even take delight in buying Sonia whatever she wants, if only to show how successful they are and how they can afford the finest that life has to offer. William might need to be careful here, however. As much as Sonia likes to feel special, she won't want to be made to feel that William is better than her. Neither does she want to feel she is in any way dependent on him – Red hates to feel dependent on anyone. If William does hold the purse strings, he might want to think about how he manages their money around Sonia so as to avoid making her feel beholden. She will hate being made to feel indebted or controlled and, if she does, may well explode in anger or emotionally detach.

Both these two will be highly stressed if money gets tight, and it won't be pleasant. They will both scoff at the idea of make do and mend. That's for others. William would rather mount up more debt than scrimp and save to make ends meet and Sonia won't want to be left behind - she may well be right there with him in racking up the credit card bills. Money is an important enabler in this relationship, a necessary commodity that will oil and smooth the emotionally tricky wheels and cogs that keep this relationship functioning.

Arguments and fights can often be fixed with gifts – which is lucky because neither of these two is going to say 'sorry'. When there's no money to keep oiling the relationship machinery, Orange and Red values in a partnership can move into very difficult territory. William may be able to convince Sonia it will all be okay, but while he can live off the energy, hope and potential of the next project, she wants it all now.

'Okay,' he says, 'I promise I'll get us back on our feet. I've got a great new business idea. It just needs a bit of investment.'

William's orange energy will then likely cause him to risk everything to try to get back on top financially, but if he doesn't manage to do it, there'll be no support and no forgiveness from Sonia.

These two absolutely love having money at their disposal and neither of them minds too much how they get it.

With Orange's cunning and Red's selfishness, this is the most likely pairing to turn 'dodgy' when it comes to money. If necessary, these two won't mind bending the rules. They'll even dodge tax or commit fraud if the rewards are too good to resist and they think they can get away with it. The MPs' expenses scandal is peak Orange at work in a Blue system. People with values at Orange and Red won't see their behaviour as criminal either. Just clever.

'People are stupid if they don't do it,' William will reason. 'Why play by the rules if towing the line means you lose out?'

Red values might even drive Sonia to commit something like benefit fraud, but William won't tolerate that behaviour for too long. Orange values are essentially aspirational and claiming benefits is neither glamorous nor ambitious enough. If these two cross the legal line, William will help Sonia find more acceptable ways of getting money – like credit cards, faux investments and pyramid selling.

On the plus side, once a person exhausts the Orange values stage they often begin to evolve upwards into the Green values stage and may start sharing their wealth to benefit others through charities – a prime example being the Bill and Melinda Gates Foundation with its $33.5 billion endowment. However until Orange starts pushing into Green, or Red starts pushing into Blue, a dodgy time-share investment is the only kind of sharing these two will be doing.

Sex

Red Alert! Red values are essentially egocentric, meaning that if your centre of self is Red then you will believe what you think and feel is true for everyone. Everything is taken personally. In other words, if your Red partner is in a good mood, everyone should be in a good mood, if Red is angry, they'll make everyone else angry, and if Red is horny, everyone must be horny! Red will love their energised and proactive Orange partner working away to make them successful, but they'll still expect plenty of attention – and, if they want it, plenty of sex. Orange is the value set that understands Red's physical needs more than any other value set. Orange can recognise that when their Red partner is angry, they often just need a good shag. Orange knows that when Red is vying for sexual attention, they must make Red feel indulged. In this way, Orange knows how to avoid having to endure hours of screaming or sulking from a cross or rejected partner.

But there are differences in how Red and Orange operate sexually, as we can see back in the bedroom with William and Sonia.

Firstly, William's Orange drives mean he will be demanding in terms of physical appearance. He may, in fact, be fairly physically obsessed and nip, tuck, pump and botox to remain sexy. But Sonia with her Red centre of gravity won't necessarily bother to maintain that level of work – her partner should desire her just as she is. But sometimes Sonia might feel William doesn't desire her quite enough.

William can get caught up in work or projects and sometimes almost satisfy his sexual needs through his business or creative pursuits. Sonia doesn't have this ability to sublimate her sexual urge in this way. The only way she knows how to fulfil her need for sex is to have sex. If this is frustrated, the only way that sexual energy will be sublimated is by way of a fight. If Sonia needs to release sexual energy and is blocked from doing so, she may well try to get into an argument. She won't necessarily know what's at the core of this aggression and could pin it on any of William's annoying little habits.

When it comes to sex between William and Sonia, he will spiral down to meet her at Red where together they can be aggressive and animalistic. These two won't just stick to the bedroom either. In order to relieve their sexual urges, these two will have sex whenever and wherever they like. Together, these two will often be very daring when it comes to sex. Whether it's on a plane, a train, in a car or a spa, Orange values motivates a need for novelty and Red values provide the courage and daring. Orange values are about variety and Red needs instant satisfaction.

While William may get frustrated with Sonia's apparent selfishness – she only ever wants sex when she wants it – he won't be anyone's slave. But neither will she. If these two don't get their sexual rhythms in tune they may end up two sexually frustrated and rejected egos.

If that happens then these two may start to look elsewhere. Both are prone to taking risks when it comes to satisfying their needs. That includes relationship infidelities. If Sonia doesn't feel appreciated, she may look elsewhere for adoration and if William can't conquer his Red partner, he might be tempted to look around for possible alternative victories. These two both love to feel wanted and desired. At the same time, neither wants to see his or her partner wanting or desiring anyone else. If either or both of them are at any point pushed to jealousy, this dynamic can get very ugly.

When it comes to being personally wronged, both these value systems share a need for vengeance. If these two cheat on each other, they both need to get a good lawyer and hide the scissors. Those designer clothes are simply crying out to be shredded.

CHAPTER 15

Red and Green

THE ONE AND THE MANY.

Dating and early romance

When two people bearing the gifts of Red and Green values first meet it can feel like the beginning of a cosmic dance of the one and the many. If there is a natural synergy between them, the sense of completion can be intoxicating. Emotions may well be intense for each of them but for very different reasons.

Keith lives by strong Red values while Serena has a clear Green value set. They met again recently after a number of years when Keith used to date Serena's best friend. They were all teenagers then, but now they are both in their thirties. Both were curious about each other all those years ago and today that curiosity has remained. They decided to start dating, bringing their Red and Green values together.

So far, Serena has been revelling in being an audience for Keith's need to tell stories of victory, past triumphs and self-promotion. Serena feels she has re-found in Keith the urgency and drive of her teenage years – an exciting time that Serena secretly yearns to return to but knows she has grown out of. Keith, on the other hand, is revelling in finding Serena an adoring and caring audience. She's always happy to listen, admire and praise him.

When a person expressing Red values goes on a date with a person at Green, they can at last relax. Red drives might cause them to initially test the water a little with their Green prospect, but they'll soon find there's no fight to be had.

Keith loves this. No judgement. No competition. Just free to be who he truly is. Currently he is basking in Serena's sweet and generous meadows where his egoistic, contracted sense of self is flourishing in her Green and fertile soil. His previous experience of dating and relationships has involved a sense that the world wants to batter him down, but Serena seems to want to nurture and feed him, allowing him to bloom.

Of course, Serena will love to share her new-found love with all her friends as soon as possible. *'Keith's amazing,'* she will tell them all.

However, she might be surprised that not all her friends will agree. They may have noticed that this new person in Serena's life not only seems uninterested in her friends but also behaves as if he's disinterested in Serena herself! There's a chance Serena may be quickly warned off Keith by close friends and family, but she won't necessarily listen. Everyone's different, she will intuit, which is a good thing. Deep down, Serena knows, Keith is sweet, vulnerable and insecure. *'If only my friends knew him like I do, then they'd understand. Why can't everyone just get along? The world would be such a wonderful place.'*

Keith doesn't care if everyone gets along and he certainly doesn't care if Serena's friends approve of him or not. What makes the world a wonderful place is when he himself feels good. He certainly feels good dating Serena right now. He wouldn't necessarily call it love – whatever that means – but it's definitely a welcome experience.

Serena is attentive, caring and doesn't get cross when he cancels a date. She seems to always understand. At last he has found someone who lets him do exactly what he wants, where he wants, when he wants and how he wants. Wow – can a relationship really be like that?

'Yes,' Serena tells him. *'I want you to be totally yourself. Don't worry about me.'*

And Keith will do just that.

'Oh, and one other thing,' she will add, *'I nearly forgot. Here's that CD you mentioned you liked the other day. I bought it for you. Hope you like it.'*

'Thanks,' says Keith. *'Should I have bought you something?'*

'No,' Serena will assure him. *'I don't need anything. I just want you to be happy.'*

And he is. For the moment.

Long-term and marriage

As we know, 'I, me and mine' will be some of Keith's favourite words. Everything belongs to Keith alone, except of course blame and responsibility. In other words, if things don't work out in Keith's favour, the blame will be on everyone else! However, there is a paradoxical problem here.

From Keith's, egocentric perspective, he believes he is in fact responsible for everything that happens in the world around him. If Serena's in a good mood, it will be because of Keith. If she's in a bad mood, it must be because of something Keith has done, as he is the centre of his own and – of course, her – universe. But here's the catch: he won't want to accept responsibility or feel guilty about having caused a problem. So as much as Keith likes to believe he is the creator of all reality, when it comes to anything negative, Keith will blame Serena and everyone else for it. Go figure.

This makes Serena, whose favourite words are 'we, us and ours', the ideal partner from his point of view. Green values are about absolute acceptance and allowing people to be who and what they want or need to be in the world. Serena wants to make the world safe and kind for everyone. No matter who you are or what you might do.

This is fine, in theory, when everyone is behaving nicely, and sharing and caring for each other. However, Keith doesn't do a lot of sharing and caring. The truth is, it will often hurt Serena that Keith always uses the word 'I' when talking about their plans. She doesn't understand why he doesn't automatically talk in terms of togetherness. *'Can you use the word "we" sometimes?'* she will ask.

But Keith is primarily entangled in the 'I, me, mine' of Red values and just can't get used to the word 'we'. It feels so unnatural. The challenge for Serena in this relationship is to truly accept Keith's self-orientated position. The danger is that she'll appear to accept his values and attitudes on the surface, but secretly store up and harbour any hurt deep inside her heart. If so, that hurt will grow and fester and cause them both great pain in the future. A future that then really won't contain the word 'we', as Keith will be long gone.

Like any relationship, Red and Green values will function very well if they remain predominantly at the healthy end of the values continuum. But it is a continuum. The healthy end for Green means being generous, open and accepting. For Red it means staying energised, passionate and creative. At the negative end Green risks becoming a martyr or victim while Red risks being selfish, arrogant or defensive. In Keith and Serena's case, the negative end of this continuum is a very dangerous place to head towards.

This pair needs to stay alert to the emotional temperature of the relationship and keep it healthy. Or more specifically, Serena needs to stay alert to Keith's emotional temperature and manage it effectively. Luckily, she is an expert at intuiting a person's needs and feelings, which will be the saving grace of this partnership – as long as Serena can still remain strong.

The ideal attitude and posture for Serena to adopt in this relationship is 'kind but firm'. If she always gives in to Keith's whims and demands, the relationship has the capacity to go from functional to dysfunctional overnight.

The thing is, if both Keith's Red sense of power and Serena's Green sense of pleasing are turned up too far, this pairing can soon go from husband and wife to bully and victim. If Serena has little or no Red values active within her own psyche and Keith lacks all awareness and empathy, they could get locked into playing out the unhealthy extremes of these two value systems. Keith asserts his power to a damaging degree – emotionally, intellectually, or even physically – and

Serena lives true to her values of not upsetting anyone, even the person who is abusing her.

This is, of course, extreme. If Serena can stand firm and tread a moderate middle path, they will find an equilibrium that will serve them both. Keith will have a place in the world where his egoistic needs are not only accommodated but accepted, and Serena will find herself with someone who will protect her from the darker side of life.

With Serena's expectation that everyone is kind and will do the honourable thing, she often risks being taken in and ripped off by others. Keith knows better. The world is a jungle and he will feel heroically bound to protect her from those out to get her. This can be a really wonderful, mutually beneficial partnership – as long as Serena doesn't become a weakened victim. If she crumbles into weakness, she may well need protection from Keith. Once that happens, Serena is in the danger zone and there'll be no one to protect her except herself.

Kids and family

In terms of human development, the Red value set begins to rise up around the terrible twos, or rather the terrible twos *is* the Red value set. As toddlers become aware that their mother, other people and the entire world are all something separate from them, it creates a surge in the development of the ego. If they aren't actually part of their mother then their mother cannot ultimately control them, or indeed their well-being. This is terrifying for a little person.

'So I have to look after myself? Protect myself from this dangerous world? Where I can fall off climbing frames and hurt myself? Where other children want to snatch toys off me and hit me? Right then, I'm not taking any more nonsense. Watch out, world. I'll have things my way.'

This stage of ego development is healthy and of course incredibly important in terms of a person's ability to cope in the world. However, for whatever historic, psychological or emotional reasons, an adult expressing peak Red values may not have fully developed out of this stage.

As a result, they are a super-sized, self determined toddler in adult's clothing. Often powerful, potentially volatile, sometimes very capable, but ultimately a tempestuous child at heart. So when they have their own children and another toddler enters their world, a person at the Red stage may not respond well to another little being asserting their own force of will. Red needs others to bend to their own will. They are top dog in this world of dog eat dog and they won't take kindly to being challenged – even by their own offspring.

So when Keith and Serena have kids, it will need to be Serena's Green values that drive all the nurturing – as long as she remembers that their 'first child' is in fact Keith.

Keith and Serena's children have the potential to grow up in the wonderful, warm care of Green values while knowing that they will be kept safe from the harsher elements in the world. This family dynamic, if it is to work, will need to accommodate Keith's Red needs. That includes the children. Keith's children must learn to pick their battles with their father – and to pick as few as possible, which Serena will help them to understand. She will teach their children empathy and acceptance and so help smooth the Red/Green family dynamics.

A parent expressing Red values, however, won't always be fiery or short-tempered. Sometimes they will be incredibly playful and creative. That's when this family will excel.

With Red's creative, passionate and fun energy along with Green's openness, acceptance and support, this family will potentially have some wonderful and memorable experiences. There'll be games and camp building and craft making and stories and jokes and lots of laughter – when Keith is in the mood!

Serena has always encouraged Keith to be true to himself, and she will do the same for their children. This is where Green and Red parenting can conflict. Where Serena will be motivated to allow the children to find their own way in life, Keith doesn't understand that there *are* other ways in life other than his way. He may become frustrated at Serena's style of parenting if he feels it is too open, accepting and, from his Red perspective, naive. Keith will either want to enforce his way of doing things onto the children or, if that meets with too much resistance, he may well disengage entirely.

That is the big danger of the Green/Red parenting relationship. A parent with Red values may try to dominate and frustrate the

Green parent's need to nurture. Fear that Keith will remove himself from the parenting role entirely may even result in Serena taking all responsibility for engaging the children, even to the extent of taking them on holidays on her own if it doesn't suit Keith to join them.

The teenage years are challenging for most parenting combinations. For anyone co-parenting with a Red partner, this is doubly true. Peak Red values won't motivate an individual to adapt to becoming a parent. Their children won't be treated any differently from an adult entering Red's home and asking to share the space with them. Of course, when Keith and Serena's children hit adolescence, this is exactly the scenario.

Serena may suddenly find herself faced with self-asserting teenagers butting up against their self-orientated father – a combination that can result in a strong battle of wills. She will need to power up her care and nurturing skills to the maximum to insure the family holds together through this hormonal time.

Knowing when to honour Keith's need for power and authority and when to give autonomy to their children will be key. If Keith always wins and dominates over the children, this couple risks their kids growing up unable to assert themselves, incapable of making their own decisions or, worse, cutting themselves off entirely. It will be Serena's loving care that will ensure as healthy a balance as possible in this parenting pairing. Which should be fine because Green values can access a limitless amount of patience, care, nurture and love.

Needless to say, Keith will be immensely proud of their children's achievements. This is where Green and Red values can blend in a mutually agreeable parenting space. Serena will be pleased for the children if they have achieved something and Keith will claim his child's success as his own. He will believe that any success will, of course, be because of his parenting style and good genes and any failure or flaw will be to do with Serena's inadequacies. You've heard that one a few times, right?

Friends and social life

Serena and Keith have quite different ideas about friends and socialising. Serena values their friends highly and would keep a date or commitment even if she didn't feel like going. If Keith doesn't feel like going somewhere, he won't, regardless of the consequences.

Serena enjoys a social occasion if everyone else had a good time. Keith enjoys a social occasion as long as he himself has had a good time. As a result, Serena may well find herself socialising without Keith sometimes. Serena understands it is better to have low social expectations of Keith and be surprised when he comes through, rather than the other way around.

Serena wouldn't want Keith to be unhappy or uncomfortable, in any case. She will go out of her way to accommodate Keith's needs when it comes to social arrangements.

Typically a person in Green partnering someone with Red values will have a clear idea of which events and people their partner will enjoy. Rather than fighting this, Serena learns to instantly assess an invitation and never commit Keith to anything she intuits he wouldn't like. What Serena could do more of is letting Keith know how much she is thinking about him and taking his needs into consideration at every turn.

Someone living Green values is not usually a great self-promoter, but when it comes to the social ducking and weaving Serena does to keep Keith happy, she would do well to remind him of it. Keith would enjoy hearing how much Serena does towards ensuring his happiness. As long as she makes it clear it's no trouble and she's happy to ease his life in any way she can. If it sounds in any way begrudging, Serena will lose ground as opposed to gaining it. No one, particularly a strong Red partner, likes a martyr.

Money

Separate bank accounts would be a good idea for Keith and Serena. It's not that either of them are necessarily irresponsible spenders (though both have the risk of being so). It's that they prioritise their spending in such different ways that it would be worth avoiding what could become an ongoing debate or argument. Basically, Keith's Red perspective will cause him to spend on himself alone and Serena will spend on others and neither of them will understand the other's money modus operandi.

If Keith has access to Serena's accounts, he will ask why she paid for theatre tickets or a meal out for a friend of theirs – again! She will explain that her friend is going through a tough time and she wanted to do something nice for them. Keith still won't understand why that meant she had to foot the bill.

'Why didn't you take ME out for a nice meal or to the theatre? That was a show I really wanted to see as well. Why didn't you want to go with ME?' he will complain.

However, Serena will understand why he needed to buy the latest in personal computer technology even though they'd just talked about saving up for a family holiday. It can all get a little one sided at times, but Serena doesn't mind too much. As long as everyone is happy.

Sex

When Green and Red values get locked in conflict, sex may well be just the remedy they need. Sometimes you just have to agree to disagree and get on with making up. If Keith can drop his pride and if Serena can get over any hurt then a good dose of bedroom action may well restore the differing values of these two lovers at a fundamental and unspoken level. Sex can restore Keith's ego and rejuvenate Serena's need for connectivity.

Red values will either motivate an individual to actively dominate in this partnership and be a forceful lover or passively dominate and wait to be pleasured. Green values will create a drive to connect with the other person in any way possible. It's the connection and the pleasing that is important to Green. Serena won't mind too much if she sometimes walks away without having reached orgasm as long as the experience as a whole brought them together. Plus, if having sex appeases any anger in Keith, Serena will be happy to oblige.

At the extreme end, and to spice things up, in this sexual partnering a Green and Red couple may well be drawn to some kind of S&M activity. They are the perfect pairing for any kind of dominant/submissive sexual role-play. With Red taking the dominant or top position and Green the submissive or bottom position. If their emotional values of power and pleasing are closely aligned to their sexual drives then bedroom action could be a lot of fun.

CHAPTER 16

Blue and Blue

THE RULES OF LOVE.

Dating and early romance

Whoever said there are no rules when it comes to love hasn't come across a relationship built on Blue values. People at the peak Blue stage might value love, but they value rules more – not for them the heady chaos of early romance. However potent this new-found love might be, Blue values will drive a person to do everything they can to keep this unsettling cocktail of hormonal chemicals in check. Order must be kept. Two people expressing and embodying Blue will do this courting thing in the proper way: one step at a time, with everything in its correct order – from first date to first kiss to first act of consummation. When there are double Blue values in the arena of love, suddenly everything makes sense to them.

Liz and Daniel are both thirty-five years old. They first met a number of years ago at an event organised by their local church. Both had been in relationships and were previously not thinking about each other in a romantic context. Daniel had a long-term girlfriend who left him after three years. (She'd had a brief fling with her entrepreneurial boss and, feeling like she needed more out of life, realised she was ready to up-spiral into living Orange values.) Liz, meanwhile, has been in and out of several short-term relationships and is tired of the dating game. It's been nothing but a bubbling soup of heightened, out-of-control emotions, uncertainty, unreliability, game playing and hurt. She has yearned for love, but she also yearned for someone who could explain on a clipboard how it will all pan out. Preferably with a graph and spreadsheet attached.

Though Liz and Daniel were previously just good friends, they both found themselves single again and started spending more time together. Their early days of dating tended towards the formal. They quickly realised that they shared the same values and that this relationship was probably the real thing for them both. Neither of them particularly loved the dating game, so after a year of fairly safe dating and some frustrating evenings of stalled passion, they decided they would do things properly and get married. After all the appropriate protocols were followed – with Daniel approaching her parents for their approval, and then getting down on one knee to ask for Liz's hand in marriage – they had a very traditional church wedding. Liz and Daniel then settled down and began to order their life in a way that suited them both.

Long-term and marriage

If any pairing has the chance of lasting the long haul, it's this one. Blue values are about honour and decency and, most importantly in the marriage game, keeping promises. This couple will do everything they can to maintain the vows they make to one another on their special day. Those vows weren't about a fabulous dress, fine catering and wedding gifts. Those vows were about forever – for better, for worse, for richer, for poorer, for whatever life in all its unpredictability throws at them. Although the person holding strong Blue values is still human and prey to weakness, vulnerability and temptation, they are also in possession of a strong framework and structure of belief that can see them through the rockiest of marital times. With two Blues together – that's one hell of a scaffold-supported marriage.

First things first for this value pairing. Let's make a plan! For people living in service of Blue values this doesn't just mean planning for next week or next year. A pure Blue couple will *start* their life together by *planning* their life together. This isn't the five or even the ten year plan. This is the lifetime plan.

These two will work out exactly what they want from life, where they're both headed and then plan accordingly. No pipe dreams of winning the lottery. Daniel and Liz wouldn't risk their life together on something so unreliable. No, they will work hard, save hard and spend only when they can afford to.

Daniel and Liz will place their trust in God or the government and believe that all will turn out as it is meant to, according to that higher power that dominates their life. All they can do is work hard and organise themselves within the set of rules that society or their belief system requires them to follow.

Liz doesn't take kindly to rule-breakers. That's another reason this partnership has every chance of flourishing. They will see infidelity as the worst possible thing they could do to their partner. If ever Daniel did stray from the marital path, he wouldn't expect, and wouldn't necessarily get, forgiveness. Unless of course, it is a religious obligation for them to forgive.

Liz and Daniel understand that there is right and wrong, good and evil and nothing in between. This relationship is absolutist. Neither party will be happy in ambiguity or indecision. Not knowing where they're going on holiday next year or what the dress code is for dinner with the boss will leave them both feeling insecure and upset. So Liz and Daniel need to keep communication channels open all the time. Which they will.

Daniel will inundate Liz with text messages, emails, sticky notes, lists, checklists, reminders, more lists, receipts, schedules and another list just in case. Liz will be just as happy to receive lists as she is to create them. Lists will make this couple feel like they've got a handle on their future. They need to know exactly how much they're saving, when they'll be able to buy a house, where that house will be, when they'll have children, how many children they will have and where those children will be educated.

Daniel and Liz's house will reflect their internal need for order. This couple will take great pride in a neat and tidy home. They will never panic about where the passports or the car insurance documents are because they'll be in the files marked *Passports* or *Car Insurance*. Together, they will revel in their hard earned and thoroughly enjoyed predictability. Neither wants to suddenly be surprised by their partner and have to cancel a long-standing arrangement with a friend. Any change of plan will be mentioned weeks in advance and so never really feel like a change of plan, just a slight and manageable adjustment.

As long as the world keeps turning, wrongs are righted and rules adhered to, Liz and Daniel will have found their perfect life. Together they will create a world of order from where they can look out at the world of chaos, united in their understanding that if only other people played by the rules, the world would be a much happier place. If anything does go wrong in their life like sudden illnesses or unexpected events, they will do everything they can to quickly gain control, plan their coping strategy and, most importantly, seek expert guidance or advice. This couple doesn't so much as roll with the punches as control them as fast and effectively as possible. If either feels incapable of getting a situation under control or their life in order it can be devastating for them. At the extreme end of stress, Liz or Daniel may buckle under the pressure and become ill or even have a breakdown. They may work hard to keep going and put on a brave face but no-one, not even a person in Blue can hold back the body's need to release emotional stress. Anyone with peak Blue values needs to watch out for unusual ailments such as heart palpitations or panic attacks. They may be signs that they are trying too hard to cope with too much.

However, when all is going well, these two will have everything organised, from anniversary gifts to their children's wedding fund to the order of service for their own funeral. (Till death do us part they promised, so why shouldn't death be just as organised as life?)

Kids and family

Liz and Daniel will have meticulously planned the arrival of children. The nursery will be ready, the newborn's nappies stacked into neat piles, and the christening gown laid out for the ceremony. Liz will love the Gina Ford parenting method – routine, routine, routine.

They will systematically help their children learn all the skills and knowledge they will need to flourish in life. They will teach them to walk, teach them their letters, teach them to swim, teach them to ride a bicycle, teach them to read instructions and eventually teach them to drive – all at the correct stage of the child's development. Everything will be done according to the book on child-rearing, a book that gives great comfort to new parents in the face of a potentially disruptive and chaotic little person entering their well-ordered world.

Liz and Daniel will tend to agree on most things when it comes to the kids. If for any reason they don't, the one thing they will always agree on is to not let the children see them disagree. They want their children to feel secure around authority and trust in the world around them. They want their children to feel safe in the fact that Mum and Dad are a united front – the higher authority on which they can depend.

If Liz and Daniel did find themselves having to separate or divorce it would most likely be because one of them had been disloyal, trust had been irrevocably broken or one of them had shifted value sets while the other remained in a rigid Blue position. Even so, they would work hard to maintain a calm, structured and united front for their children.

Divorced parents living Blue values can even go on to marry new partners but still share responsibility and effectively parent their own children together. They understand and embrace self-sacrifice for the good of others. They know that swallowing their pride in the short-term will make everyone happier in the long-term.

Mind you, when the children are out of earshot, estranged Blue parents won't hold back in making it clear that their ex has done them the worst kind of wrong imaginable by leaving them and breaking up the family home.

Friends and social life

A Blue couple will often be friends with other Blue couples. Rather than seek novelty in their friendships, they seek dependability, reliability and predictability. Liz and Daniel will find their friends through work, sports clubs, committees and their children's schools. They will be drawn to people who are doing the same things, at the same time and in the same way as them.

As Blue values are about shared commitment and community, a couple living peak Blue will usually enjoy socialising very much. Their calendar will be full of dinners, fundraisers and community events – many of which they will help to organise, though they will often stick to places, wines and food that they know. These two won't want to risk trying something different when they already know what they enjoy, unless they become friends with a restaurant, wine or food expert in which case they will be very much lead into new territories. If a wine expert says the 2007 gewürztraminer is good, or a Michelin star chef says the new Vietnamese on the high street must be tried, then it must be. Liz and Daniel will always trust the experts.

A true Blue couple will have a real sense of where they are in their own social hierarchy. They respect the structures and etiquettes of social position and will enjoy making friends with people who hold positions of authority. For example, if an MP moves into their street, Liz will be falling over herself to be the first to meet them. Though they might not like to admit it, Liz and Daniel love a bit of social climbing. Even though they respect the hierarchy and know their place in it, they also enjoy the respect that being near the top brings.

Daniel will accept a seat on the board of governors or the local council with great pleasure and a healthy display of humility to boot. They'll often claim they are only accepting a certain honour in the name of doing good and so that they can be of service to others, but secretly they'll embrace promotion with relish. Blue only recently came through Red values and that ego is often still thumping away below the surface.

Liz and Daniel are, of course, very loyal to their friends and will stand by them through any family, career or emotional difficulties.

Go easy on the emotional though; Daniel can only take so much blubbering before he'll advise you to pull yourself together and work out how to move forward. However, as much as a true Blue couple will make friends with people like them, if those people suddenly stop going to the same church, mosque, temple, synagogue, house group or sports club or start working for a competitor or relocate their children to a different school, the Blue couple will find it challenging to maintain that friendship. They like people like them.

The less their friends seem to be people like them, the less they will find themselves being invited to Liz's homely soirees. She doesn't want to seem mean but 'those' people just don't fit any more. Consequently, these two are capable of very suddenly cutting people out of their lives. If any friend or acquaintance of theirs commits a crime or cheats the system in any way, Daniel and Liz will agree to instantly and permanently turn their backs on them. As for seeing a friend of theirs cheat on his or her partner, you can be very clear who they will side with: it won't be the cheating heart.

Money

Money matters will be open and ordered between Liz and Daniel. They are unlikely to get into financial difficulties. If they do, they will know it's coming and have a back-up savings plan in place.

This couple will be very comfortable with joint bank accounts and will often have a number of them for different purposes as well as a healthy level of savings for that drizzly day that may never come.

This value set can sometimes come across as a bit petty when it comes to money. If Daniel has lent you ten pounds one evening in the pub, he will expect it back quickly. Don't think offering to buy him a drink next time you're out together is adequate payback. If he lent you ten pounds, it's only fair he gets exactly ten pounds back. Anything less and this couple will soon be talking to each other about how terrible that was of you and that they'll never lend you money again.

'Couldn't he see that a drink would come to no more than five or six pounds – even a glass of champagne is only eight pounds. So he's basically

borrowing a tenner off me and stealing a fiver. I mean, what is that? I'm so cross,' Daniel complains.

'You didn't accept his offer, did you?' Liz enquires.

'No, of course not. I told him quite clearly that I'd take the ten pounds in cash, thanks very much. That's the last time I ever lend him any money. People are so unreliable. Oh, by the way I've finished all the Christmas shopping and got your family the things they wanted on their Amazon wish lists.'

This is in July.

So, nothing to worry about when it comes to Liz and Daniel and their finances. They will be fine with money. Just like the good old reliable Blue banking system before Orange charged in and collapsed the global economy. If only they'd listened more to Blue.

Sex

Sex in Blue is generous, considerate and mutually satisfying. It ticks all the boxes Blue values need ticked.

Extroverts embodying Blue drives can even make clear to their partner what particular box they want ticked and tickled. Being Blue means sorting this sex thing out and getting it right, not just for themselves but for their partner. This can be excruciating for a more introverted partner who may have never discussed sex in their lives and thought they'd just switch the light off and slip out of their nightwear for a few minutes.

An extroverted Blue partner is a great counter to this shyness as they'll want to establish the right way of having sex in the same way they establish the right way to arrange the contents of the fridge. There's a way, there's a system and sometimes it takes a little work and a little practice to master things, but they'll be more than happy to put in the groundwork and reap the rewards of what could turn out to be a well-researched and very satisfying sex life.

That's the great thing about Blue on Blue action: they'll keep working at it. If their rutting rhythms don't seem to be in tune, they are more likely than other pairing to seek the advice and wisdom of an expert sex counsellor. This couple will approach sex like any other project – they'll find out the facts and work hard to master it. It might not be very innovative, but it will function well, relieve the sexual urges and serve its purpose as the glue that can hold this loving all-Blue relationship together.

Once they've mastered it and worked out what each other needs, these two will often establish a routine in the bedroom – and I do mean bedroom. That's where sex is supposed to happen, after all. Peak Blue values don't manifest in a need to strip off in the kitchen and start pumping over the gas hob. That would just be uncomfortable, not to mention dangerous. I mean, what if Liz's bottom pressed down on the gas release for too long? One false move and they'd go up in flames. It doesn't make any sense and anyone who does have sex over a hazardous kitchen appliance deserves what's coming to them.

No, sex feels safer in the bedroom, with the door shut and the lights dimmed or turned off.

The bedroom is where they can bed in their routine, because they will soon work out when and how their partner wants to have sex. They may even establish 'sex nights', just so long as everyone is clear where they need to be, what they need to be doing and how long they'll be doing it. There's a schedule to keep to, after all.

One sure sign of a partner exiting their Blue values and heading up into the Orange altitude can be sexual frustration and the need for more sexual adventure. This is when politicians, vicars and suburban housewives or husbands begin to tire of the rigidity of their world. One minute it was all committee rotas and coffee mornings, the next thing they know they're being caught pants-down in the neighbour's basement, a cumquat between their teeth, being whipped to the sounds of Iron Maiden. A Blue exit into Orange can be dramatic for all concerned.

CHAPTER 17

Blue and Orange

PUSH AND PULL.

Dating and early romance

Let's contrast and compare the following individuals: Peter likes to control impulsivity in himself and others, he always observes the rules and is easily made to feel guilty. Sara likes to be spontaneous, enjoys novelty and innovation and is untroubled by her conscience. Peter will sacrifice his own needs for the promise of a reward later. Sara would sacrifice Peter for a reward right now!

Doesn't seem like a great start to a date. Please welcome to the dating game, Blue and Orange!

Peter (Blue) and Sara (Orange) work at the same bank. Peter is a finance manager and Sara is a trader. They are roughly the same age and both single. They have met a few times through a mutual work colleague, and the last time they did, Peter suggested they might have a drink together sometime. Sara called Peter a few days later and suggested lunch: *'There's this new place I want to try.'*

We join them towards the end of their first date at a restaurant called The Modern Pantry.

Peter: *How was your salmon?*
Sara: *Great. I wasn't sure if the raspberry jam was going to work but, hey – that's why it's worth trying new things.*
Peter: *I've had a really nice time. We should do this again sometime.*
Sara: *Me too. How about dinner tonight?*
Peter (choking on his espresso): *Er, I was thinking next Friday. Maybe a drink?*
Sara: *Oh, okay. Yeah maybe, though I might be in Paris. Or Barcelona.*
Peter: *Oh, you have a holiday booked?*
Sara: *No, just sometimes I take off on a Friday afternoon. You know, lastpossiblesecond.com.*
Peter: *Oh right. Wow. Just like that?*
Sara: *Yeah. I went to Thailand once for the weekend. I was knackered, but what a two days.*
Peter: *Goodness. I've always thought Thailand would be great. You have to get all the inoculations months in advance, don't you?*
Sara: *Do you? I didn't.*
Peter: *Anyway, we should leave or we'll be late.*
Sara: *I take as long as I want for lunch. My boss is cool with that.*
Peter: *Oh, well, mine isn't. So, I'll see you Friday, then?*
Sara: *If not before. Nice suit by the way. Is that D&G?*
Peter: *No, M&S. Bye.*

Peter wants the dating part of this relationship to go perfectly and will give it all the time it needs. Sara just wants it to get going. When it comes to dating, getting it right and being polite is important for a person expressing peak Blue values, whereas for Sara, in Orange, if the first date goes wrong then she'll just move along. Life, as well as love, is a fluid, ever-changing playground. Where Peter needs rules, structure and certainty, Sara figures you can simply make up the rules as you go along – if indeed you need any rules at all – and if the game you're currently playing ceases to be fun, then start playing another one – asap.

But for Peter, love isn't a game. Love is not to be played. Love is to be found and cherished forever. Peter is looking for the perfect partner who will fit into the definitive set of rules he has decided life should be lived by. Sara, by contrast, is looking for a partner with whom she can create a whole new way of being, based on nothing other than what she decides.

So while these two are dating, Peter is constantly looking for signs that his new partner will fit with his way of thinking. For him, it's almost as if the ideal partner is already out there. All he now has to do is to find them.

In contrast to this approach, Sara has no pre-prepared boxes to tick. She will simply enjoy Peter's company and get what she can from the relationship. Sara doesn't have a gap in the jigsaw of her life that is waiting to be filled by a Peter-shaped piece. But then again, Sara doesn't have a jigsaw at all. She will flexibly adapt to whatever comes along. Peter might not be the sort of life partner she envisioned for herself, but that won't stop her entering into a relationship with him. If Sara is benefiting from the pairing, having fun, feeling good and – even better – making money then she'll be happy. If Peter has money then marriage and commitment just got a whole lot more attractive to Sara. If the match immediately benefits her Orange values, she might even put up with a few things that annoy her.

These two could have a lot of fun while they date. Peter will suddenly be introduced to a whole new range of ideas and experiences. While this may seem a little daunting, Sara will be a reassuring presence. This isn't like dating an unpredictable, irrational Red partner. Sara is motivated by values that drive her to think things through and undertake a little risk assessment before taking the plunge.

So, though a sudden trip to Malaysia to do a bungee jump and eat roast bull's penis might seem like a dangerous business, Sara has done her research. There have been no bungee accidents at this particular resort and no reported deaths by bull penis. Well, certainly not through eating them anyway. That's not to say she wouldn't still go ahead if the risks were high, but at least Sara will be aware of the facts. That's important to her, and it's also important to Peter.

Sara and Peter could actually be a very romantic pairing. For Peter, a certain amount of wining and dining and flower buying will be deemed necessary and appropriate. Sara, on the other hand, likes the finer things in life, so romantic experiences definitely fit into the category of feel good, peak life experiences. Peter's gestures of romantic expression may be fairly traditional: red roses, smart dinners and Valentine's cards. Sara will prefer adventures: balloon trips, exotic meals and reservations on the first Virgin Space flight as a token of love. Both will appreciate the other's romantic gestures, though, with Sara finding Peter safe but cute, and Peter finding Sara quirky but thrilling.

Deep down, Peter is looking for a long-lasting fit, while Sara knows that everyone is replaceable. However, if they do get on – if he feels secure enough and she's excited enough – then these two could make for a very successful long-term partnership.

As for any marriage proposal, if Sara is doing the asking the scenario could be anything from a double parachute jump to popping the question while racing down the M1 in their new soft-top sports car. If Peter is proposing, it will have been planned weeks ahead and the father of the bride will have been approached and consulted well in advance.

Long-term and marriage

A healthy Orange and Blue relationship will be based on a balance between stability and change, with Sara in the driving seat and Peter making all the safety checks. In this pairing, Sara will impatiently rail at the sky at the injustice and incompetence she feels surrounds them, while Peter will be a dependable and solid structure when life's many tornadoes threaten to tear apart the happy home.

However passionate and irate Sara might become, Peter will often be able to remain composed and stoical in the face of the most difficult of challenges. He will try his best to put his emotions to one side, do the right thing and sacrifice his own needs for the sake of the whole. When Sara has rushed headlong into a new idea, business, project or social group and got herself into a bit of a mess, Peter will naturally put things back in order and deal with all the admin and fallout.

'*But Sara,*' Peter will say as he helps her get her accounts in order, '*if we just lived according to the rules all will be well and we'll be happy.*'

'*I don't agree,*' Sara will reply. '*If I create my own life according to my own rules, that's when I'll be well and happy.*'

'*You mean that's when WE'LL be well and happy,*' says Peter.

'*Yes, sure,*' she frowns, '*though I can't be the author of your happiness, can I? I can only be responsible for myself.*'

And with that final phrase we really go to the heart of the fundamental difference between these two. Orange values have up-spiralled, having transcended and included Blue; they've played the responsibility card and they either didn't like it or found it limiting. Peter is still very much in the value set of responsibility to a higher order, be it the family, the community, the church or the nation.

While part of Sara may respect his sense of honour and duty, she knows that self-sacrifice is often unrewarding.

'*Who's doing the rewarding?*' she will ask. '*And for that matter, who's doing the rule-setting? No,*' Sara tells Peter, '*you keep your rules if it makes you feel better. What makes me feel good is doing things my own way.*'

But while these two have their differences, they also have plenty in common. Both Peter and Sara may very possibly have a strong sense of shared purpose and meaning to their lives. Both respect the qualities of confidence and assertiveness, and if they don't already have these qualities themselves, they will seek them out in others.

Both will have little sympathy for weakness. In fact, if Blue and Orange values are energised to work on a project together, not only will the deliverables be reliable and on time, the product or service will be faster and more innovative than any competition. The combination of these values will ensure quality *and* quantity, style *and* substance.

Many people refer to romance as playtime and marriage as a business. When it comes to business, Blue and Orange are the 'must have' values for any successful company the world over: Orange to innovate, Blue to regulate.

One thing to bear in mind if you're living Orange values with someone at the Blue stage: don't forget to tell your Blue partner what a good job they've done. While you might be happy to silently wallow in the results of a successful union, Blue very much values appreciation and approval. They would probably even like a certificate, acknowledging and qualifying them in 'Advanced and Superior Marital Skills'. Never stop reminding Blue how well they're doing and how proud of them you are. It's the key to their heart, mind and soul.

Domestically too, this can be a fantastic partnership.

Sara's Orange values will motivate her to choose the holidays or shop for gifts for family and friends on Christmas and birthdays, but she will be very happy to leave Peter to do the bookings, print the tickets and itinerary, wrap the presents, write the cards and make sure everything arrives at the right time for the right people. Which suits Peter just fine.

As long as Sara doesn't bring shame or guilt to Peter's honourable life, these two can create a highly successful, loving and mutually respectful partnership.

Kids and family

When Blue and Orange values are dominant in two parents, there will be a system and a strategy to raise their children to be the best they can be. Peter will want their offspring to be responsible, polite and well educated. Sara will want them to have every opportunity that life can offer.

It's not uncommon for a new parent to go into peak Blue values – even if that hasn't been a dominant value set for them previously. Parenting can be a time when one partner suddenly starts edging into Blue or becomes even more driven by Blue than they were before. However, a new parent in Orange might down-spiral into Red and just want to escape the whole thing. Particularly if their Blue partner has suddenly taken over the house with sterilising timetables, sleep schedules and infant learning charts. Orange will feel suffocated without a role, not to mention disinterested.

'He had a feed at eleven a.m.,' says Peter, *'and then one at three p.m. He's due a sleep now and then we'll bath him at five-thirty p.m. Ahhh.'*

'I'm bored,' Sara replies. *'When will he start being interesting?'*

While Sara will dutifully care for her infants in the early stages, she may not be particularly useful or interested in the children outside the necessary functions of feeding and clothing them, that is until the children themselves become useful or interesting to her. She's not likely to be the doting mother gushing about how wonderful it was to give birth and how beautiful her blood-stained progeny looked as they emerged from the torn remains of her birth canal. Unless, of course, any of her important colleagues and associates wants advice or to talk about kids, which will then motivate Sara to become an expert, delighted to have baby knowledge to share, and beautiful, well-behaved children to show off.

Sara may have a lot to thank Peter for in the early stages of parenting. Whether Blue values are expressed by the mother or the father, it is the partner motivated to act in service of Blue values who will have more patience and stability to offer the children. It is they who will give the children the best chance of a good, solid foundation and stable mental health – if they can remain relatively open-minded that is.

Blue parenting values can tip into fundamentalism, where their way is the only way. When Blue values become extreme, they can begin to stultify growth by insisting on enforcing laws that don't allow children any flexibility or space to express themselves. Blue might believe they are acting in the best interests of their children but too much control can have the opposite effect. So while Blue values can be incredibly useful, they ideally need to be counterbalanced with a more fluid and open attitude. This is precisely where Orange values come in to play. Strict yet spacious, authoritative yet creative, traditional yet original, stable yet spontaneous. Peter and Sara's children really can get the very best that a capitalist society has to offer.

They will both work incredibly hard to provide for their family. Well, Sara will be mainly working hard to provide for herself, but she's aware that when she succeeds, the entire family benefits. However, Sara will shift and change her plans according to her own whims – even if that means risking family stability and financial security.

But Peter will do whatever it takes to make sure the family is provided for. He might hate his job, but he'll stick with it if the family is depending on him to bring home the bacon. He'll work hard, long hours and then rush home to read the all-important bedtime story to the kids – because he promised he would. Sara, however, would almost do the opposite – leave a job she hated without looking back and avoid being at home for the mucky, boring, feed, bed and bathtime bit.

As the children grow up there may well come a time when Sara is better equipped to deal with them. The teenage years won't necessarily fall into Peter's neat plan! This period of adolescence could cause him a great deal of stress. He will feel like he has given his all, done everything he could to show his children the right way to live, and now they seem to be going all maverick on him. This is when Sara's Orange attitude suddenly comes into its own in the parenting arena.

'Calm down, Peter. I drew on my bedroom walls when I was a kid. Yes and I stole stuff too. So what if Thomas has a black eye and Gemma's got a tattoo of Tinkerbell on her bum? It's normal. They're expressing themselves.'

'But we want Thomas to be an accountant,' says Peter, *'and he hasn't touched his maths homework in weeks.'*

'Maybe he doesn't want to be an accountant,' Sara retorts.

'But he has to be. These are uncertain times. Our children need to find jobs for life,' Peter gasps.

'Job for life? There's no such thing any more. That's a delusion,' Sara smirks.

'But . . . but . . . how will it all turn out? It's all gone off plan.' He splutters.

'Look it's okay, let it go,' Sara reassures him. *'You can't plan and predict every little thing in life. You can only live it. The kids are bright and confident. You did an amazing job. It will all work out. You'll see.'*

And sometimes, when they put their mind to it, Orange will find just the right words for Blue.

Friends and social life

When it comes to socialising, these two complement each other perfectly. Sara will be brilliant at arranging dinner parties, cooking fabulous food (or hiring a fabulous chef), ordering amazing wines and entertaining the guests with dazzling wit and repartee. Peter will make sure no one important is left off the invite list, organise the logistics and clean up after the party. Orange and Blue are the perfect social team.

A couple expressing peak Blue and Orange values will often enjoy being members of prestigious clubs or groups. Both of them are very keen to be around other people who lend them even more status. While Peter is happy to sip his champagne and admire – even fawn over – those further up the hierarchy, Sara is busy working the room. She knows exactly who she needs to talk to in order to get a promotion, get their kids into the right school or university, or make sure she and Peter get planning permission for their new extension. While Peter obeys the system, Sara is working it.

Peter will be happy with the social group this couple has formed around themselves and may be disturbed when Sara suddenly announces that they're moving on. He has just settled in and found his place in this new social scaffolding, but Sara's work here is done. This group has served its purpose and she now has bigger social fish to fry.

'But I like these people,' Peter will say. 'They're smart and funny and, what's more, decent.'

'Yes, that's the problem,' Sara will reply. 'They're all too set, too fixed in their ways. We need to be mixing with movers and shakers, not dinosaurs.'

So that's how Peter and Sara's social life will continue – Sara wanting it to change, Peter wanting it to stay the same. However they work it out – perhaps with Peter keeping a set core of friends regardless of Sara, and Sara having her own social nights of the week – these two can make the socialising they do together a very successful affair, as they can in every other area of their life. As long as they understand that the reasons they are both there and that their expectations from the occasion are different, these two will rule the events calendar.

Money

Now, let's be honest: most couples argue over money. While this couple both have the capacity to earn good money, they also have one of the strongest opposing forces; this couple are in a constant stand-off between save and spend.

While Peter desperately wants to save and assess, Sara is all about spend to impress. Having been through Purple and Red, Peter now understands he needs to secure the future, save for old age, insure for the worst and wait for the best. Peter is very comfortable with a twenty-year saving plan, but Sara wants to cash in the pension, roll the dice and take the high risk for instant high return option.

Both these attitudes could bring this couple financial wealth. There's no right or wrong underlying these decisions, only personal values. Peter is all about the direct debits, standing orders and settled debts. Sara has more of a tendency towards building endless credit, final reminders and juggled debts.

When times are financially hard, Peter will get frustrated with how much Sara spends. He will feel they must both save together against an uncertain future. There's no way of knowing if the economy will remain strong. Sara knows better, though, and will tell him in no uncertain terms that the only way the economy can remain strong is if they spend! It's their *duty* to spend.

Spending money is the key to future safety and security. Now *that's* going to confuse Peter's Blue driven thinking! Sara has a point but everything in moderation.

So, if Peter really needs that feeling of safety, then the best thing he can do is to secretly bank a security fund. It's not always a good thing for these two to know exactly how much money the other has. Peter might be horrified to learn Sara has absolutely nothing saved and Sara might be tantalised to learn Peter has some investable savings floating about. So, Peter must stay firm and remember, it's strong Blue rules around money that will keep their finances thriving.

Sex

Celebratory sex will feature high on this couple's agenda. Both of them are driven by values that like to celebrate feeling good or a job well done. Even though on the surface it looks like Blue and Orange are quite different values – Peter seeking cohesion, Sara, independence – they both enjoy the feelings of achievement and status. These two will find each other very sexy after a successful company dinner, a recent promotion, an exciting business deal or an up-ladder house purchase. So, one of the best things for a Blue and Orange couple to do is to find lots of things to celebrate. Then these two can look forward to a truly glorious sex life. If both have healthily integrated their egoistic Red stage, they'll both share an ego-driven sex drive, to at least some level.

Sexually, Peter might find Sara's need for variety challenging. He is far happier finding a way for the two of them to have sex that seems to work for them both and then sticking with it, but Sara seeks innovation and change.

The last thing Peter wants is for Sara to go off seeking change elsewhere.

By tapping into the values that they both share, this couple can keep celebrating and deepening their love, and by thinking of their sex life as a celebration of their continuing, committed life together, Peter can give Sara the novelty and newness she desires while still serving the security and stability he needs. If Peter thinks of sex as a gift or a reminder of his strengthening love for his partner then he might try something new and so Sara will get all the surprise and excitement she craves.

CHAPTER 18

Blue and Green

HIERARCHY AND EQUALITY.

Dating and early romance

Suzy is an ex-police officer who now works for the housing department at the local council. She's confident, organised, structured, law abiding and extremely polite. Darren is a freelance web designer by day and musician by night. He is mild-mannered, kind, loves music and the arts and is a little disorganised.

They first met when Darren found Suzy's mobile phone on the pavement outside the wine bar where he plays guitar on Wednesdays. He was just about to hand it to the bar manager when it rang. After interrogating him for a full five minutes, Suzy was relieved to discover Darren was not a thief and instructed him to take care of the phone until she arrived. He offered to take it to her if she gave him her address. She quickly refused his offer and insisted that he hand it in to the bar manager from whom she would pick it up. When she arrived she was so delighted that her phone was safe that the attractive guitarist was her saviour. She rewarded Darren by buying him a drink and within moments they were in love.

When two people expressing peak Blue and Green values meet and spiral into love, there will be an enormous amount of love in the room. This meeting will feel like an incredibly important moment.

The moment Suzy and Darren met, he was completely carried away with a feeling of deep connection and Suzy understood the significance of meeting a kind and honest man like Darren.

This may well be what God and his sidekick, fate, had in store for them. Both of which are to be listened to carefully.

Blue and Green values are both in the 'we' position and, as such, Darren and Suzy are very people orientated. So they should be a perfect match, right? Hmm, maybe. Possibly. Sometimes, but not always.

Yes, they both like people and will sacrifice their own well-being for others, but while Darren will do that for everyone, Suzy will only do it for people who share her values, ideas and beliefs. Sure, there's plenty of common ground but there are also a couple of adjoining plots of land that are definitely not shared.

For example, on their first date, Suzy didn't appreciate Darren taking her to that new Mongolian restaurant without checking the reviews first. Darren feels Suzy is a little closed-minded to new experiences, but the overriding factor about this pair is that they realise they'd much rather be together than apart.

Neither Darren nor Suzy are people who need too much time to themselves. They'd rather be with each other than sitting on their own. Both hold values that drive them towards communion, openness and honesty and neither likes to play mind games. Darren is fine with ambiguity so doesn't see the need to play mind games with a potential partner. Suzy on the other hand absolutely hates ambiguous game play. For her, things are either right or wrong, good or bad, black or white. Suffice to say – there'll be no manipulative mental chess between these two lovers.

These two won't necessarily indulge in talking about themselves, but they will love to talk about the world at large and how it should operate. Together they'll have some wonderfully in-depth conversations about life and how they feel about it. They may find themselves still up at four in the morning, sitting in front of the fire, putting the world to rights. Not that they'll always agree.

Suzy won't understand Darren's insistence that everyone is equal and he won't understand her need to rank people in what he feels is an artificial hierarchy. On the downside Darren judges everyone to be equal and Suzy simply judges everyone. On the upside, Suzy and Darren are always thinking about each other.

Long-term and marriage

In the long-term, this couple have a very good chance of creating a happy life together. Neither is prone to passionate or selfish outbursts, so this partnership is unlikely to be turbulent.

Darren and Suzy are looking for equilibrium, stability and calm. They both love a happy home and will do all they can to create one together. Both of them like to take care of other people and they'll look after one another as much as they can. When Suzy gets sick, Darren will be there by the bedside feeding her soup, reading her favourite book aloud and reassuring her she'll feel better very, very soon. When Darren gets sick Suzy will look up his symptoms in the *Family Medical Encyclopedia*, work out precisely the best thing to do and exactly what medicine he must take. Darren might be concerned that the medicine isn't a homeopathic remedy containing Belladonna but Suzy will insist that Paracetamol is just what the doctor ordered. After all, a qualified doctor knows better than Darren's yogic spiritual guru who, as far as Suzy can make out, has no qualification other than an unnaturally bendy spinal column.

When it works, Darren and Suzy's relationship is filled with kindness, thoughtfulness and generosity. Both are able to sacrifice their own needs or feelings for the other or for the greater good of the relationship, which they will do, all the time they feel like their partner is committed to making this partnership work. But they need to watch out. They will often fall into the trap of thinking they are on the same path, holding the same values, with the same goal in sight. Both of them want to believe this of their partner.

They don't want any differences to come between them, but there are differences and it will serve Suzy and Darren to recognise them early on, before any conflict catches them unawares. The problem is how this couple interprets 'committed to the relationship'.

Darren can be incredibly committed to this relationship while also being able to share himself with a diverse range of friends or groups or interests. Suzy can feel he is neglecting what's important. Suddenly Darren may seem far too general and not at all committed to the partnership. They have agreed the nights they'll spend together, but Darren just keeps saying yes to other invitations.

'We haven't sat down and compared diaries for nearly two weeks,' Suzy complains. *'The lawn didn't get mown on Saturday like it's supposed to and I still haven't been able to cross "Fix bathroom lock" off the to-do list on the fridge. Darren, you need to be more responsible – we need to get the system back in place.'*

This can make Darren feel hemmed in, and Darren doesn't work well when he feels hemmed in. He wants to go and play guitar with a few friends. Why can't Suzy understand? It doesn't matter if the lawn is mown another day or if they don't lock the loo door for a while – it's only the two of them after all. Darren sees experience as more important than chores or order. This drives Suzy nuts.

'How can you enjoy an experience knowing we're in chaos here? And those guitarist people you hang out with – I'm sure some of them are on drugs.'

'What?' Darren responds. *'Drugs?'*

'Yes,' Suzy says, *'they've got an air of marijuana about them.'*

'Suzy, you can be SO judgemental and exclusive. They're nice people. If only you'd get to know them.'

'I don't need to get to know them to know they're not decent people,' she retorts.

Darren's Red begins to rise and he now does something he very rarely does: storms out of the house. Even a person with Green values can down-spiral and need some space to cool off.

When he returns home, he'll face a very cool reception. Even though Suzy loves him, her Blue values will cause her to withdraw some of that love if he doesn't meet her expectations. Only temporarily, of course, but it may take a while for her to forgive him, and she may never forget. Every argument is another black mark that will be neatly documented in Suzy's internal filing system that can be found in the folder marked *Why I was wrong to marry Darren*.

Kids and family

If Suzy and Darren bring children into the world they will not only want to teach their children how to *get* the best from life, they'll want to teach them how to *give* the best to life. Both of them will give their kids the clear message that life isn't just about taking, it's also about giving back. This is the common ground upon which Green and Blue parents stand strong, firm and utterly united. Suzy and Darren will be kind and generous, but they also want to instil a strong work ethic in their children. This set of parents doesn't believe life owes anyone a living.

Young people need to learn to be responsible and take care of both themselves and others. Pocket money won't simply be handed out, there'll be jobs and chores to do before cash is given over. It's no good little nine-year-old Lily moaning. Darren will only tell her that we all have to do things we don't like, if it helps other people or the environment, while Suzy will tell Lily it's all character-building. Suzy loves the phrase 'character building' and will use it frequently when her children find themselves doing something hard or unpleasant. Doing the washing up, tidying bedrooms, trudging in the rain on long family walks or camping in a thunderstorm with only a sheet of tarpaulin for protection – are all considered by Suzy to be character-building.

'You'll be glad that you cycled fifty miles uphill in this sleet,' Suzy will tell them. *'A little suffering now and you'll enjoy the relief later. It's all character-building.'*

'But, Mummy, I already have a character,' little Lilly will weep, *'and I wouldn't need relief from the suffering if I didn't have to suffer in the first place.'*

Sounds logical, but logical or not, letting Lily give up doesn't fit into Suzy's own systemic rules so Suzy will have none of it. *'Mummy didn't have time to moan when she was in the police force.'*

This may be where Darren and Suzy's Green and Blue values begin to diverge. Whilst Darren is all for teaching the children to do good to others, be kind and work hard, he draws the line at rigid dogmatism. This is can become a discrepancy between Green and Blue values when they parent together.

In a nutshell, Darren is easy come easy go; Suzy is not so easy come, not so easy go. He thinks people can be ruled by what their hearts tell them. She knows they can only be ruled by what the rules tells them. Suzy and Darren's children will quickly suss out this very important difference between their parents – Daddy can be manipulated a lot more easily than Mummy. It's no good asking Mummy for that eighteen-rated computer game or for those three-inch-heeled stilettos. Suzy has very clear rules on what's allowed or not allowed. But Darren? He doesn't have a clue. Darren and Suzy's children will wait for an opportunity when Mum is away to get things they want out of Dad. Green values are far more willing to please.

For a parent expressing Blue values, there's a way to parent – a way they will have probably learned from their own parents, a parenting guidebook or a higher deity who, when writing their religious bestsellers thousands of years ago, sprinkled them with a number of handy parenting tips. Such tips might include *'do not provoke your children to anger'* or *'do not withhold discipline from a child'* after all *'if you strike him with a rod, he will not die'*.

'Hmm, I'm not sure,' Darren will point out to Suzy, *'but at a guess I'm thinking striking Lilly with a rod will probably provoke her to anger. Rule books can be so confusing. Why don't we just let the kids find their own way in life?'*

But this is even more confusing for a person living Blue values than a confusing set of rules. *'There have to be some kind of guidelines, even if they're not one hundred per cent clear. We can't all just go round expressing ourselves and our individuality as we feel like it. There'd be anarchy,'* Suzy will protest.

'No!' Darren will say, *'it won't be anarchy. It will be beautiful. Let them find out who they are in a free and open way. By the way, I'm taking Lilly on a walking holiday of self-discovery in Nepal.'*

'*What?*' Suzy will cry. '*She's only thirteen. Who's in charge of this hippy-wandering? Where will you sleep? What's the itinerary? How much will it cost?*'

'*Calm down,*' says Darren. '*Your Red's coming through and we don't want the kids to see that, do we?*'

'*No!*' Suzy says through clenched teeth, '*Quite right. We don't. I . . I . . .*'

'*Need a nice cup of tea?*' He interjects.

'*Yes, thank you. And maybe a biscuit. They're just behind the spare Post-it notes.*'

Remember, if you want your Blue partner to accept change or adventure, don't forget to keep bringing them back to a safe, familiar place every now and then.

Friends and social life

Darren and Suzy both value being in company, and will quickly fill up their diaries.

Suzy is more likely to have filled hers up in advance and know exactly what's in the schedule from now until Christmas, whereas Darren is happy to be spontaneous and accept invitations on the spur of the moment.

Not only do they have different approaches to their social lives, Suzy and Darren also have different criteria towards their social circle. While Darren is happy to be friends with anyone and everyone, Suzy will tend to be a little pickier. She likes people who are more like her. Darren just likes people. Suzy has an inbuilt Blue filter system when it comes to friends and acquaintances and she'll weed out anyone who doesn't fit with her code of living. Suzy's Blue values drive her to seek to define the parameters of her social life, whereas Darren, in Green, will seek to expand them. She may well come home to find him playing host to a whole bunch of eclectic people sitting around the house.

'*Hi Suzy, this is Henry – he's a modern-day philosopher; this is Sally – she runs her own cupcake company; this is Tony – he's an actor; and this is Gillian who – doesn't like to define herself.*'

Suzy will smile and be polite but has already decided that tonight might be a good time to sit down with Darren to review and revise a few of the household rules.

Money

When it comes to money, Suzy will, as usual, hold the purse strings, but while this might frustrate people with other value systems, Darren may well be incredibly relieved that Suzy has taken charge of the finances. He finds keeping a check on incomings and outgoings all a bit left-brain and corporate, not to mention boring. Peak Green values don't generally motivate people to relish detail-orientated tasks, whereas Blue values revel in them.

Darren wants to focus out on ideas and big picture thinking. Suzy wants to focus in on facts and figures. So people with Blue and Green values can be a very happy pairing, financially.

Another good reason for Suzy taking charge of the money is that these two have very different understandings of what money is for. For Darren, money is all about 'give, give, give' and for Suzy money is all about 'save, save, save'. These two attitudes simply don't go together. Unless, that is, Suzy arranges it so that Darren give, give, gives his money to her so she can then save, save, save it.

While Suzy and Darren have less chance of becoming millionaires than some of the other more ego-driven, dynamic pairings, they have every chance of financial comfort and security for the rest of their lives. Darren doesn't crave material goods and Suzy will only enjoy spending money they can afford to spend. Neither of them finds a thrill in over-extending mortgages or credit card limits to buy flash pads or iPads that will be paid off on the never, never. Suzy knows, when it comes to loans and credit cards, the never, never really does mean never ever. She will get so much more pleasure from buying something they've saved hard for and Darren is happy to fix the old TV and not keep buying new ones – it's so much better for the environment.

These two are happy to make do and mend. That's not to say Suzy doesn't enjoy iPads and laptops, or that Darren isn't at all interested in high tech solar panelling, or a new guitar but they'll only spend when they've planned to and when they can afford it. At which time both of them will thoroughly appreciate the extras they've earned through hard work and determination.

Sex

When it comes to sex, Darren is very open to new experiences. Wanting to please his Blue partner, he will be keen to hear what Suzy likes when it comes to sex. If Suzy is confident enough, she'll tell him exactly what pleases her. If she is less confident, she may try to make it clear in other ways when Darren has hit the right button or pulled the right lever, as it were.

But be warned – of all the value systems, Blue is the most likely to feel it improper to make explicit their sexual demands. If you are with a more shy Blue and don't help them open up about their bedroom preferences, they may well spend their whole lives sexually frustrated. In extreme cases, sex can become a problem as the Blue partner begins to feel they may be frigid or impotent.

In fact, they probably need to express their true desires. This isn't always easy for someone at the Blue stage as they quite often carry a sense of guilt, shame, shyness or impropriety around sex. However, a Green partner will have the patience, tact and understanding to gently ease Blue into a sense of sexual security. Blue needs security in the bedroom in the same way as they do when it comes to their bank account. Even if the Blue partner is entirely comfortable with sex, the partner at the Green stage may well be able to take them to a whole new level while still making sure they feel loved, respected and considered.

The fabulous thing about sex and expressing Blue values is that when a person living in service of Blue is presented with a new way of doing things, they'll want to master the task, get it right and be the best they can be at it. This is great news for Darren, whose careful, sensitive approach will pay off big time when it comes to long-term sex with Suzy, as long as he understands that he will only get the best from Suzy with a softly, softly approach in the bedroom. Suzy like rules. It's no good Darren suddenly suggesting something wild to her, but if he patiently bends the rules little by little, he may see a side of Suzy that he's never seen before. The wild side.

Never underestimate what lies below the surface of Blue values and if anyone can get a Blue lover to the wild side, it's someone expressing Green.

CHAPTER 19

Orange and Orange

THE GAME OF LOVE.

Dating and early romance

Personal preparation for the double Orange first date will be meticulous. These are two people who are hungry for a new experience, striving for autonomy, exuding material abundance, playing to win and loving the competition. So, each partner will want to be suitably preened, hair coiffed and make-up perfect. People motivated by Orange values truly understand what it means to both create and take advantage of peak experiences.

The most up-to-date, must-be-seen-at venue will have been booked for this initial meet and preen. As both these individuals express peak Orange, they will probably agree on what constitutes the latest hot spot. If not, they'll be very excited to try something new. If one of them suggests somewhere the other hasn't heard of then chocolate Orange brownie points are already in the bank of cool, and Orange loves anything being in any kind of bank account with their name on it.

Let's take a look at a couple who are both at the peak Orange values stage – Cheryl and Jason. Cheryl likes a date to be electric. In fact, if she describes a date as 'nice', 'okay', or 'pleasant', what she's actually saying is 'I'm bored out of my mind', 'like dating a corpse' or 'fell asleep in my spaghetti vongole'. Orange is not a forgiving value set.

Jason doesn't so much date people as audition them. He's not searching for someone with whom to share his life, he's looking for a charismatic co-star to cast in the movie of his life. Jason is constantly in the process of creating the perfect lifestyle. He works hard to make it happen, but he wants results as fast as possible, so he's looking for someone who is up and running in terms of the required skills and attributes. Jason doesn't want to have to mentor and coach a partner, he wants ready-made, unambiguous perfection – someone fabulous and exciting who won't be too demanding. If Jason finds someone attractive, his first question will be, *'Are you ready to leap?'* The next will be, *'What can you do for me?'*

Individuals in Orange are ideas people whose first position is often: 'Ready! Fire! Aim.' They are interested in establishing only the basic facts, obtaining the minimum of required knowledge and information, putting together a quick strategy and then just doing it: *'Let's get out there before anyone else and we'll fix it as we go.'*

Once Cheryl and Jason both recognise the worth of the shared values each of them will potentially bring – this new relationship becomes rocket-fuelled. Every time they share another matching experience or mutual interest, these two lovers will metaphorically high five each other in celebration of their own fabulousness.

Both of them will probably have already achieved and experienced so much of life, both of them will be looking to the future and see so much potential in their life ahead. Now they have teamed up with each other, ideas for their future together will be boundless – Orange values are all about reaching out towards infinite possibilities; they certainly have the personal energy and attitude to take advantage of them.

If the first few dates go well, the conversations between Cheryl and Jason will be fired up with exciting and mutually beneficial stories of business ventures, foreign travel and exotic or daring experiences. As each of them revel in sharing tales of their exciting lives and even more exciting plans for the future, they will also be listening out for key nuggets of information from this new potential partner opposite them. What do they have to offer? Not necessarily emotionally, but intellectually, creatively, socially, energetically and financially?

People in peak Orange are often very good at elaborating and augmenting their own talents, but they can also be adept at spotting the same traits in others. The values that drive Orange also facilitate an acute capacity for detecting bulls**t. Cheryl and Jason will both put this ability to good use as they seek to make sure this new potential partner has financial fluency, a home of their own (or a large inheritance), good taste and their own business network.

Both Cheryl and Jason will want to be reassured on a number of important factors before they proceed any further. They will listen attentively – not through empathy or altruistic interest in the other person, but so as to carefully sift through each other's language style so as to ascertain the truth. As they are at peak Orange and interested in growth and success, both will likely be familiar with communication techniques of neurolinguistic programming, so their focus will be on how they each use speed, tone, rhythm and pitch to express themselves.

While Jason is all about creating and living his own life story, he's not about to recreate the story of Cinderella. He definitely doesn't want financial or social dependents. He wants an independent partner who will journey with him in life and ideally help support or even increase his own success and wealth. Once Cheryl has decided this is the right partner for her, she will do whatever it takes, say whatever she needs to say, and go wherever she needs to go in order to win over the object of her desire.

But if you're dating someone like Jason or Cheryl, watch out. For Orange lovers, the thrill can often be in the chase. Life is a game and that includes relationships. Like the Red values before them, Orange values will drive a person towards the conquest, but, unlike someone with a Red centre of self, Orange values do not require absolute submission to satisfy them. They are satiated by a strategic approach to victory: they will take you prisoner then revitalise you and inspire you to use your strengths for their advantage. As long as you are useful everything, will be fine. If you flounder, you might get acknowledgement and understanding about the level of your incompetence, but no empathy.

Orange expects everyone to take care of himself or herself. Life's a game remember, if it's treating you unfairly then you're obviously not playing it very well.

So, back to Cheryl and Jason on their first date where both parties are playing exactly the same game. Both are auditioning the other and being auditioned at the same time. These two will probably suss out long-term incompatibility quite quickly. That's not to say the date will then be over – if they fancy each other they may well decide to go home, have amazing sex and even enter into a full-blown fling.

But if their individual paths are headed in very different directions, neither of them will waste any more time than required to satisfy an immediate need. They'll assess the situation pretty quickly and decide whether this will be a one-night stand, a whirlwind fling or something with more long-term promise. If it's the latter then watch out father of the bride, this wedding is going to cost a pretty penny. Think Posh and Becks and you're on the money. Which is exactly what anyone contributing to this lavish Orange ceremony will need to be.

Long-term and marriage

If these two hook up for the long-term, they have a very good shot at a successful partnership. They both know how the game of life works, so with two people expressing Orange values there can be a level of understanding that will usually make prolonged game play unnecessary. In other words, these two can cut through the crap and cut to the chase very quickly. They know how destructive conflicting values in relationships can be and how draining negative emotions will become.

They don't have time for this in their lives. They need all their energy aimed at success and would rather use the independent strength of this partnership to focus any game playing outwards onto the rest of the world, not on each other. When it comes to their core relationship, they'll both want a low-maintenance, high-reward emotional investment. There's only one reason to enter into a business merger: if it's going to improve the success of the original business.

When it comes to living together, Cheryl and Jason's home will inevitably be more style than substance. The home inspired by Orange values will be awash with an eclectic mix of the latest furnishings, artworks and kitchenware. There will likely be a plethora of pictures of the happy couple in various exotic locations around the world, smugly throwing tantric shapes, while wearing a range of designer garb. Reading widely but not necessarily well read, Jason and Cheryl prefer to be generalists in a broad range of subjects rather than specialists in any one. These two will tend to absorb up to date Twitter soundbites and Facebook trends rather than delve into great detail on any one subject.

On the coffee table you will find magazines like *GQ*, *Forbes*, *Vogue*, *Wallpaper*, *Hello* and maybe even *OK*. On the bookshelf – yes, there will be bookshelves – you're likely to spot anything from the *Dukan Diet*, *150 Years of Couture Design*, Bill Bryson's *A Brief History of Everything*, to *The Diary of a Sex Addict*. Flitting from one latest fad to the next – whether it's in management styles for business, novelists, TV shows, salsa classes, cooking, parenting, dieting, exercise regimes or holiday destinations – as long as it's new, it's on Jason and Cheryl's agenda, though not much of it will actually reach their brain cells.

Orange values drive a need to accumulate but not necessarily assimilate information. It is often the buying habits of people expressing Orange that result in the Amazon statistic that only one in ten of the books bought online are actually read. It's not because they're dumb – far from it, Cheryl and Jason are incredibly astute – but a book or an idea may not hold their attention if something more novel, innovative or exciting suddenly crops up.

This partnership understands that about each other and both will be comfortable with sudden changes of plan, or indeed of mind. Both are on the look-out for the next bigger and better idea, product or way of life.

As soon as they see something they admire, they will want it for themselves. Unlike people expressing peak Red, Orange values won't necessarily manifest sulky behaviour, nor will they drive a person to sink into jealousy if someone has something better than them. A person at the peak Orange stage is far more likely to admire your possessions and aspire to get the same or better for themselves. In this case, the Orange response will be: *'Great! If you can do it, then so can I. Now, what's the quickest route to me achieving and exceeding what you've achieved and what can I learn from your mistakes?'*

Orange values share Red's perspective that the world is a jungle and everyone is out for themselves, so it may take some time to establish trust between Jason and Cheryl. As much as they recognise themselves in each other, they may both always hold a slight reserve when it comes to giving their trust entirely. Which can serve them well. When life throws unpleasant experiences at them, or if one lets the other down, they won't crumble into a heap of sobbing incredulity. Their Orange values will inspire them to rise up and face whatever needs to be faced head on, with a sense of expectancy and inevitability. This is why an individual at the Orange stage can love but never fully trust; for all the planning, all the strategies and all the vows of ever lasting love, from an Orange values perspective, they believe that other people are just like life: unreliable.

On the upside, Orange values are about passion for adventure and possibility. These two will love sharing holidays, business ventures and new ideas. For Jason and Cheryl, the prospect of success is almost as exciting as actually having achieved success. Anything is possible as far as these two are concerned, and that includes a life-long partnership. As long as they both remain in peak Orange, these two will give anything a go. They'll stretch their finances to afford a bigger home, they'll learn to fly planes, they'll invest every last penny they have. If any of it goes wrong, they won't have to pick up their partner and mollycoddle them. Orange values are demonstrated through an attitude of *'Get back on that horse'*, *'What doesn't kill you makes you stronger'* and *'Feel the fear and do it anyway'*. For these two, it's not about failure, it's about trying.

They know that if they try often enough, they'll eventually succeed. The same goes for their relationship.

A great way for an Orange couple to build both their careers and their marriage is to combine the two, to become 'co-preneurs'. An Orange couple in business together will be a formidable team.

However, working and loving together will have its drawbacks. Any disagreements in the home will need to be parked during working hours, which will be difficult if they are working from home. Although it's almost impossible for these two, they would do well to define the work/home life boundaries and have an agreed set of do's and don'ts, and on and off limits. Boundaries will become important for the health of this relationship as they can both be workaholics.

Constant and open communication is at the core of every successful marriage and no more so than for the co-preneur, Orange partnership. Learning how to manage and resolve conflict will be vital. Orange is fundamentally independent and resourceful, so the temptation to walk away seems an easier option than to most other couples. But fortunately, Orange values include communication, so both partners should have the capacity to hold a rational, objective and strategic dialogue around any issue. It's just whether they choose to, but as time-consuming and 'emotional' as difficult conversations are, open, rational communication will ultimately be the glue that will hold these two together.

Kids and family

Rearing children may be tricky for Cheryl and Jason. If both are working full-time – allocating household chores and childcare responsibilities in a fair way will be vital. If one partner has to stay at home and take care of the kids, the dynamic can become even more complex. Stay-at-home Orange parents will not take kindly to their successful, working partner coming home with stories of deal-clinching pitches and networking lunches. It will only make them feel dissatisfied and wonder how they can start to build their own career again.

Studies have revealed that females in male/female partnerships are still often left with the bulk of childcare and housekeeping duties and this can be particularly challenging for Orange-driven females. Not because it's any harder for them than any other woman, but because a mother with peak Orange values will not only be rearing the kids and running the house, she'll be stressing about her body, her looks, her career, her success rate, her social rating, the stock market and generally how she is being judged by the outside world. Often a new parent will down-spiral into Purple or Blue when they spend the first few months or years at home with their children, but those who remain in peak Orange may pile excessive pressure on themselves in a bid to be and to have it all.

Orange females may spend many a late night poring over articles, trying to discover the secrets and tips for how modern, successful women manage.

'Should I be on a macrobiotic diet like Madonna? Should I be working out at five a.m. every day like Hilary Duff? Should I be running a multi-million global business like Nicola Horlick? Should I be writing a blog about motherhood like Gwyneth Paltrow? Should I be a UN ambassador like Angelina Jolie? I've only slept three hours and my boobs feel like the weights I should be lifting in the gym. I'm moody, tired and about as creative as a plank of wood, but I've been at home three weeks now – shouldn't I be setting up that new business I was planning before getting pregnant? Am I doing enough? Am I enough?'

Orange motherhood is exhausting. What's more, Mother Orange needs it to look effortless. But why do you think Victoria Beckham never leaves the house without super-size sunglasses? It *is* exhausting. It *does* take a lot of effort. On the plus side of motherhood, Cheryl will have no time to eat and loses her pregnancy weight in no time. Which could be the start of a whole new diet business: the 'Faux-Baby Diet'. Every time you want to eat, an electronic crying noise wails out from your Faux Baby gadget. By the time you've deactivated the noise you'll have forgotten you ever needed to eat in the first place. It might just be the next big thing. However tired Cheryl gets, she'll always come up with creative solutions and ideas that will energise and propel her to the next stage in her life.

In the meantime, Jason and Cheryl's children will be dressed in top brands from Armani Junior to Mini Boden via Baby Nike. Parenting for this couple will be like maintaining a collection of highly prized pedigree dogs, but these pedigree dogs will soon learn to become self-reliant and highly competent. Orange parents will encourage their offspring to take responsibility for their own needs as soon as possible, and Cheryl and Jason will reward behaviour that demonstrates self-reliance.

If one looks at parenting from a traditional standpoint, on the surface, parenting doesn't entirely suit these two. However, Jason and Cheryl aren't particularly interested in the traditional standpoint. They both thrive on finding new ways to solve old problems. Both are strategic thinkers who will quickly find an effective solution to any child-rearing problems as they arise, at least for the short-term. If they both decide to maintain their careers, they will face the challenge of how to support each other's career development, while managing childcare, housekeeping and maintaining their personal relationship. But if there's one thing these two will excel at, it's communicating and creatively resolving issues.

There's no better way for these two to tackle an issue than to start by having a creative brainstorming session to surface every crazy, inventive, whacky yet possible solution to their latest difficulties. Yes, family life can be challenging, but if these two stay healthy, keep talking and sharing ideas, they will come up with the most innovative and unprecedented solutions to make both their lives and the kids' lives easier, happier and increasingly successful.

Friends and social life

When it comes to a social life, Jason and Cheryl can get incredibly busy. The charisma and energy generated by their Orange values will often make them very popular. They may well find themselves flitting from cocktails to dinner to late drinks at the club, all in one evening. As they have transcended and included Red's drive for attention along with Blue's ability to organise themselves, Cheryl and Jason are willing and able to pack their social life like no other couple. Plus, they have the skill of knowing exactly which invitations to prioritise, while still keeping everyone happy.

Cheryl is an expert at the social story. She knows that perception is everything and that telling people what to think about her creates the reality she desires. She will never reveal insecurities or worries just to feign empathy with someone else expressing those fears. Cheryl's

Orange value set drives her at full steam ahead with confidence, certainty and vision. That's what makes this Orange squared partnership such a social powerhouse.

People love to believe anything is possible, and this pair will make them feel just that. On top of that, they will do all they can to show a united front in public; even if they've just had a row before leaving home, these two will smile for the cameras. Like a Hollywood couple who walk the red carpet arm in arm on Thursday and announce their divorce on Friday, they understand the power of telling whatever story suits them in any given moment, even if that narrative will change tomorrow. It's not about consistency, or even truth, it's about consciously creating the impact you choose. This couple is the king and queen of self-branding and personal PR.

When it comes to friends, these two will value useful and yet casual acquaintances above close and trusted friends, but this will be driven by a strategic rather than emotional need. A brand new connection can potentially introduce them to new and exciting opportunities, whereas a tired network of old friends and neighbours may have run its course.

When Cheryl or Jason are done with a certain way of being, neither will hesitate to dump an old story and move on. This couple will take great delight in reinventing themselves, both within the relationship and outside it. They will support each other in fashion and self-presentation choices. They will also stand united in their need to keep the social wheels moving into new and useful territory. This tends to mean their social and business life will very much intertwine. In fact, their social life can frequently become totally centred around meeting new business colleagues and building their business networks. As is so often the case with people expressing Orange values, this couple's boundaries between personal and professional may well begin to blur.

Because of this personal–professional blurring, these two need to keep a close eye on each other when it comes to each other's business 'friends'. Business and pleasure are the same thing in an Orange world. A business meeting can turn into a business dinner, which can soon turn into a business nightcap which can then turn into a business deal which may ultimately call for further celebration between the sheets of a fancy hotel suite! Unless these two agree on an open marriage, they need to make sure that business means business and that they save the pleasure side of things for their own bedsheets.

Money

When it comes to money and two people with dominant Orange values, risk is a key strategy, and they will have few qualms about borrowing money in order to get what they want. As a result, these two can become burdened down with credit card debts. Though, at the same time, they also have a greater capacity to tolerate stress than other value systems. So even if they do get into large amounts of debt, they will experience less anxiety or arguments than say someone in Blue might. This is because they know anything is possible. These two are endlessly resourceful when it comes to creative ideas for making money.

'Any day could be the day that changes everything,' they tell each other whenever one of them gets a little anxious about the future. *'All we need is a new idea.'* There'll be no shortage of ideas, dreams and aspirations these two can concoct to imagine their way out of debt and into fame and fortune. They both know that any future success all starts with imagination. Have the idea, believe that it's possible and at some point it may very well happen.

For Jason and Cheryl, there's no such thing as failure, only another building block to success. They will cite the law of probability which suggests that the more business attempts they have, the more likely it is that one will take off. Plus, if these two have been through an adequate amount of Blue values, they will quite often have just enough sense of order and control to keep at least half an eye on their finances.

The extreme manifestation of unhealthy Orange values can be seen in the fraudulent businessman or trader. It's not that Orange values inspire criminality, it's just that the lure of millions of pounds and a life of ultimate luxury is something that people at peak Orange value so highly that sometimes they just can't help themselves.

But when money is healthy between these two, it's very healthy. When their combined skills lead them to the business jackpot, they will both absolutely love living the Orange high life. Holidays, gadgets, the best restaurants, designer clothes, custom designed cars . . . you name it, Jason and Cheryl will order it.

Peak Orange is peak capitalism – make a huge amount of money out of the system and then spend a huge amount to keep the system going. Even if they're not making any money, Orange understands you still need to spend it. As their debts mount, people at the Orange stage will tell you they're just trying to keep the system going. That's the way the world turns. If you know how to play the game then, win or lose, you can still win!

Sex

When it comes to sex, these two will constantly seek change and variety, so this sexual union can go almost anywhere. Remember, when it comes to satisfying Orange drives only the most daring survive.

Life is a theatre for these two so they will find a great thrill in role play and costume drama in the bedroom. They may even include a few extras! Having transcended and included Blue values, the Orange stage is about breaking out of the more honour-, duty- and tradition-bound values. Orange is ready to experience guilt-free, sexual freedom. Not just with anyone, however. Orange drives a discerning and choosy attitude when it comes to sexual partners, because they demand the best of themselves and they expect the best of others.

Jason and Cheryl will very much appreciate it if each of them stays in good shape. While someone with more Green values might find someone's heart or soul attractive, physical appearance is primary at the Orange stage.

This couple will be proactive and energised when it comes to their sex life. They'll be hunting out all the latest sex fads and orgasm aids available. They'll want to know what all the celebrities are doing to retain peak sexual attraction in their relationships. These two will even pay through the nose to stay in hotel rooms where famous people have previously had sex. Jason and Cheryl will love nothing more than to reach peak orgasm in the same bed that Brad Pitt and Angelia Jolie may have made love. A romantic holiday for these two would be staying in the villa where Casanova supposedly had his most lusty and outrageous sexual conquests.

As for the latest gadgets, from the rose bud vibrator to the backward bum beads, these two might well be up for trying anything.

They're highly innovative and if either one of them becomes prudish or conventional when it comes to sex, then they may well have physically down-spiralled into Blue. That means their partner has gone too far for them and this couple has just found their sexual limit.

This can be the moment the more adventurous partner goes looking elsewhere, but even if one of them does get temporarily distracted and have a moment of infidelity, they may feel slightly troubled about it afterwards. Unlike people at the Red stage, a person living Orange values can experience some feelings of guilt. They also understand the benefits of long-term investments. They'll hope not to get caught, but if they do, they may well find themselves right back at the beginning of the dating process – trying desperately to win back the person they know is far more valuable to them than anyone else in the world: their Orange partner.

CHAPTER 20

Orange and Green

PEACE AND PROSPERITY.

Dating and early romance

My first question is: how on earth did these two meet? Wherever it was, they must both have been there for very different reasons. Was Rachel (Orange) somewhere she doesn't usually go? Or had Josh (Green) been asked along to an occasion by someone else and didn't feel he could say no? Perhaps they ended up working for the same organisation or taking the same course? Which, if they did, it certainly wasn't with the same goals in mind. Put it this way: if Josh and Rachel meet at a lecture on neuroscience, he is there to further his understanding of the human race and she is there to work out how she can psychologically manipulate a tricky business colleague.

As it seems so unlikely they would have either met or been attracted to one another, when they do Green and Orange can feel that their new-found relationship is in some way very special. It must be. It was all so unlikely. As they begin to date, they will marvel even more at how different they are and yet how much they like each other.

Rachel will initially have liked Josh because he will have made her feel successful and marvellous. Josh will have initially liked Rachel because she had so much to tell him about her projects, ideas and experiences. Josh loves to learn.

Rachel will take Josh to the hottest bar in town and he will be delighted that the hottest bar in town happens to be an uber-ecologically sustainable bar in Shoreditch, lit only by recycled tea lights and built entirely of cardboard. But again, Josh and Rachel will enjoy this experience for very different reasons. Josh loves how sustainable and forward-thinking it is; Rachel loves how last week Wills and Kate were spotted on the cardboard corner-couch sipping fair-trade kiwi margaritas from recycled paper pouches.

But somehow Rachel and Josh can rub along. Yes, she may be only concerned with her latest business venture and being seen in all the right places, but fluid, flexible Josh will go along with whatever she wants. They only see each other twice a week anyway because Rachel is so busy and this gives Josh plenty of time to fill up on the deeper meaning of life elsewhere with other people. Also, Josh is secretly, or even subconsciously, looking at Rachel and the way she lives in the same way one might look at a younger sibling who has a little more to learn. As Josh cosies up on the cardboard-couch and bites into his economically equal enchilada, he sagely assesses his enthusiastic, success hungry date.

'Yes, I've been there,' he thinks, *'and what you seek will bring you material wealth but it won't bring you the deep, internal happiness you really need. For that you must see the world as one interconnected organism that you no longer need to exploit, but care for.'*

Josh is nothing if not idealistic, but Rachel sees the world as she sees it: a competitive market where only the quick thinking and innovative survive. What's more, she may well see it that way till her dying day, so Josh may be disappointed in these early days of dating if he wants Rachel to come to that spiritual yoga retreat or run a marathon to save the pandas.

A couple can often be blinded by the heady rush of falling in love and not see the fundamental differences in their outlooks. Rachel might find Josh overly optimistic, but oh, how cute is all that idealistic enthusiasm. Josh might find her a little cynical, but there's nothing like the power of love and enlightenment to wash away all that mistrust.

So Josh and Rachel may well make it to the long-term, particularly if they can avoid discussing politics!

Long-term and marriage

If Josh and Rachel do make it down the aisle or into a long-term relationship, it can make for an interesting and dynamic pairing – as long as they agree to differ. This is not a relationship built on similar values and understanding. If they can appreciate the complementary nature of each other's strengths, they can be incredibly useful to each other.

Where Rachel might sometimes overlook people's needs or feelings when in pursuit of her personal goals, Josh can help her see that taking a little time to listen to people and get to know them can be incredibly productive. It might even improve her bottom line. Not that *her* bottom needs improving, Josh is quick to reassure the body-conscious Rachel. He means her profit margin.

Suddenly Rachel is all ears. *'Did you say increase my profit margin?'* She enquires, while furiously typing a business email one Sunday morning.

'Yes,' Josh replies. *'Research reveals that understanding your business colleagues and employees and tapping into their intrinsic values and drives often means they'll go the extra mile for their boss.'*

'What? So you really think asking my team what's important to them, or talking about their family or what they did at the weekend could really make me more money?' She mocks.

'Yes,' he says. *'People work harder and put in more discretionary effort for people they like, or for people they think care about them.'* *'In fact,'* Josh adds, peering over her shoulder at the computer screen, *'I hope you don't mind but it might be an idea to think about starting your business emails with something like, "How are things going with you?"*

rather than "Why aren't you picking up your bloody phone? I don't give a damn that it's Sunday."'

Once Rachel gets over the fact that Josh is coaching her in business etiquette, she retorts, *'But I don't give a damn that it's Sunday. He should pick up the bloody phone.'*

'I understand,' Josh coos. *'So, let's see if we can find a different way to get him to take your call.'*

For Josh, sharing and transparency is vital for a sustainable relationship. His Green values can help to soften the edges of Rachel's self-protective expression of peak Orange. Josh is different from anyone she's dated previously. He not only doesn't want to compete with her, he wants to give to her, add to what she already has, support her, and do whatever he can to make her happy and successful. More to the point, he has the capacity to do so.

Rachel will like that Josh doesn't pose any threat to her. She has had enough competition out there in the world. It's nice to come home to someone who's not demanding, but to also find someone who adds something to her life. This side of Josh is very appealing to Rachel.

Josh will love to spend hours cooking for Rachel and creating a safe haven for her to come home to, but on top of this, he has seen the world, literally and metaphorically. Having lived through the other four value sets, he has useful knowledge and insightful understanding to offer up. So what if Rachel only has three minutes to digest both Josh's insightful understanding and his casserole before she needs to get on a late night call with her accountant? Josh is very forgiving. Which is going to be key in this relationship. Rachel might sometimes say and do things that sensitive Josh will find tough to hear. He may find himself wishing she could be softer towards him, more caring and gentle, but that's not how Rachel gets results. She gets ahead by calling things how she really sees them, not wrapping the facts in cotton wool.

What's more, once Rachel has surfaced her thoughts or feelings, the moment has passed. She won't necessarily hold grudges. She doesn't dwell in the past. She lives and works for the future.

When there is discord between these two, Rachel will quickly be ready and willing to move on, keen to work out how they can both create the next part of their exciting future together. Knowing this, Josh and Rachel can enjoy a powerful collaboration.

Josh is brilliant at helping individuals realise their potential – and Rachel very much wants her potential realised. Though Josh lives in service of Green values, he is realistic. He wants change, but knows it's hard to beat the system. He also understands that if you want to create change, you must bring something new to the table that makes the old system redundant. As the current system is Orange, his new entrepreneurial partner might know key people in key places that can affect change for a better world. A little Orange in service of Green might be just the ticket! Living and loving with Rachel could be Josh's chance to get a little more eco-preneurial. It's what the future's all about and if there's one thing Rachel and Josh will share, it's a concern about the future. Yes, perhaps for very different reasons, but remember how these two first started dating? Doing similar things for very different reasons is nothing new to Rachel and Josh. Anyway, Rachel is always on the look out for new ideas. Who knows, Green might just be the new Orange.

Kids and family

If and when Josh and Rachel have children together, the wonder of human creation is overwhelming for them both, though once again for very different reasons.

Josh will be bowled over by this new, first-hand, visceral experience of nature doing what nature does. As he takes his newborn into his arms and looks into their eyes, the natural process of the earth has suddenly become even more personal than ever. The Green values that Josh holds suddenly now surface overflowing feelings of love for the wonder that is all human life.

Rachel, too, will be overwhelmed with this newborn baby. It distorted her body for nine months and then finally she endured the dangerous and painful process of giving birth. It wasn't always fun, but no creative or business process ever is. The results are so often worth it, though. Rachel loves seeing her projects, innovations and ideas come to life. As she looks down at her latest creation, she will probably overflow with the realisation that this baby may well be the greatest and most challenging project she will ever have to manage and complete.

Becoming a parent can be invasive for someone like Rachel and her Orange style of life. If post-natal depression kicks in for her, it will only confirm all her worst fears: 'This was the biggest mistake of my life. I don't want this thing dependent on me. I am a free agent able to spontaneously create my own life.' However, if she is lucky enough to be bathed in a post-natal cocktail of oxytocin and oestrogen, she may well feel that nothing will ever live up to this feeling again. Either way, Rachel will finally find herself somewhere between the two positions – loving and proud, but still independent and self-motivated. Rachel's challenge will be to not get too distracted with work projects and the pursuit of life achievements. Time moves so fast and this new baby project has so many fascinating stages for her to experience. If she is able to remain engaged and present.

Thankfully, Josh will help her do this. He will usually be incredibly present and emotionally engaged with their children. Josh will worry if he feels Rachel is absent or detached for too long and do everything he can to reconnect the whole family unit. Josh loves everyone to be connected as much as possible. As the children grow up, he will be most happy when everyone is in a shared open space in the house getting on with their homework, business reports, drawing, playing or cooking. Josh will feel sad when the family members all disappear to their own rooms and close their doors. In fact, he will not only want their own children in the communal space in the home, but will encourage them to bring all their friends round too.

Josh will be exceptionally welcoming, which Rachel will usually love, and as long as he takes charge when it comes to the children and their friends, Rachel will be very happy to dip in and out of the fun and buzz that Josh helps create. She will love that their home is 'vibey' and popular where young, energised people want to be. They may even splash out on a barn conversion or games den to make it clear they can provide a happy, playful and creative space for their children and their children's mates. Rachel knows this will also keep their children engaged with the family for longer. The truth is, if the house suddenly became empty, Rachel would secretly miss all the energy, excitement and stimulus of having all these young people around.

As much as Rachel will want the children to have fun and be happy, she also wants them to be realistic about how the big, wide world operates. This can be an area of tension between Green and Orange parents. If one of their young children comes home upset at having fallen out with a friend, these two parents will have very different advice.

'*I hate her, she's so mean. She called me Football-head,*' says twelve-year-old Vicki. '*So I called her Etna-face.*'

'*It's okay, darling,*' Josh will reassure her. '*I'm sure you both said mean things. The best thing is if you talk to her tomorrow and both say sorry. Tell her how much she means to you and that you didn't mean what you said, as you're sure she didn't mean what she said. I'll tell you what, I'll bake you some of my special bonbon brownies and you can share them with her at lunchtime.*'

'*Or you could ignore her and move on,*' pipes up Rachel.

'*Sorry?*' counters Josh.

'*Ignore her.* Rachel continues. '*She'll come round. And if she doesn't, it's her loss. Here's the truth, Vicki: the world is full of mean people and you mustn't rely on any of them. Only ever rely on yourself.*'

After Josh has made light of Rachel's comment and sent Vicki off to find the cocoa powder, he will probably question Rachel's advice, but she will remind him that they need to make their children aware of the reality of the world. As much as he may believe life is one big love-in, there are ill-intentioned people out there and it won't serve their kids to be unprepared as to how to deal with them. Josh and Rachel will never see eye to on their Realism vs Idealism stand off.

Friends and social life

Josh and Rachel's criteria for choosing friends and acquaintances couldn't be more different. Rachel loves to network and Josh loves to socialise and there's a huge difference between the two. Rachel will soon realise that few of Josh's friends are necessarily of much use to him or her. None of them will be forthcoming with introductions to any serious venture capitalists and most of them won't even carry a business card.

When it comes to socialising for pleasure, Rachel really only has time to play when the latest deal has been done and the latest success assured. Even then, relaxation or celebration will be brief. While Josh is happy to spend long lazy weekends brunching with friends from their yoga class, Rachel will soon tire of the conversation and need to get on and do something else.

Rachel will not necessarily be able to relax in company the way Josh can. She is very likely to be highly energised and constantly tapping her fingers, ready to move on to the next thing. Josh will feel they have only just started to get to the heart of a certain friend's current emotional issue, when Rachel will leap up and say it's time to leave. Whether they have a proposal to deliver in the morning or *Dragons Den* is on TV, anything will be more productive than hearing Josh's best friend Sophie whinging on again about not being able to find a boyfriend. *'Why doesn't he just tell her to sort her life out, lose a bit of weight and get a decent hair cut?'* she'll think.

It's at times like this that Josh finds Rachel a little selfish and callous. Josh's perspective is that people should be allowed to be who and what they are and behave as they choose. Whether Rachel agrees or disagrees with this position, she will respect someone who owns his own opinion. All too often, however, Josh's Green values will drive him to suffer in silence, unwilling to upset Rachel. If he only knew, she isn't afraid of being upset by him she's more afraid of losing respect for him.

Money

When this couple manages money well together, it can lead to phenomenal philanthropic initiatives. Money that is made and distributed in service of Green and Orange values can warm the heart and restore one's faith in human kind. Think Bill Gates, Warren Buffet, Oprah Winfrey, *Secret Millionaire* and the Sainsbury's Trust – money well earned and well spent. That's when Orange and Green finances are at their healthiest. A combination of Orange's desire to earn money and Green's desire to do good with it.

Even without being a millionaire couple, Orange and Green can still be recognised as a force of generosity and benevolence. A person expressing Green values will enjoy this recognition because of the good work it does and an Orange-motivated person will enjoy the attention of everyone thinking they're impressive.

If Rachel and Josh have enough money and are healthily expressing their value sets then everyone around them and possibly even a number of global charities will benefit. Plus Rachel can still have her designer kitchen and Aston Martin Virage all to herself. However – and it's a big however – when money goes wrong with Orange and Green, it can go terribly wrong.

Orange values can cause a person to be a huge risk-taker and with no Blue structures around to keep them in check, they may just gamble everything. It cannot be over-estimated how financially disastrous Orange and Green can become. It's down to weakened Green government bodies deregulating the Blue financial systems and reckless Orange stockbrokers running rampant in the global betting shop that we're in the worst global recession of modern times.

Before Josh and Rachel buy a house or open a joint bank account together, they'll need to sit down and work out exactly who's responsible for what and how much they are going to put into a safety account that's off limits for risky investments. Rachel and Josh will need to create some structure around their finances, and maybe think about getting a financial advisor. Unless they get a reasonably solid Blue financial strategy in place, they risk facing their own mini financial meltdown.

Sex

Together, these two can rewrite the Karma Sutra. Well, Rachel will rewrite it and Josh will be the test pilot. Sex for this pairing can happen anywhere, anytime, in any position and in any attire. Rachel wants to try it all. As soon as it feels like a routine has settled into place, she will suddenly surprise Josh with a whole new position.

'It's called froggy style! It's the latest thing. Everyone's at it,' she will say, suddenly delighted that Josh has done all that yoga. *'Lucky you're so bendy.'*

'I'm not sure even a frog could do this!' he protests.

Green values are about accepting all perspectives – however uncomfortable that may be at times. Even if froggy style is a little, erm, challenging, never mind, anything is worth a try as long as it doesn't harm anyone. You never know, Rachel might be into tantric next and Josh will just love that. So all can be fun and frolics in the bedroom, with Rachel in the role of sexual artiste and Josh playing artist's muse.

Now, at this point would usually come the warning about people motivated by Orange values liking a conquest and to be forever challenged. They see the world and every member of the opposite sex as part of the big competition they have to win. But this time, Rachel is with Josh, and that changes things slightly. It doesn't change her need for novelty, but with Josh in the mix, it might change how she gets it.

In brief, Orange values strive for novelty and Green values seek to accommodate and please. This means Rachel and Josh win the award for couple most likely to be part of a swinger community. If they're up for it, swinging can be perfect for this couple and even keep their relationship together. No other values pairing share this combination of selfish need for new excitement or conquests and an all encompassing understanding and acceptance. Rachel won't believe her luck. Josh being happy to go swinging will make for a very happy Orange partner.

'What, I can have my cake AND eat it?' Rachel will say. *'And you'll still love me and only me?'*

'Yes,' Josh will assure her. *'I'm happy to do this because it makes you happy – and I love you so much.'*

Even if this couple doesn't go as far as swinging, the openness and acceptance that Josh offers Rachel is incredibly exciting and liberating for her. These two lovers are a highly creative force. Both will be open to new ideas and both will be happy to try them out. No judgements, no patronising comments, just a forceful combination of curiosity, willing, energy and play.

On top of which, jealousy isn't high in Josh's list of emotions. Even if Rachel is more subversive in her need for novelty and has an affair, Josh is the most likely partner to try to understand.

More than any other pairing, the Green and Orange partnership can weather quite a lot of marital storms. Green values can somehow keep forgiving. Even though their partner can sometimes be thoughtless and get caught up in a moment, Green knows their partner still loves them. People expressing Green can tolerate more than most and will understand their partner's needs – having been through Orange themselves. Together, a couple embodying Green and Orange values will keep innovating and recreating this relationship, making it one of the most dynamic, exciting and yet, at the same time, stable of all the pairings.

CHAPTER 21

Green and Green

ALL YOU NEED IS LOVE.

Dating and early romance

The stomach flips even thinking about the early dating days of two people living Green values. Think soft focus, hazy days of summer, staring into each other's eyes and finding the joy in every tiny, atomic aspect of life, all underscored to the sound of a soaring, selfless ballad. These two will feel they have never known a love like this before. Where have they been all each other's lives?

Gina and Anna met on the second day of an enlightenment retreat, during a hatha yoga class. They began talking after class over a pot of green tea and found themselves still together hours later, sitting up all night asking questions about each other. They discovered that they both love to learn and love to love. So, once heightened emotions and physical attraction kicked in, they became utterly transfixed and fascinated by each other. There was so much to talk about: life, the world, religion, beliefs, values, the universe and what it means to be human, not to mention a gay woman. These two quickly became lovers and poured themselves into each other, holding nothing back.

Although Green values are about being responsible and thoughtful towards other people, friends and family, Gina and Anna's early dating period brought out some less familiar behaviour.

So caught up were they in their new-found, overpowering love, that they almost lost all sense of time and space. Indeed, friends and family did not see or hear from them both for days as they spent this initial and intense time together, filling up on each other and their wonderful new shared experience.

Unlike previous value systems, at the peak Green values stage a person won't necessarily be motivated to prioritise business appointments or deadlines over the new person in their life. Quite the opposite. Green values are very people and emotions orientated. Anyone living Green will often drop everything in favour of an important person or relationship in their life.

By day three, both Anna and Gina's mobile phones were ringing from their numerous friends and family members, worried that they haven't heard from either of them for such a long time. *'Where are you? We've been so worried. We've got the peace rally tomorrow and haven't heard from you in three days.'*

Gina and Anna will be full of remorse respectively.

'Three days? Where did the time go? We completely lost track . . . When I say "we" – I can't wait for you to meet someone. I think I've found my soulmate. Well, we found each other. This is the one. You'll love her as much as I already do.'

A person embodying Green values can be so open, trusting and even naive when it comes to love, that when they fall, they can fall very hard and very fast. When it's a question of two Greens in a new relationship, it can be overwhelming and intoxicating.

By the end of week one, as a newly formed couple, Gina and Anna were talking about moving in together, discussing living room colour schemes, and even contemplating children and pets. Both of these two Greens will very much want to please the other during their first few weeks of dating . . . and indeed for the rest of their lives.

The challenge for Gina and Anna long-term will be that with so much focus on pleasing each other, they may be unable to actually make any concrete decisions. When it comes to choosing a restaurant, an outfit or who will drive, these two could get caught in a stalemate of niceness. The phrase 'I don't mind – you choose' is a common theme when Green values are predominant in a partnership. But what do decisions matter when these two are spiralling into the kind of love only mutual Green values can experience together?

You can spot Green couples fairly easily – they're the ones who suddenly stop in shop doorways or down a busy street to simply stare into each other's eyes and remind each other how lucky they are to have met. It's all very touching and very beautiful, but for anyone single, dumped or divorced looking on it's sick-making. It's just too good to be true and everyone else wants some of it as well.

Long-term and marriage

Gina and Anna have every chance of making their relationship sustainable in the long term. They may well consider marriage, or the equivalent, as both will be overflowing with optimism and idealism. They know the stats on marital success aren't great, but they believe they will be different.

The modern world is no doubt tough on relationships, but from the Green altitude, Anna and Gina can see beyond the modern material world. Reaching the Green values stage means someone has transcended and included Purple's need for belonging, Red's need for autonomy, Blue's need for rules and Orange's need for material wealth. Therefore their personal vow to each other may sound like this: *'We promise to do everything we can to make it through to the end of our lives together. Not just with the requisite planning, organising, contingency or marital strategy, but with genuine love.'*

Gina and Anna will join together in the full belief that neither will ever let the other down. If one or both partners are wealthy they may be advised by friends and family to get a pre-nup or see a lawyer in regards to who owns how much of the house, but they will both shake their heads and sigh.

'You're so cynical. It must be terrible to live like that. You go and do your own pre-nup. We don't need it. We have found inner peace and trust together. A trust that goes beyond lawyers and contracts. We have the deepest trust in each other and the human ability to find the good, the true and the beautiful in life.'

That's all great as long as things are going well. A Green partnership is wonderful when it comes to mutual support, trust, friendship and interests, as well as learning and growing together. Long-term, however, Green faces challenges when the rest of the world comes crashing in to their Green-tinted peace podule. Suddenly they are once again confronted with the confusing reality that not all of humanity is loving and kind.

Individuals with Green values can be far too trusting. They risk being taken advantage of and manipulated by others expressing the 'I' orientated Red or Orange values. When two Greens get together, they double the risk and vulnerability of being taken in by supposed new friends who are simply out for themselves. It can then become difficult to avoid spiralling back down in response to the negative feelings, thoughts and behaviours of others and end up entangled in a web of confusing Red and Orange emotions.

However, a couple expressing peak Green values will find each other a great support when people hurt them or let them down. When Anna discovers that a work colleague has tried to sabotage her career prospects, Gina will be an incredibly empathetic ally.

'I can't believe it,' says Anna. *'She seemed so supportive of me and my career development, and then I find out all the time she was bitching about me to my boss. She was so nice to my face and then made sure she ruined my chances of promotion just so she could step in and take it herself.'*

'I know,' Gina will empathise. *'People can be so surprising sometimes. Only last week I gave my bank details to one of those charity street workers. I assumed they were legitimate. I didn't think to check. I've just had two hundred pounds taken from my bank account. It's so upsetting.'*

'It really is,' Anna will say, in a sympathetic and loving tone. *'Why are people so mean? If only they understood the truth of human oneness.'*

While the sympathy and empathy flows between our Green lovers, neither of them necessarily have any practical advice or solutions to give – acceptance is the way, the truth and the light. Although they are both great listeners, they both know it's best to simply keep an open and trusting attitude. Keep filling up the karma bank and all will turn out well. It's no good telling this Green partnership to go out there and fight their corner, they need to be true to who they are. They'd be miserable pretending to be anything else.

Together, Gina and Anna have the beautiful potential to nurture and help each other grow and self-actualise throughout their entire lives. They may well share in a life-long journey towards spiritual growth, which could see their bond strengthen and enrich over the years. Both will allow the other to express their inner most feelings, helping them to understand each other at the deepest level. This relationship really is give, give, give.

However, for all the talking and idea sharing, people in Green have the potential to stay in the 'discussion,' 'sharing' and 'opinion forming' phase of a project for a long, long time. So when it comes to any major decisions in their life, home renovations, important purchases, holidays, etc. – they can often prevaricate and procrastinate, for fear of not making the right decision for all involved.

As they are both at a more mature stage of ego development, they will go to any length to avoid upsetting anyone, especially their partner. If they do cause any upset, it can go one of two ways. They will either truly express Green values and be able to calmly see the other person's point of view as well as fully embrace their partner's right to say how they feel, or, on the other hand, they may down-spiral and their latent Red, Blue or Orange may suddenly spring forth.

It's important to remember that being at the Green stage means, at some point, they have both been through and exhausted the other value stages. However, sometimes that powerful Red energy inside them both will need expression. No one can be perfect and calm all of the time.

While this is true for all the other values, it can be the most surprising for a Green partnership to experience one or the other expressing Red energy as they both very much want to live a life of peace and love.

They need to watch out that they're not too hard on themselves, though. They are human after all – and it's very human to be cross or annoyed sometimes. If they mistakenly believe they should never express their negative feelings, any anger may well be displayed as passive aggression. The anger will be there, but people living Green values can sometimes have a habit of hiding it under the guise of reluctant self-sacrifice – the martyr complex.

It is vital to acknowledge that within us all is a whole rainbow of values to be expressed. The important thing is to take care not to become totally hijacked by just one set.

Another thing Anna and Gina may need to watch out for is to make sure they prioritise their own relationship. They can have so much love to give that they will often happily spread it around, way beyond the home and close circle of friends. While that can seem like a wonderful quality, they might need to be a little careful that they don't inadvertently neglect each other.

Unlike Purple, Green doesn't naturally prioritise the family unit. They prioritise the whole of humankind. They value pleasing people and find it hard to say no. Someone needy outside of the relationship can suddenly demand and absorb time, energy and affection. It is worth both Green partners recognising if they have this pattern and to draw some boundaries. Of course it's great to help and support people from all walks of life, but Gina and Anna just need to be careful they keep finding time to nurture each other. Green values are firmly in the 'We' position. A Green relationship is not a relationship of total independence – it needs to be one of inter-dependence, but in this pairing, there are less Red or Blue values to demand attention or set the relationship boundaries.

Individuals living in service of the sharing, caring Green values are less interested in ownership or possession and that includes being possessed by a partner. So people are always surprised when a couple with Green values breaks up because one of them met someone else.

'But they're supposed to be caring and kind and all about people,' friends and family cry.

They are! But there are a lot of people in the world to love. That doesn't mean that they will cease to love their current partner, but it does mean that Green's love may be open, available or even polygamous. If they do find themselves in an 'open' relationship, a Green lover will still need to feel engaged with and attached to their partner. The bonds that unite them might not be about loyalty, dominance or success but rather a deep, unique bond around an energised, forward-moving and idealistic way of life.

Kids and family

When it comes to having children, Gina and Anna will make wonderful parents. Their home will be bursting with love.

There may not be a great deal of structure at times, but what this family unit lacks in order and rules, they make up for in warmth and self-expression. Their home will often be a little chaotic but very caring. There won't necessarily be many rules – other than everyone should do their thing, but also share and be kind. Even if the few rules that exist are broken, Gina and Anna are unlikely to come down too hard on the kids. Green will usually value the natural evolution of individuals, not the harsh discipline of authority. So when it comes to parenthood, a Green couple suddenly have a whole new focus for their Green idealism – the next generation.

For someone in Green, children are the shining lights of the future of the human race. Green parents love to see their own and other's children growing strong, playing collaboratively and developing their own new ideas about the world we live in. They will believe that this new generation of children could be the generation that dissolves prejudices of every kind, cures all cancers, eradicates poverty and brings about world peace. Green is all about the children being our future. They represent the hope that Green clings on to, even in times of seeming despair. It's important that this new generation carves out their own way of being - free from old rules or prejudices.

That's all very well if they adopt or give birth to easy going, naturally well-balanced children, then letting each child find and express its individuality is all very rewarding. But it's easy to forget that not everyone comes into the world with Green genes. Some might argue that kids benefit from strict guidance and structure at a certain stage of their development, but Green parents would often rather do things in their own less disciplinarian way. They will organically find the parenting style that suits them and expect to be left alone to parent as they see fit – just as they leave others alone.

When it comes to schooling, Green parents will often want to send their children to an establishment where the little ones can explore their unique creative talents unhindered.

They will often favour Montessori nurseries and schools that have a humanist or pluralistic approach to education. If they can't find a liberal or open enough place for their children to be schooled, they may well consider home schooling.

At the Green values stage, people have invariably let go of strict doctrines. They have come to understand that each and every belief is an expression of the same thing, and that all beings are interconnected. No belief is absolutely right or wrong.

Everyone, in a way, is right. Therefore it's very important that children learn there are many approaches to life and that everyone has the right to express and live in service of their own worldview.

The Green parents at your kids' school are usually the ones wearing organic clothing and holding a petition to ban all competitive sport and academic ranking. These parents are incredibly kind, though their kids will rarely find them 'cool'.

It's often only later in life that kids of Green parents fully appreciate their parents' choices and values. Children have a lot of Purple, Red, Blue and Orange energy to get through before fully appreciating Green.

Friends and social life

This couple needs to be around others. Not only because they like to have fun but because mixing with other people also provides them with a basic sense of well-being and happiness. Gina and Anna are both very people orientated and will seek a fair amount of social contact in their lives. For these two, being able to make friends is important to both their psychological health and the health of their relationship.

Although this is a strong partnership, both will find it very natural to also seek emotional support from their friends.

A male at the Green values stage will have transcended traditional – or cultural – gender role expectations and be more likely than males at any of the other value stages to talk about intimate issues with their close, male friends.

Between them, Gina and Anna will probably have a great number of friends and acquaintances – male and female. Both will accept each other's friends – even if they don't particularly like them. In fact, if one of their friends were to upset either of them, their Green values are likely to stop them making a big thing about it. These two can be very forgiving because both have a very open and trusting attitude to the outside world and other people.

'But, Anna, she took money off you and never paid you back,' Gina insists

'I guess she needs the cash,' Anna replies.

'But she turned up uninvited and has been staying rent free for two months.'

'I guess she needs somewhere to live.'

'She slept with your ex while you were still with her.'

'I guess she needs love.'

'She stole underwear from you.'

'I guess she . . . needs help?'

Green values will drive a need in Gina and Anna to make the world a better place, because they themselves want to live in a better place. A safe, kind place. That's why they want to make their friends and social circle happy.

If anyone needs anything doing – a helping hand, a volunteer, a charity event assistant – Gina or Anna will be right there, giving up their time and love to a good cause, or even a friend's good cause, or even a friend of a friend's good cause. As long as it is a good cause, they will feel their time has been well spent.

Money

Green values are not orientated around money. That's not to say Gina and Anna won't enjoy money if they have it, but it's unlikely to be a strong motivating factor in their lives. In fact, they will often want to avoid dealing with money altogether. Based on their worldview, from the Green altitude, talking about money can feel ugly and uncomfortable, but unless they choose to move out of a Western capitalist context, someone in this partnership will need to focus on the finances. If not, this pair risks getting into financial hot water.

The biggest risk they face isn't overspending on themselves, but overspending on each other and everyone around them. Green values can be overly generous and charitable. Typical behaviour for these two is to go out with a friend, pay for a taxi or a take-away and tell their friend not to worry about paying them back.

They enjoy the feeling of being generous, but the end of the month can be stressful when they realise they didn't budget for all their friends' social lives plus birthday presents for every child of everyone they've ever met. Generosity is wonderful, but so is the relief of being able to comfortably pay your own bills.

The truth is, for Anna and Gina living in Green, friendship and acceptance are far more important than material wealth and, of course, they are right on one level – money can't buy you love. However, it can buy you future security and a few less sleepless nights. This partnership would do well to work out who, between them, has the most active Blue values as a secondary driver and put them in charge of bills, taxes and piggy banks.

Sex

From the perspective of a values-based approach to life and love, traditional or cultural gender roles are almost redundant. So, when two people of either gender live genuinely Green values and become lovers, they will both put all their focus on the giving – but at some point someone needs to take! A gift isn't a gift unless there's a receiver, and preferably a receiver who thoroughly enjoys the gift they're given.

Sometimes Green needs to lie back and learn to enjoy receiving a little. It might feel selfish, but relax! Your Green partner loves being generous too, so everyone's a winner, and you love it even more when everyone's winning, right?

At the peak Green values stage, people can sometimes deny or reject the other value systems, but the bedroom is the perfect place to embrace and express all the previous values. Having transcended passive Purple, power-hungry Red, rules-orientated Blue and success-hungry Orange, it's now important to include and integrate the healthy expression of these previous value stages. Sex and the physical self are the most basic and fundamental human expressions. For all the goodness, kindness and generosity expressed by Green values in their everyday lives together, the bedroom might be a very important release for any unexpressed anger, basic sexual urges, irritation or worry that they both may be holding.

Sex between these two will either be open and explorative or, alternatively, all become a bit ambiguous and uncertain – maybe even fade away to non-existence. That's why it's important that these two find a way to play with the dominant/passive dynamic in their sex life, because if they are unable to confidently communicate their needs and desires then sex can disappear from this relationship altogether.

The bedroom is the perfect opportunity for two Green lovers to learn every detail about each other's sexual desires and to use that knowledge to explore this relationship's sexual potential and beyond.

CHAPTER 22

The *Rainbow* Perspective

You should now have a clear understanding of how the five values are expressed in feelings, thoughts and behaviours, as well as how they meet and match in the fifteen relationship combinations. You can see how the pairings of different value systems each create a unique dynamic between both people in the partnership. Every values fusion has its own strengths and joys, as well as its more challenging aspects. Simply recognising where each value set thrives together and where they risk pulling apart is a huge step towards creating a deep, rich and long-lasting relationship.

Looking at your own Spiral Profiler results, you can identify where your own values' centre of gravity sits. The values with the highest scores are those you are currently expressing. These will be driving your behaviour and attitude to life and specifically to your partner. Once you've both completed the Spiral Profiler, you might like to compare each other's scores.

The first step is to identify where your values match. Any same value set within two points of each other could be thought of as a strong match. For instance, if you've scored twelve in Green and nine in Red and your partner has scored ten in Green and seven in Red then you are sharing very similar value sets.

However, if you've scored twelve in Red and three in Blue, and your partner has scored two in Red and eleven in Blue, then you may benefit from understanding and managing the gaps. If you have been finding areas of your relationship challenging, then the next step might be to explore whether these challenges may be rooted in a mismatch of both your values.

It is also important to understand that couples in the examples I have outlined are expressing one value set each at a peak stage, but this is not how we always function in real life. Although most of us will live by a dominant value set at any one time, we will often express a combination of all five values at different times, in different situations and with different people. Therefore we need to apply our new understanding of each of the value stages – how they manifest in feelings, thoughts, beliefs and behaviours – and view them from what can be called the Rainbow Perspective.

From the Rainbow Perspective, you can consciously recognise which value set both you and your partner are expressing at any one time. Once you have recognised the dominant value systems, you can then manage and support each other so that both of you get exactly what you need from your relationship. In this way, you can learn to maximise each other's happiness and allow your love to expand and grow every day. This is when you can truly start to spiral into love.

So, it's time now to take an in-depth look at the spiral of values from 'The Rainbow Perspective.'

When a fierce storm is over, if we're lucky, we may see a rainbow in the sky. This multi-coloured miracle of nature is a wondrous sight and signifies a break, or even a change, in the weather. As we gaze at the spectrum of colours, we may feel a magical glow and think about the old adage of the pot of gold waiting for us at the end of the rainbow. In fact, this may be a useful analogy for the potential benefits to taking the Rainbow Perspective within a relationship.

Imagine if whenever your relationship became challenging and erupted into conflict, a rainbow appeared over your heads and helped you to end the storm. Well, that's just what the Rainbow Perspective can do.

Learning to take a Rainbow Perspective means being able to see how all the value systems, from Purple to Green, connect as a whole system of human values and drives. Understanding where your own – and your partner's – personal centre of gravity sits in terms of your values will help you both to take an objective view of how you feel, think and what you do in any given situation. In other words, shifting your experience from being hijacked by emotion and then habitually reacting from your own value position towards being able to take a perspective that sits outside all the values.

For example, you and your partner might sit in a strong Blue value set most of the time but suddenly you find your relationship is breaking down. Perhaps they have been caring for an elderly relation or been overstretched at work and have found themselves increasingly tired and busy. Suddenly they are short tempered and difficult. It might be that they have been neglecting themselves and are now compensating by spiralling down into a Red ego position.

By recognising what has happened you can now understand why your Blue, rules-based values are having an unusual effect on the dynamic. The last thing your partner wants is to be told what to do. They feel put upon and burdened with responsibility. They want to take back some control. Your partner is now in Red so if you continue to react to them from a Blue, rules-based perspective, you risk further damaging the relationship.

This is the moment to take a Rainbow Perspective and talk to your partner from a healthy Red values perspective. Make them feel strong. Make them feel empowered. Then they can relax. There's no fight any more, only acceptance. In time, they will shift back up the spiral to their usual dominant Blue value set but with the wonderful knowledge that in this relationship it is safe to express every aspect of themselves. They are wholly loved for the whole of themselves.

The Rainbow Perspective means you can see, hear and feel how the value systems can be integrated in a relationship of natural flow and growing love. Being able to recognise your partner's values profile is potentially the beginning of a wonderfully rich and life-long relationship.

In 2003, two psychologists, Neff and Karney [16], ran a fascinating test that explored the connection between a couple's happiness and their awareness of the other's perspectives and values. Individuals were asked to write open-ended paragraphs about issues in their marriages. Some of them recognised that there can be two sides to every conflict and that compromises are possible. Others wrote only about their own perspective, failing to recognise that other perspectives are valid or even exist. Guess which individuals were then rated as being in the happiest relationships? You guessed it – the ones who could recognise that there was more than one perspective in the room.

This isn't about the gender divide; nor is this about becoming someone you're not or communicating in an inauthentic but supposedly appealing way. If you're not someone who oozes empathy or does straight talk, then you may never and should not be expected to change! But still, you want to be able to reach your partner in a way that will help them to understand your needs as well as help you to understand theirs.

The way to do that is by understanding their values and drivers. When I look back on past relationships, I am certainly guilty of not having seen a partner's perspective. When the disagreements or breakdown in communication became unbearable, I walked away from every one of them. But it's never too late. I now know how important it is to be aware and awake to the deepest values driving your partner.

Whether or not those past relationships would have lasted, who knows – but no wonder they didn't when there was only ever one perspective in the room. That might be hard to admit perhaps, but it's true.

Today I understand how to take the full Rainbow Perspective within a relationship. My eyes, heart and mind are fully open. I have now found a wonderful partner with whom I've learned how to spiral into love. I won't be walking away from this one! I guarantee the Rainbow Perspective can help you spiral into love too.

The Rainbow Perspective reframe

When you recognise, respect and nurture your partner's values, the love between you will grow and strengthen into something truly astounding. When a human being feels heard, understood and loved, there is no limit to the love they can return. But if you have a high understanding of your partner's values and use that information to manipulate or torment them, the relationship will quickly become toxic. As Francis Bacon said, 'Knowledge is power', but if you use this knowledge for evil then your power will lead to nothing but hurt and misery. Use the knowledge you have gained to support and develop your love for one another. It's easy to use knowledge about a loved one to hurt them. It takes strength, intelligence, creativity and foresight to use that information to build the next layer of the rainbow that is your love together. You have everything you need to create the very best and avoid creating the very worst.

Ask yourself, are you pointing out the negative aspects of your relationship or reaffirming the positive ones? How are you using the information you have about your partner's needs and values? You do have a choice.

Many people inadvertently fall into what I call the Phase Two trap without even being aware they had a choice to avoid it. The relationship Phase Two trap comes right after the initial euphoria of Phase One.

Phase One is all about having fun, falling in love and getting to know your new partner. You love everything about them, even the annoying things.

You believe you will always feel that way, but before you know it, the two of you are bickering about the small things and chipping away at your love by constantly reminding each other of your faults. As an ex-boyfriend of mine once put it, *'You spend your first year with your partner finding out as much about them as possible and the rest of your life using that information against them.'* And that is the

Phase Two trap.

But happy couples don't do that. When happy couples are asked to rate which specific aspects of their relationships are most important to the success of their partnership, they generally point to whatever aspects of their relationship are most positive. Individuals with this tendency are the ones who are the happiest with their relationships overall.[17]

It can be frustrating when our partner has habits that we don't like, though again it's interesting to keep reminding yourself that these habits bothered you little in the initial stages of your relationship! As my partner said to me when I complained about shaving residue around the bathroom sink, *'Just think how much you'd miss it if I was no longer here.'* What he meant, of course, was think how much you'd miss me if I wasn't here. A fairly Red statement, I grant you! But he was right. It really made me stop and think. From my perspective, I want my partner around, I want him to be at peace, I want him to energise and enforce our life together. I want him to be able to be who he is. I want him to feel comfortable and free. I want him to know he is enough. He doesn't lack anything. I don't want him to feel less than he is, because that's not when he's at his best. He's at his best when he most fulfils either my often Green needs for harmony and collaboration or my Orange needs for innovation, ideas sharing and productivity.

There are countless things my partner does for me every day that makes my life full of fun, creativity, laughter and love. What future life would I be creating if I headed down the route of nagging him about supposed faults or irritations every day? How helpful are those niggling comments in nurturing and growing our love?

How much would *I* want to be around someone who reminded me on a daily basis exactly what I was lacking and why I am such a disappointment?

If we focus on the negative aspects of our partner's values, how surprised can we really be if that relationship begins to lose its charm, if communication breaks down, or if the relationship self-destructs entirely? We're creating the relationship. Every minute of every day. So what choices are we making about what we say and do in response to our partner? What aspects of their value set are we choosing to focus on? We always have a choice to focus on the positive or the negative.

Of course, those positives and negatives will vary depending on the value set combination. For example, if someone with peak Blue values were in a relationship with a more Red partner, they might need to look at the value set in a slightly different way from someone with more Green values. Where someone in Green might look at Red's creativity and fun and see how valuable those aspects were to the relationship, Blue might better appreciate looking at Red's power and self-determination to get things done. If Blue focuses on the negative, they might find Red's independence rather daunting, but by focusing on how Red gets results and doesn't put responsibility on others, Blue can once again open their eyes to why they feel so much love for Red.

Abi and Jeff have been together for eighteen years. Abi expresses mainly Orange, aspirational values. Jeff expresses a rules-based Blue value set. Abi and Jeff's relationship had lost its sparkle. Abi felt they were bickering on a daily basis, and even at times avoiding each other. When asked what Jeff was like, this is what she said:

Jeff is really fussy. Everything has to be just so. There's no room for error or a change of plans. He gets frustrated with me if I suddenly land something on him like having to go to a work function or even a friend's for a barbecue at the last minute. He'll go, though he's initially quite reluctant. He doesn't like change. We've lived in the same house and he's been in the same job for fifteen years.

As I've got older, I realise I want more from life than Jeff seems to, or certainly different things. We constantly bicker about his lack of get up and go.'

Abi has understood Jeff's Blue values. She knows what is important to him and yet has almost exclusively focused on the negative aspect of those values that annoy her. The more she looks at Jeff's Blue values from a negative perspective, the more dominant that perspective will become for her. Until 'fussy, staid old Jeff' is the only perspective she has on the man she supposedly loves.

Abi doesn't like that perspective, but she's the one who's created it! So what if Abi started to focus more on the positive aspects of Jeff's Blue values? What if Abi looked at how Jeff's Blue values support and complement her Orange values? She did just that and from her Orange perspective that reframe sounded like this:

Jeff can be quite a perfectionist. He loves to plan and get things in order. He wants the best for me and the family. He needs things to be organised before he's comfortable enough to try something new. He creates an incredibly stable environment, which allows me to be freer in my own life. Jeff can get a little irritable when I suddenly land an impromtu social or work event on him. However, we always have a good time and end up laughing about the fact that he didn't want to go! He's very popular and likes it when people ask his advice. I feel proud of him in company. Jeff would never let me down and always supports my ideas.

I realise, however, that if I want change to happen in our lives, I need to make Jeff feel safe. Rather than expecting him to lead the change, I need to assign him the more organisational aspects of a project and take the lead myself. He's a great support, whereas I'm more of a go-getter. I can see now that I've been frustrated with Jeff for not doing the things that I could have been doing all along! For example, moving home. Jeff made some really sensible decisions to stay in the house. Although I've always wanted to move, Jeff insisted we stay put. He said this area was up and coming. He was right. We've made a lot of money on the house and I know I can now persuade him to retire somewhere really fabulous in the sun. When I look around, I realise some friends of mine haven't got such stable, thoughtful and caring partners. Without him I could have gone wrong so many times. I'm pretty lucky.'

The ability to use the Rainbow Perspective totally changed Abi's outlook on her partner. She was able to understand and really see how Jeff's Blue values served and nurtured her own Orange values. Rather than looking at where she felt they clashed, she could see where she and Jeff harmonised and collaborated. Abi pushed back against Jeff's Blue values because she saw them as representing rigidity and authority. This clashed with Abi's need for freedom and change, but by understanding that Jeff didn't need change in the same way, Abi could stop being so frustrated with him and start to find a way to lead the changes herself – and still keep Jeff feeling secure.

Taking a Rainbow Perspective on your relationship means looking at your partner's values and seeing how they serve and nourish both you and your relationship. It all starts by shifting your perspective from the negative to the positive as the Rainbow Perspective chart lays out.

The Rainbow Perspective chart

VALUE PAIRING	NEGATIVE PERSPECTIVE	POSITIVE PERSPECTIVE
Purple to Purple	We're so stuck in our ways	We're so safe together
Purple to Red	I sometimes feel alone	I feel so protected
Purple to Blue	You put rules before family and love	I always know where I am with you and where we're headed
Purple to Orange	Sometimes I don't know if I can trust you	You always want to bring the best to the family
Purple to Green	You seem to love everybody; sometimes I don't feel special to you	I always feel I belong with you; you bring out the best in me
Red to Red	You always have to have the last word and life feels like we're always fighting	Look at us – we're both so powerful, independent and decisive and yet together we could do anything
Red to Purple	You're too needy	I know you are always there
Red to Blue	You're always bossing me around	You've kept me out of trouble
Red to Orange	I don't always trust you	You totally understand me
Red to Green	You're naive	You totally accept me for who and what I am
Blue to Purple	You're too lead by your emotions and instinct	You're very loyal
Blue to Red	You're a total nightmare	I can rely on you to take action and get things done
Blue to Blue	You always think you're right	You respect the rules
Blue to Orange	You're selfish and manipulative	You're a great strategist
Blue to Green	You're flaky	You're incredibly kind and caring
Orange to Purple	You're so unadventurous	I can always rely on you
Orange to Red	You're dangerous	You energise me
Orange to Blue	You're uptight	You're my rock
Orange to Orange	I feel like we're always competing	Together we can rule the world
Orange to Green	You're not living in the real world	You give me hope
Green to Purple	You're so narrow-minded	I feel we're so connected
Green to Red	You're terrifying	You make me strong

Green to Blue	You're so inflexible	You have such integrity
Green to Orange	You're so wrapped up in yourself	You're so creative
Green to Green	We're so indecisive	We're so supportive and forgiving

Finally, once you've shifted your internal perspective on your partner to the full Rainbow Perspective, it only remains to talk to them in a way they will understand and respond to positively.

Of course, when all is going well in your relationship – great.

Enjoy every moment of it. Just stay awake and alert to areas of conflict – they can catch us unawares. That's not to say conflict is always a bad thing. I'm in no way suggesting the Pollyanna approach to life of skipping through the metaphorical meadow pretending everything is fine when it clearly isn't. Conflict can be healthy, invigorating and energising – a renewing and refreshing force. A bust-up doesn't have to mean a break-up. Conflict can be important in a relationship. It can temporarily bring us down from the peak feelings of love that in reality are unsustainable. When we argue, we break the untenable tension of joyful love. We need to. Sometimes we need to release energy and express our negative feelings. We can do this in a positive, awake way when we:

1) understand our own values
2) understand our partner's values
3) have the tools and techniques to help each other spiral back up to the peak experience of love.

When conflict arises within your relationship, ask yourself what's motivating your partner to say the things they are saying. When you get caught up in the moment those words can feel extremely personal, but if you put that feeling aside for a second you can start to ask yourself what is underlying this emotional release of energy.

For example, let's take an argument over jealousy. Along with money, communication and domestic chores, jealousy is one of the most common points of conflict in a relationship, but the root cause of jealousy will vary depending on what values underlie this damaging emotion.

For a Purple partner, it will be the sense of family betrayal – *'How could you break up our home?'*

For someone expressing Red values, it will be an outraged ego – *'How dare you humiliate me?'*

For Blue, it will be that their partner broke the rules, vows or promises they had made and brought shame on the partnership – *'But you promised.'*

For Orange, it will be a sense of competition – *'What have they got that I haven't got?'*

For Green, it will be hurt and pain but at the same time a selfless love – *'Do what you need to do, I want you to be happy more than anything else.'*

By understanding the values at work beneath everyday conflict, we both start to resolve it, and also use it to move the relationship forward.

Always remember a value clash is a two-way street – it's as annoying for your partner as it is for you!

Managing the values

So whether you're on your first date or your forty-year anniversary, how can you tell which value is dominant in your partner? Let's take a look now at what to listen out for in order to recognise which value set is present in your loved one as well as what language to use to manage those values.

Here's a look at the language patterns and triggers of all five value systems in terms of:

▶ What they might say – some typical phrases to identify the value set being expressed.

▶ What they don't want to hear – words or phrases that will push their buttons, wind them up and drive them up the wall.

▶ What they do want to hear – phrases that will calm them down, build an emotional bridge towards them and make them feel understood, safe and ready to talk.

▸ When's a good time to ask – quite simply, when might be a good time to influence your partner or ask them to do something for you.

▸ What they need – the core essentials to keep this value set loving you deeper every day.

How to manage Purple

What they might say

Everything happens for a reason.
We need to talk about the family.
It's our tradition.
My family/parents think . . .
My sister/brother says . . .
It's a bad omen.
We always do things this way.
Are you part of this family or not?
That will come back to haunt you.
My mother was right about you.
That's not how we do things.
Why does anything have to change?
But we always go there.
I'd need to talk to my family about that.

What they don't want to hear

I don't care what your family thinks.
Let's go through this step by step, totally logically.
You need to be a bit more independent.
You rely too much on your parents.
We're not inviting your family.
Your superstitions are stupid.
You shouldn't listen to your sister so much.
Get a mind of your own.
Your grandmother was a loony.
You need to cut the apron strings.
You should be more adventurous.
I've never felt part of your family.

What they do want to hear

Let's not fight – give me a hug and let's forget it.

We don't need to talk about it – I love you.

Let's invite the family over.

Is there anything I can do for your parents/sister/brother/cousin?

How do you feel about this?

Let's go back to your favourite restaurant/holiday destination.

You're safe with me.

Charity begins at home.

Family comes first.

If that's the way you've always done things, that's fine with me.

Let's keep it simple.

As long as you and the family are happy.

Blood is thicker than water.

I love your family.

Let's keep things the same.

Let's ask your mother/father/sister/brother/cousin what they think.

Your family's important to me too.

When's a good time to ask

When you have the support of the entire family or community or your partner feels safe, secure and loved.

What they need

Reassurance

Stability

Sameness

Strength, but not dominance

Direction

Tradition

Secure parameters

Predictability

Sense of belonging

Unity

How to manage Red

What they might say
I'll do it when I'm ready.
I'll win.
I'd rather do it alone.
I don't care what you or anyone else thinks.
I'm going to do it my way.
I'm in charge.
I'm not doing that.
Don't tell me what to do.
I want this.
I'm going with or without you.
Leave me alone.

What they don't want to hear
You're pathetic.
I don't respect you.
You've disappointed me.
What's so special about you?
You're wrong.
You're an embarrassment.
It's your duty.
We need to do this together.
You can't just do what you want.
Do what I tell you.
You're not in charge.
So and so does this so much better than you.
Everyone else thinks you should do this.
What will people think?
Calm down and we'll talk later.
Grow up.

What they do want to hear
'You' (not 'we').
You're the best.
You're so strong.

Do whatever you like.
You decide.
No pressure.
I trust you.
I wish I was like you.
You can do anything.
It's totally up to you.
I'll never leave you.
For me, there's no one else but you.
Can I borrow your brilliance for a moment?
Take me to bed.

When's a good time to ask
After sex.

What they need
Independence
Space
Admiration
Praise
Power
Status
Sex

How to manage Blue

What they might say
We need to do the right thing.
I'm fixed on this – I won't change my mind.
That's not what we agreed.
We need to get this organised and sorted out.
There's no other way to look at it.
We made a promise.
There's a time and a place.
That's not in the plan.
We mustn't do the wrong thing here.

Can we stick to the agenda?
I don't want to say anything I'd regret.
Those are the rules.

What they don't want to hear
Let's break the rules.
You need to loosen up.
Let's just see what happens.
I don't care if it's not right.
There's more than one way of looking at it.
You're narrow-minded.
I don't agree with your rules.
I know it's wrong but sod it, let's do it anyway.
I can't give you any specifics.
Anything could change at any minute.
Just go with the flow.
Let's jump in feet first.
I've reorganised your things for you.
You got that wrong.
You can't apply logic to this, it's just how I feel.

What they do want to hear
Let's stick to the guidelines.
Can you show me how to organise this?
I want to do what is right by you.
Help me understand where we went wrong.
You're absolutely right.
Let's bring some order to this chaos.
Let's sort out this mess we're in.
Tell me the right way to do this.
I value your opinion.
Shall we take some of the emotion out of this?
I need your expert advice.
Let's consult an authority on this subject.

When's a good time to ask
When everything else is sorted, organised and tidy

What they need
Structure
Order
Integrity
Honour
Rules
System
Regularity
Codes of conduct
Procedure

How to manage Orange

What they might say
I've got a great idea.
I've got a better idea.
Let's just deal with this and move along.
Anything's possible.
I'm in to win.
Let's take the risk.
I can see where you're coming from but I think you'll find I'm right.
I've thought about this and I know what to do.
I'm bored with this.
Let's just go for it.
Let's try something new.
I have my own strategy.

What they don't want to hear
You need to stop dreaming.
That's not possible.
I don't want any more change.
It's bound to fail.
You're not in their league.
You don't have what it takes.
There are other people to consider.
It's too risky.
You need to calm down and play safe.

Life isn't a game.
Why can't you be more consistent?
You're so manipulative.

What they do want to hear
You can do it!
I'm up for anything.
Let's do it your way.
How can we benefit from this?
Let's innovate.
Can we look at this strategically?
Let's use this to our advantage.
I have a surprise for you.
You're so exciting and fun.
I love how unpredictable you are.
So we screwed up – let's learn from it.
We just get better and better.
I'm proud of you.
You're the best.

When's a good time to ask
After they've received a gift or won a deal.

What they need
Flexibility
Spontaneity
Freedom
Energy
Creativity
Independence
Opportunity
Possibility
Vision

How to manage Green

What they might say
What do you think?

Whatever you like.

How can I help?

Let's do it together.

I understand you and I want to make this better.

Let's share this.

Let me take care of you.

I hear exactly what you're saying.

We can do whatever you need.

I really don't mind.

Whatever's right or easy for you.

What they don't want to hear
I don't care.

I'm only interested in myself.

You need to stop being so nice to everyone and toughen up.

You're naive.

People are generally horrid.

This is going to end in a fight.

Recycling is a waste of time.

Human rights laws have created more problems than they've solved.

People take advantage of you.

Humans are fundamentally selfish.

There's no point.

You're a mug.

You're far too idealistic.

What they do want to hear
We're all in this together.

Thank you for helping me.

You're so understanding.

I couldn't have done this without you.

I'll never forget you.

We're stronger together.
You've been so kind and thoughtful.
My life wouldn't be the same without you.
We're such a great team.
What's mine is yours.
I'm right there with you.
Tell me how you really feel – I want to be better.
Let's agree on this.
Nothing's more important than our relationship.
We're both right.
It would help me if you were totally honest with me.
Let's help each other.
You've changed people's lives.
You have so much love to give.

When's a good time to ask
After they've helped someone

What they need
Acceptance
Cohesion
Unity
Social contact
Potential
Growth
Learning
Love
Harmony
Peace
Generosity

CHAPTER 23

Making It Happen

We're now at the end of our rainbow and I hope you find that this book serves as your pot of relationship gold.

We've looked in depth at how understanding your own values and those of your partner can help both of you spiral into a beautiful, long-lasting love. However, something needs to drive those emotions. Something needs to fuel them.

That something is, quite simply, energy. You can have all the intellectual and emotional understanding of the values that it is humanly possible to have, but if you are physically exhausted and energetically deficient then you'll be running on a very empty tank.

When we're tired, we can't be bothered. When we can't be bothered, we don't take care of our own or our partner's needs. That's not to say there won't be times when your energy levels are low. Of course, there are periods in your life when you don't have the energy to fuel your relationship or give your partnership exactly what it needs to flourish. You need some downtime. You need to recharge. That's normal. But you also need to ask yourself whether you always tend to expend your energy outside of your relationship and whether the love between you and you partner is constantly being starved of the fuel it needs.

If you're eating poorly, overworking, sleeping badly, not exercising and generally neglecting yourself then your tolerance levels will be down, your irritability up and your willingness to do anything about either of those things at a rock bottom.

In the same way that it is always essential to ask whether you are creating as much of your own happiness as possible, it's important to ask whether you're maximising your relationship's chance of success. Positive action takes positive energy. Do you have enough personal energy? Can you maintain, find and create the energy that a successful, loving relationship needs?

Spiralling into love isn't just about having the ability to understand your relationship, it's about having the energy to put that knowledge of your partner into positive action.

The beauty of the *Spiral into Love* is that it goes to the very core of who your partner is and what's important to them in order to help you communicate effectively and build the affectionate, loving, respectful relationship you desire. Spiralling into love is all about co-creating the life of love and happiness that you know is waiting to happen.

You are now awake and aware. You now have the power to constantly create the ongoing feeling of love in our relationship.

By appreciating what is most important to you and your partner – the values that make you who and what you are – you can now begin to spiral into a lifetime of love.

Good luck, enjoy and be happy.

ADDITIONAL THEORY NOTES

The eight levels of Maslow's Hierarchy of Needs

1. **Biological and physiological needs** – food, water, shelter, warmth, rest and physical contact
2. **Safety needs** – security, order, law and stability
3. **Belongingness and love needs** – affection, family, relationships and bonding
4. **Esteem needs** – achievement, personal mastery, independence and status
5. **Cognitive needs** – knowledge, information, purpose and meaning
6. **Aesthetic needs** – beauty, creativity, innovation, natural balance and form
7. **Self-actualisation needs** – self-fulfilment, personal growth and peak experience
8. **Transcendence needs** – seeking to help others to grow and develop to their full potential

Dr Reiss's Sixteen Basic Human Desires

1. **Acceptance** – the need for approval
2. **Curiosity** – the need to learn
3. **Eating** – the need for food
4. **Family** – the need to raise children
5. **Honour** – the need to be loyal to the traditional values of one's clan/ethnic group
6. **Idealism** – the need for social justice
7. **Independence** – the need for individuality
8. **Order** – the need for organised, stable, predictable environments

9. **Physical activity** – the need for exercise
10. **Power** – the need for influence of will
11. **Romance** – the need for sex
12. **Saving** – the need to collect
13. **Social contact** – the need for friends (peer relationships)
14. **Status** – the need for social standing/importance
15. **Tranquility** – the need to be safe
16. **Vengeance** – the need to strike back/to win

Clair Graves and Dr Don Beck

Do check out the work of Clair Graves and particularly Dr Don Beck (http://www.spiraldynamics.net/) if you're interested in how Spiral Dynamics is attempting to understand human development and find innovative solutions to global needs.

SPIRAL PROFILER

Answer each statement in a way that indicates what is true for you generally. Put your score in the white box to the right of the statement.

3 = Strongly Agree   2 = Agree   1 = Moderately Agree   0 = Disagree

		1	2	3	4	5
1	Family and staying faithful to the values and beliefs of my culture are most important to me.					
2	I have clear guidelines about what is good and evil and right and wrong.					
3	In a relationship I will balance my moods and try to keep the peace for the benefit of all.					
4	I always keep up with the latest fashions and trends in clothing and culture.					
5	The world is a jungle full of threats and predators where only the strongest and fittest survive.					
6	I prefer to spend my free time with my immediate and/or extended family.					
7	When entering into a relationship I like to make the ground rules clear.					
8	I believe ecological sustainability is vital for our future so we should all be taking care of our environment.					
9	I am independent, ambitious and I like new challenges.					
10	My needs come first and I will get what I want, regardless of the consequences or cost to others.					

11	Emotions, sensitivity, and caring are much more important than cold rationality when dealing with people.					
12	Children should be taught to obey rules & authority because laws, regulations, & discipline build character and moral fibre.					
13	I insist my partner allows me the space to do what I want, how I want, when I want.					
14	My life's priority is the pursuit of wealth and status.					
15	I need to feel I belong to a family, community or a team.					
16	I believe in delaying gratification in order to receive my just rewards in the future.					
17	If I were in power I would spread resources and opportunities equally among all people around the globe.					
18	I often act on impulse without feeling guilty or remorseful.					
19	It's important to me that my family like and accepts my partner.					
20	I like my partner to be organised, tidy and reliable.					
21	I am optimistic, risk-taking, and self-reliant and I deserve success.					
22	I am fairly superstitious and I like to read horoscopes.					
23	I believe everyone's point of view is valid and right at some level.					
24	When I think about relationships I always ask – what's in it for me.					
25	I am competitive, strategic and play to win.					

Add up the scores in each column and enter them into the corresponding columns in the box below.

	TOTALS				
	1	**2**	**3**	**4**	**5**
PURPLE – Family & Tribe					
RED – Personal Power					
BLUE – Rules & Regulations					
ORANGE – Ambition & Success					
GREEN – Community & Sharing					

Looking at your final numbers, the highest score represents the value set you are most dominantly expressing at this time in your life. The second and third highest scores indicate which values are supporting your dominant values, and the lowest scores are values that you have either transcended and included, denied or passed over altogether.

For example:
Green: 11
Orange: 6
Blue: 5
Red: 1
Purple: 7

If this was your profile, you would be living in service of Green values in your relationships with a solid, underlying, family-orientated Purple. If you have values scoring equally, you may be in transition between two spiral sets or have found an integrated balance of all the values and be at or entering the Rainbow Perspective. The Rainbow Perspective is not assessed here as it is not defined as an additional 'value set.' Rather it is the ability to recognise all the previous value sets.

From this perspective you can meet your partner wherever they are. You know when you are operating from the Rainbow Perspective when you are aware of adapting your behaviour or approach depending on your partner's value needs rather than remaining fixed in your own.

FOOTNOTES

Introduction

(1a) Don Kulick *Language Shift and Cultural Reproduction* (Cambridge: Cambridge University Press, 1992), 119.

(1b) Elinor Ochs Keenan, 'Norm-Makers, Norm-Breakers: Uses of Speech by Men and Women in a Malagasy Community', in Richard Bauman and Joel Sherzer (eds.), *Explorations in the Ethnography of Speaking* (Cambridge: Cambridge University Press, 1974), 137.

Chapter 1

(2) Agnew and Lehmiller, 'Marginalized Relationships: The Impact of Social Disapproval on Romantic Relationship Commitment', *Sage journals – Personality and Social Psychology Bulletin* (January 2006), vol. 32, no. 1, pp. 40–51

(3) American Express Spending and Saving Tracker Survey, June 2010

(4) Pew Research Center, *Cohabiting Couples and Their Money*, D'Vera Cohn; November 22, 2011

Chapter 2

(5) Andreas Bartels and Semir Zek, The neural basis of romantic love, *Wellcome Department of Cognitive Neurology NeuroReport*, September 2000

(6) Fisher, H. E. Brown, L. L. Aron, A. Strong, G. and Mashek, D. 'Reward, Addiction and Emotion Regulation Systems Associated with Rejection in Love', *Journal of Neurophysiology* (Vol. 104: 51-60, May 2010)

(7) Tallis, Frank, *Love Sick* (London: Arrow Books, 2005)

(8) Neff, L. A. and Karney, B. R., 'To Know You is to Love You'. *Journal of Personality and Social Psychology* (2005) vol. 88, no. 3, pp. 480–97

(9) Neff, L. A. and Karney, B. R., 'To Know You is to Love You'

(10) Neff, L. A. and Karney, B. R., 'To Know You is to Love You'

(11) Neff, L. A. and Karney, B. R., 'To Know You is to Love You'

Chapter 3

(12) Horwitz, A. V., Videon, T. M., Schmitz, M., and Davis, D., 'Rethinking the Relationship between Twins and Environments: Possible Social Sources for Presumed Genetic Influences in Twin Research', *Journal of Health and Social Behaviour*, (2003) vol. 44, no. 2, pp.111–29

Chapter 5

(13) De Klerk, F.W. Nobel Peace Centre in Oslo; April, 2011

Chapter 6

(14) Amabile, T. M., 'Motivational Synergy: Towards New Conceptions of Intrinsic and Extrinsic Motivation in the workplace', *Human Resource Management Review*, (1993). no. 3, pp. 185–201

Chapter 13

(15) Luanda in Angola now tops the list of most expensive cities in the world with rents costing $10,000–15,000 a month to rent and over $1 million to buy. After the relative stabilisation of the civil war in 2002, unhealthy Orange values of corruption and profiteering have spun out of control. To the extent that, in early 2011, a Frenchman tried and failed to sue a Luandan grocer for charging him $100 for a watermelon. The case was thrown out of court through lack of evidence – the original watermelon.

The Frenchman had eaten it. You can read more in this article: **www. economist.com/blogs/baobab/2011/02/expensive_angola**

Chapter 21

(16) Neff, L. A. and Karney, B. R., 'To Know You is to Love You'. *Journal of Personality and Social Psychology* (2005) vol. 88, no. 3, pp. 480–97

(17) Neff, L. A. and Karney, B. R., 'To Know You is to Love You'. *Journal of Personality and Social Psychology* (2005) vol. 88, no. 3, pp. 480–97

SOURCES

Beck, Don and Cowan, Chris (1996) 'Spiral Dynamics'. UK: Blackwell Publishing

Dillner, Luisa (2009) 'Love by Numbers'. London: Profile Books Ltd

Tallis, Frank (2005) 'Love Sick'. London: Arrow Books

Reiss, Steven (2000) 'Who Am I?'. New York: The Barclay Publishing Group

Reiss, Steven (2008) 'The Normal Personality'. New York: Cambridge University Press

Reibstein, Janet (2006) 'The Best Kept Secret'. London: Bloomsbury Publishing Plc

Kirschner, Diana (2009) 'Love in 90 Days'. New York: Hachet Book Group

Atcheson, Lucy (2006) 'Your Relationships – A Work In Progress'. London: Hay House Uk Ltd

Gray, John (2008) 'Why Mars and Venus Collide'. London: Harper Element

Cameron, Deborah (2007) 'The Myth of Mars and Venus'. New York: Oxford University Press

Wilber, Ken (1996) 'A Brief History Of Everything'. Boston: Shambhala Publications Inc

Maslow, Abraham (2011) 'Hierarchy of Needs: A Theory of Human Motivation'. www.all-about-psychology.com (16 Jan 2011)

The LoveGeist Report 2010-2011

Neff, L. A. and Karney, B. R., 'To Know You is to Love You'. *Journal of Personality and Social Psychology* (2005)

Amabile, T. M., 'Motivational Synergy: Towards New Conceptions of Intrinsic and Extrinsic Motivation in the workplace', *Human Resource Management Review*, (1993).

Horwitz, A. V., Videon, T. M., Schmitz, M., and Davis, D., 'Rethinking the Relationship between Twins and Environments: Possible Social Sources for Presumed Genetic Influences in Twin Research', *Journal of Health and Social Behaviour*, (2003)

Fisher, H. E. Brown, L. L. Aron, A. Strong, G. and Mashek, D. 'Reward, Addiction and Emotion Regulation Systems Associated with Rejection in Love', *Journal of Neurophysiology* (Vol. 104: 51-60, May 2010)

Andreas Bartels and Semir Zek, The neural basis of romantic love, *Wellcome Department of Cognitive Neurology NeuroReport*, September 2000

Pew Research Center, *Cohabiting Couples and Their Money,* D'Vera Cohn; November 22, 2011

American Express Spending and Saving Tracker Survey, June 2010

Elinor Ochs Keenan, 'Norm-Makers, Norm-Breakers: Uses of Speech by Men and Women in a Malagasy Community', in Richard Bauman and Joel Sherzer (eds.), *Explorations in the Ethnography of Speaking* (Cambridge: Cambridge University Press, 1974),

Don Kulick *Language Shift and Cultural Reproduction* (Cambridge: Cambridge University Press, 1992),

Lightning Source UK Ltd.
Milton Keynes UK
UKOW05f0614080114

224153UK00002B/64/P